IN THE WHEEL
OF LIFE

VOLUME II

CENTRUM Publishers

IN THE WHEEL OF LIFE

VOLUME II

Wanda Pratnicka

Translation: **Krzysztof Kwiecień, Marlena Romanczuk**
Copy-Editing: **Kirsten Volkert**
Cover: **Łukasz Rutkowski**

Printed in Poland on acid-free paper

Library of Congress Cataloging-in-Publication Data is available

CENTRUM Publishers
P.O. Box 257
81-963 Gdynia / Poland
Phone: + 48 58 522 9497
Fax: +48 58 550 6812
E-mail: office@WydawnictwoCentrum.pl
Web: www.WydawnictwoCentrum.pl

ISBN 10: 83-60280-52-5
ISBN 13: 978-83-60280-52-2

CONTENTS

INTRODUCTION

Once again, I welcome you dear reader. In the first volume of this book I presented the soul's journey coming down to earth. I presented the soul as though it was making this journey for the first time. I couldn't present it differently, because many people believe that they were born on earth for the first time and the life they lead in their physical body is their only life.

In volume II, I expand on this and present life from various perspectives. I hope that this revives latent inner knowledge we all have so that you can decide for yourself what you should believe in. I will lead you in this quest not just from birth to death, but beyond death to the point where you make the decision whether to remain in Heaven or return to earth.

You will come to appreciate how important your current physical life is (how much it influences life after „death") and realize that it doesn't simultaneously end with the loss of your physical body. After „death" we continue living, but in more subtle, higher worlds. That is why in volume I I described subtle bodies in detail; so that you would understand they are essential instruments of our inner being.

SOUL'S DESCENT ON EARTH

In Nature and the Divine Order of Things nothing happens by accident. For a soul to fulfill its desires, it looks for conditions conducive to the realization of these desires. Among these supportive conditions would be parents, siblings, distant family and friends, material and health conditions, culture, skin color, climate, country, city, and/ or even an environment that would facilitate the soul realizing its desires.

The quest for these conditions is simply about the soul seeking out desires in others similar to its own desires. On the one hand a soul attracts to itself parents who would fulfill its specific desires and needs, and on the other hand, the parents who fulfill these conditions, would be attracting to themselves a soul that meets their specific desires. If the parents are not in mutual agreement then one of them can also attract a soul unilaterally. Where a child has to be an orphan or partially orphaned in later life, the soul would chose parents or a parent that would depart soon. If the incarnated human has to be sick or handicapped throughout his entire life, he would be born into a family where souls desire that experience.

You are wondering if this makes any sense? Who would want to raise a handicapped or sick child? Nobody would consciously decide to do that? Believe me, that involves the subconscious and it is always a choice made by one or both parents. If only one of the parents chose that, then the other parent will in some way remove themselves from those conditions. I analyzed many such cases and each time I discovered what caused that to happen. And, after realizing their desire to have a sick child, the child miraculously got better. How is this possible? It's because the desire changed to wanting a healthy child. Of course, the parents or a parent had to forgive themselves for their previous choice and also ask the child for forgiveness. Usually the child embraces this opportunity.

In many cases, people wanted for their child to be simultaneously healthy and sick, which obviously is not possible. In most cases, and this surprised me, sickness was chosen. I will return to this later.

Most often the process of a soul being attracted to parents is the moment of a child's conception or the period just preceding it. Think about it, dear reader, what kind of soul would be attracted to parents who don't talk to each other for weeks, or are full of hatred, are pretentious, or who after violent physical fights „make love" to „make things better". And, many people „make love" to each other just for fun, often drunk or high on drugs. Not to mention situations where kids are conceived due to rape, orgies, prostitution or through sexual relations with random partners.

In such cases the soul would enter this world with so many lessons to pass (or karmic burdens) that it would echo, like thunder, not only on the parents, but on the entire environment. People often say – „Such a good family, but such a lousy child" in these situations. You have probably heard people talk about the black sheep of the family.

Given the above, before conceiving a child, young couples should think about what they want in a child and ask for such a soul in their future child. It's about being fully engaged in the entire process, because future parents should not only think about and attract an adequate soul, but they should also adequately prepare their plans and implement them. Alternatively, parents rely on „chance" or blind fate. The consequences of such an approach could affect parents for the rest of their lives.

If we want to have a good, loving child then a reason for the sexual connection through which the child is conceived must solely be love. Everything born from a loveless relationship negatively impacts the coming soul, and this negativity flows back to the parents like a boomerang. Therefore, it's very important for prospective parents to discuss such topics. Within society today, this knowledge and approach is practically unknown, including among young people. Few people know what a great influence the moment of conception, the course of the pregnancy and/or the conditions at birth are upon a child's entire life. We also don't talk about the importance of each day of our stay on Earth or that only love protects us from harming ourselves and others. Most people think that these things are trivial because the fetus is not yet formed or is still growing. Whether worrying about these things is important is demonstrated from the examples below. And I have a countless number of similar examples.

Many aspects of sex are discussed, for example, how to prevent unwanted pregnancies. However, not discussed is the fact that we determine what kind of children we have and the fate that awaits both them and us. I will try to show you this, dear reader, through the example, not of a bad soul, but a good one, and how the carelessness of a young couple affected her life.

A few years ago I met Jack and Barbara, two wonderful people who were smart and growing spiritually. Currently, they are well-known in the artistic world. They were both calm and balanced individuals. Therefore, they were totally confused as to why they had horrible physical fights that often led to damages to their home. After such fights Jack often called me for help, because Barbara would want to commit suicide. I spoke with them multiple times and each time I saw in them a loving couple. I was surprised that after these fights there was no hatred between them, as usually occurs. They both genuinely cared for their relationship. We wondered what caused their sudden, dramatic attitude changes when they fought. Initially I suspected they were influenced by ghosts. But when I checked in on them in between fights there were no ghosts. Yet, during arguments there were plenty of ghosts around them. What concerned me was whether ghosts were provoking these fights or they were attracted by the fights. Each is a fuel for ghosts.

They were both very tired, resigned about the situation, and despite really loving each other, there were thinking of separating. They felt that they were not directing their own lives, that there was something that was „steering" them, over which they had no control. „Mrs. Pratnicka, I would gladly end this life, but I have wonderful kids" – a resigned Barbara said after a fight. „Are you crazy?" – I said. „Suicide is not a solution. Every person who commits suicide has to experience everything that made them end their life over and over again". Ghosts of people who committed suicide tell me that this is a thousand times worse than what they experienced in their physical body, and there is no way out of that. I believe them, because the feelings of our astral energies are multiple times more direct, because we don't have that protective barrier anymore, our physical body.

„Listen Barbara, nothing happens without cause" – I said. „There is always a cause; it has to be researched in your past sometimes. Don't wait for Jack to do this, just start with you". „Mrs. Pratnicka" – she said – „Do you think that I am doing nothing, that I am not looking for a solution to our problems? Do you know how many rebirthing sessions, regression and therapy sessions I went through – both normal and including hypnosis? And yet I have found nothing". „Probably you did not search where you should be searching. I think you should take a closer look at the time of your conception" – I said. „Ask your mom or dad, maybe they will tell you something about it, although I doubt. If you are ready and want to take a look at that moment yourself then I can help you and guide you through it. She agreed to this right away.

We started. Almost immediately she saw a moment during which her young, beautiful, dressed up mother with increasing impatience awaited her husband who was running late. „Mrs. Pratnicka, I not only see her," – Barbara said surprised – „I also feel her agitation and great sexual arousal. Finally dad came, stood by the doorstep seemingly undecided, as if he was afraid of something and didn't know whether to come in. My mom was happy when she noticed him and begun to be flirtatious, coquettish, and was tempting him from far, I have the feeling she could not wait to have sexual contact.

This is very unlike my mom; I have never seen her like this in my life. Dad sensed her behavior and aroused, he gladly moved closer to her. Only then did she smell the alcohol and noticed that he was drunk.

Instantly, mom's desire for sex went away, she became upset and being terrified she started to withdraw. Fully aroused dad was pressuring her more and more and mom became enraged and started pulling away from him. This resulted in a struggle and mom pulled away, started to run away throwing whatever she could at dad. Dad really wanted to catch her and he finally did. Simply, he forcefully raped her."

Barbara for quite a long time sat with her mouth wide open. When she bounced back she said in amazement – „Mrs. Pratnicka, I do exactly the same thing my parents did back then in my marriage. I allure and then I push away, I fight and simultaneously want to be raped. When I don't get this, because my husband would never come up with this unilaterally, I become despondent. Now I understand why I wanted to commit suicide so often. I don't receive what I subconsciously expect".

„Now you definitely know the cause, but this doesn't solve the problem" – I said. „In order for that situation to stop influencing you, you have to forgive your parents what you saw today. Do this for as long as it takes for you to start seeing changes for the better".

Suddenly her blood froze and she asked – „Will my kids have the same problems if they were conceived in a similar way?". „Most likely yes, but this is not always the case" – I explained. „Don't worry in advance. If in the future, after your children are grown up, they are faced with a similar situation, then you already know that they can be helped. However you can only tell them when they need to know and certainly only when they are ready for such a confession, otherwise telling them could harm them".

When Barbara returned home she didn't tell her husband what she saw during the session. After some time passed Jack told me with some degree of surprise that for some reason unknown to him the situation at home started to radically change for the better, as if suddenly he and Barbara had no reasons to fight anymore.

Now I will give you a different example – I would like to show you, dear reader, how giving birth has influenced a life and how a truly loving confession could change the course of events. When years ago I sensed that I was pregnant I went to see my mom to share this news with her. But I couldn't get a word in edgewise, she immediately told me – „I am dying of cancer. Basically, nothing can be done about it, I have metastasized all over my body". My blood froze. At that moment I was ready to give up my pregnancy so that she could live. I know that is horrible, but that is exactly what went through my mind. And when my daughter just started to speak, she immediately asked me why I didn't want her. Constant reassurances that she was very much wanted and anticipated (because she was) and that I love her, did not get through to her.

Years passed and she constantly repeated the same thing. This seemed very unfair and tiring to me. I got mad and resentful. I thought – „Doesn't she feel the great love I have for her? Is she blind and deaf to my constant reassurances and explanations?" And she didn't recover from it even after she became a teenager and got a boyfriend. „God" – I thought – „Will this never change? What did I do for her to constantly oppress me with this? Did I do such an evil thing at the moment I was trying to save my mother at the expense of two weeks pregnancy? What else can I do?" I was forgiving myself so many times and was asking her soul for forgiveness… „Can't she forgive me? Perhaps the reason for her experiencing it so much is the great stress related to my mom's serious illness and death during my pregnancy? Maybe this stress caused her some emotional harm?" Often I felt great guilt. „I help others, and I am incapable of helping my own daughter" – I thought. I wanted to make up to her for this, but in her case nothing worked.

A solution came at the least expected moment while we sat in a crowded restaurant. „Tell her about giving birth and she will come to understand her problem" – my intuition told me. „About giving birth?" – I thought puzzled. „Yes, when you were going to give birth to her" – my intuition said. Suddenly I saw images which I had completely removed from my memory and I froze due to the sensation. „Alright, I will tell her once we return home" – I thought. „No, tell her now" – my intuition demanded –"Now is the right time, she will come to understand and it will heal her". My daughter's school friend was with us in the restaurant. My intuition suggested – „This is the best moment, because his presence will urge her to hear you out seriously".

„My daughter, you know at this very moment I understand why throughout your entire life you felt unwanted" – I then started to explain how she came to this world. „When I sensed that I was pregnant, I found out that very day that my mom was dying. Every day I went with her to the hospital for treatment: laser light treatments and chemotherapy. I didn't want her to die in a hospital. It was like that for the entire nine months of the pregnancy. The day you were born I came back home very tired. I had barely undressed myself to go to sleep and then suddenly, before my due date I started to go into labor. I was alone at home so I called for an ambulance. „We don't have any ambulances" – they told me – „all of them are out". At the last moment came, straight from the car repair shop, an old, dirty, falling apart piece of junk. At the hospital, when a doctor noticed that you would come into the world at any moment, she pulled my hand to go to the hospital immediately. With lights flashing we left for the hospital. It was late in the fall season and I was dressed in pajamas and shaking because I felt very cold.

The doctor didn't give me an opportunity to take anything with me, and there was no blanket in the ambulance. We were in the ambulance and the doctor was constantly screaming to me „I never delivered a baby before. If you start giving birth now, I will stop the car and run away, you will be left alone on an intersection". During that ride I experienced true terror – I was shaking from the cold, and through holes in the car's body fuel fumes were entering the cabin of the ambulance. I had problems breathing and the doctor was screaming loudly – „Don't you dare give birth". It was a superhuman effort to stop the labor. I succeeded not only because she told me to, but because I did not have the courage to bring my beloved child into this world in such horrible conditions. I recognized then, that both of us deserved something better and I asked God to help us. And He did. After almost half an hour we got to a hospital, where I was put on a stretcher and quickly taken to the labor ward; soon after you came into this world. You were weak and livid from the prolonged labor and the fuel fumes. You were reanimated for almost an hour, but with all thanks to God you made it".

My daughter was rebelling and constantly interrupting me while I was talking – „Mom, why are you saying this now, can't you wait until we are home alone?" When I was finished she was sitting sheepish, distant and completely lost in thought. I noticed something wonderful though; in front of my eyes her entire energy suddenly started to change, I was looking at this phenomenon and I was captivated with her. Since then my daughter has calmed down, is more beautiful, has gained inner radiance and does not feel unwanted anymore. She now feels wanted and expected. She has stopped fighting to be loved and accepted.

As you can see, dear reader, even traumatic experiences which we went through before we appeared in this world can influence our life. If you are a parent and you have problems with your child, consider whether your child is influenced by some sort of trauma coming from the period before his birth. If you reach a conclusion that it is yes, then you have to work through that event. When a child grows up and is capable of understanding, you can help him to correctly interpret his experiences. The most important thing is forgiveness (no matter how unforgivable a situation may seem). One should also ask a child's soul for forgiveness. This should be done until you get the feeling that you have nothing left to seek forgiveness for and positive changes appear. Sometimes there could be a situation where you work through everything yourself, but your child is not ready to embrace changes.

BLACK SHEEP OF THE FAMILY

We often hear – „Such good parents, but they have such a terrible child". Here I am referring to parents who are in anguish because they extend great effort in raising their children but they are ashamed of them, because of what they do and who they are.

But, if you didn't consciously teach your child something bad then you aren't responsible for his temperament. A child, like any other person in the world, has to pass though his own learning process. This doesn't mean (even though sometimes this has to be done) that you should leave him on its own, leave it up to fate and not worry about him but rather just take care of yourself.

You can only advise your child, guide him in the right direction. In other words teach him how to dismiss the sphere of „evil". However, the decision to live by the guidance you provide depends solely on him, or actually upon his soul's

desires. Sometimes it seems that a soul is fundamentally „bad"
and we cannot do anything about it. However that is a mistaken
perception, because the idea of a bad soul doesn't exist. Each
soul is good and ultimately will find itself on the path to understanding.

Sometimes (although rarely) developed or even highly
developed souls behave „badly". They do differ though in terms
of their intentions. A less developed soul commits so called
„evil" as a means of learning to differentiate. On the other hand,
a developed soul came to the world to live in low vibrations and
would not allow itself to get tarnished by these low vibrations.
Bad souls don't exist. No matter what, each human entity has its
own, goals known to itself, and what it does has a deeper meaning along life's intersecting paths. The entire secret lies in
recognizing why our paths intersect and appreciating what we
should learn from such meetings.

I think it should now be clear why commands or prohibi-
tions don't work with some children, why you are not able to
force your child to do anything he did not want to. If you have
had this experience remember that your child's soul has its own
desires, often different from yours. These desires are the reason
he came into this world and they form the basis for his experiences. You might not like the way your child gets these experiences, but you cannot do anything about it. If you want to
convince your child about anything, remember that your child's
soul must have the same desires. Perhaps, you yourself have not
yet processed what you are trying to instill in your child.

It is also possible that before your child's soul came
to Earth it was clean and perfect. Perhaps it came down to
earth to learn about low vibrations in order to understand
them. If that's the case, then instead of trying to put your
child on a „good path", remind him nonstop that he is a good

soul and allow him to have his experiences.

When you come around to understanding this, you will no longer be worried or have sleepless nights. It would be much easier for you to enjoy life and take care of your health. Instead of constantly trying to fix what is beyond your scope of influence, you would be busy developing your own soul. If you do not comprehend this in time, the soul that you are trying to „fix" could pull you down to its level. Then you may be unable to do anything to help yourself or the other beloved soul. This is very similar to rescuing someone from a marsh. If you want to help someone who is stuck in a marsh you cannot jump into the marsh and pull him out of it, because you would harm yourself as well and would not be in a position to help the person you are trying to rescue. Only, when you are giving someone a helpful hand from „above", from a firm, „higher" ground, would you have a chance for success.

What is the „marsh" in a practical sense? The „marsh" is the negative emotions you experience with regards to a „bad" child. It is the shame and unfulfilled aspirations which cause anger and sorrow and even a willingness to punish yourself and/or your child. This is the source of the guilt which brings on the perceived need for punishment. Constant anger, sorrow and feelings of guilt all become seeds, which as a result of constant frustration and unfulfilled aspirations could grow in intensity. They could grow to the extent that they become your soul's desires and start resembling the desires of your child's soul. Your child's soul already had these desires before it came to this world (I will write more about this later in this book).

Perhaps you would not recognize this and as a result become as „bad" as your child. That is why you must be very alert now, while you still have control over the situation. Know that spiritual development is the same as mountain climbing; the higher you go, the steeper it gets and the easier it is to fall, and fall fast. It is always easier to fall than to climb up.

How to get out of such a vicious cycle? Most of all, forgive your child and his soul that it chose such tough experiences through which you must both pass. Next forgive yourself that you attracted to yourself a soul that tough to live with. However don't feel sorry for yourself (this is a negative emotion), but realize that nobody but you has desired to learn through such a tough experience. If you don't like this experience then wish for something else and maintain that desire until things start changing for the better. Also, allow your child to experience and learn from his own mistakes. Always remember the old saying – „What doesn't kill a human makes the soul stronger".

Even though this might be tough to accept, you would see that both you and your child are able to breathe again. When you stop attacking your child constantly, demanding he change and improve his behavior, the fighting between the two of you would disappear. Then your child would resist less, and who knows maybe the resistance would disappear completely based on the adage – there is no attack, then there is no need for defense. At the beginning your child would be surprised with such change, however he won't remain neutral, quite the opposite, he would start to look at you and listen to what you have to say. Only then would your child notice your positive characteristics, notice who you are, and start treating you seriously as a role model. This is the best gift you could give to your child. A child would gladly accept such „help". However he would only do so when he is ready to embrace this change.

It is a fact that parent's good upbringing of a child is not all that matters. There are a lot of people in the world who had terrible conditions for personal growth, lived in destructive families, and yet grew up to be upright and smart individuals.

They came to earth to learn amongst the many ills of human life and did not allow the negatives around them to become part of their experience. There are also children from good, upright families who grew up to be a disgrace to humanity. I repeat again – the essence of a human does not depend on his parents or their upbringing, but on the choices of his independent soul. I return to this later.

CHOOSING OUR OWN PARENTS

A child's soul, long before coming into the world, choses parents and quite often is near to them. Therefore parents, especially mothers, long before getting pregnant start to hatch plans about eventual motherhood. It is at that exact moment we should start thinking about what kind of child we expect, whether it is exactly like the soul that is next to us. If you are afraid that you won't sense such a soul then know that this is a completely unnecessary fear. How could you think about a child if his soul wasn't around you? It would not be possible. Do you think that a mother who has given birth to a child didn't think about him before giving birth? Every woman who is giving birth did think about the child before, but not every woman wants to acknowledge these thoughts. This could even be verified with childless families, where a woman is unable to get pregnant. In those instances, there are also thoughts about a child, but they are „empty". This does not result from closeness of a soul, but from environmental pressure (for example: grandparents or a husband who desires children), or fear (for instance, of the would-be mother's age). Everyone around could desire to have a child, except parents themselves. In order for us to understand this situation well consider the following,–on a conscious level parents could try to have a baby, perhaps even try very hard. They go through testing and treatments, making many attempts. The failure to get a positive result is not caused by physical shortcomings (for example: there is no right kind of sperm), but rather by the reluctance of the parents' souls. Most likely their souls do not want children to participate in their experiences. This could be changed; it would require working to reach inside to your subconscious to understand what is causing the child-lessness. It is only then can you start to work on effecting change. Sometimes, the reluctance to have children is due to decisions from previous incarnations. This may have been caused for example, by superhuman work with children because there were many children in the family. Perhaps, the children were bad, sick or died early, etc. To have children now, you should reach past these causes of your childlessness and decide differently. Once you do this, a child would suddenly appear in your life. Another possible reason could be you were once bad parents. If this is the reason then you must awaken a desire to have children. And, new desires could only be awakened in us when something is hard to achieve.

You have to take into consideration that even when a soul finds an appropriate physical body for its birth, various obstacles could change the situation. Sometimes future mothers keep changing their desires. One day they want to have a child, and the next day they change their mind. They claim that they aren't ready for motherhood or they are afraid of the experience. The child's soul could then find a different mother from similarly vibrating parents. The undecided mother would then miscarry or have an abortion.

It is also possible that a mother is fully prepared for a child, but the soul of her future child turns back from its earlier chosen path. Then the childbirth would end in a miscarriage or a crib death. If a soul turns back then nothing in this world would stop it (even if the mother had been in the hospital for nine months). Analogically – even if such a child was watched over in the most comprehensive way he would still die. Although this rarely happens, almost all young mothers are afraid that their child would die this way. I hope that this knowledge would help rid them of this paralyzing fear which prevents them from fully experiencing the happiness of the blessed state of childbearing. Death isn't an accident. When newborns and small children die it allows us to go through very important lessons (I write about these lessons later). Such children are our teachers. They teach us values, priorities and above all love. Often we accomplish the most important lessons at the most difficult moments. If a child is supposed to live then nothing or anyone is capable of stopping him. The child would live (and this could be a very good life), even if he had no parents.

Each miscarriage or abortion is a sort of agreement between a mother and the coming soul. A miscarriage happens when the child's body wouldn't be properly formed and the soul's plan requires experiences in a healthy body. The birth of such a child would mean a wasted incarnation because the child wouldn't be able to manage the tasks planned for him in his upcoming life. Another possible cause for a miscarriage is changes (sometimes on a global scale). Plans on earth are changing and this could mean that it is not yet the right time to fulfill goals which a soul has chosen. On a smaller scale this could possibly mean that the situation in a family is changing (or would change in a future), for example: the departure of the mother or father, and the child's goals require their presence.

I hope that this knowledge provides some consolation to parents who have experienced a miscarriage or a child's death. You do not need to suffer, because you would meet each other again. You certainly wouldn't want to make a soul unhappy by forcing the child to come into this world. Therefore, forgive yourself and the child's soul and live with the knowledge that everything would be alright.

I would also comment on abortions. When I was young, abortions were very common; it was like a substitution for contraception. Many women were getting abortions without thinking about the consequences and many of them suffered greatly. Many years have since passed and still some of these women feel shame and extreme guilt. This doesn't only apply to women, because men often suffered or suffer equally. Even at an advanced age some people feel as though they have murdered their own children. These intense feelings of guilt can cause possession by ghosts during physical life or failure to go to the other side of death's curtain after physical death. This is unnecessary… (and that doesn't mean that I support abortion). This is often associated with a rigid catholic upbringing which makes it difficult to overcome the feelings guilt and shame. You have to understand that not all beliefs are true. Old, established perceptions and ridiculous superstitions make it more difficult to attain new knowledge, even though (or rather because) they are incompatible. I return to this later on. At this juncture please understand, dear reader, a soul cannot be in any way killed or harmed, because a soul is immortal and imperishable. Also, a soul cannot be stopped if it wants to come to this world, it would always find a way to get here. I know of many cases where after a miscarriage or an abortion the soul returned to the same parents in their next child's body or was born to a family close to them in order to learn its own lessons. A deep understanding of what I wrote above would prevent much suffering in this and the other world. I constantly deal with these problems and know how unpleasant and even tragic the resulting consequences can be.

I repeat one more time that I am not a fan of abortions. However I want people who went through this experience to rid themselves of their intense feelings of guilt. This intense feeling of guilt is a lot worse for the soul's development than anything done in the past. People must absolutely forgive themselves and ask the soul of the unborn child for forgiveness (it does not matter whether the soul is in this or the other world).

A soul doesn't enter a body at the moment of conception. In that moment only a „reservation" takes place. From that point on, no other soul could take that growing body. During the pregnancy, the soul gradually establishes a stronger and stronger connection with the child's body. The ultimate connection occurs shortly before, during or right after the birth. Certainly, a soul that reserved a body can get in and out of it, in the end nothing limits it, but a soul doesn't do that. I write later about why that happens after we have discussed new life after the death of the physical body.

ENTERING THE WORLD

Finally you are ready for your experiences and you are born as a child. You managed this with much thanks to your parents. You should be very thankful to them, especially as not every soul is afforded this opportunity. Many souls wait a long time for this opportunity to present itself. Parents should also thank the child for choosing them specifically. You thank them and they thank you as you concurrently have this experience that is, *What You Are in Essence.*

As a Godly spark, the divine part of your humanity is clean, innocent and perfect. You are a wonderful, polished diamond with thousands of facets. You remember perfectly who you are, from where you came and why you came into this world. You are fully aware that you are a free spirit and soul. And while you gain experiences, you are in a way „imprisoned" in a human's body. You would like to move and communicate far more than you could, but it would not be possible because you are in the underdeveloped body of a small child. Your spirit would be impatient and want to do more but it needs to wait until your body is grown and is capable of gaining experiences. Because of this, you feel as though you are in a prison; uneasy, vulnerable and at the mercy of adults.

Once I wanted to check whether a small child actually remembered, *Who He Is* and where he came from so I asked my grandchild. I was shocked at how he reacted with his eyes in a mature manner. It surprised me. His eyes looked normal, like any other newborn, until that point. However, when I started to talk about God, he looked deeply inside my eyes and started to make strange sounds, even though he had not even started to babble yet. When I was finished, he became quiet and his visual acuity returned to normal. Later, I repeated these conversations and every time the reaction was the same. I also talked to my newborn granddaughter and she reacted the same way. Later, I had a chance to experience this phenomenon with other newborns and I always observed the same reaction.

When we begin our existence on earth and learn how to live here, the people around us are our teachers. Our first teachers are our parents, family, friends and neighbors. Later we learn from our teachers, priests, friends, neighbors and television etc. We learn by imitating others and it seems that by being around people the way they do things, which may not always be the correct way, is forced upon us. God however very wisely set up this world. Even though, everything that we come into contact with tries to influence us and teach us something, it solely depends on us what we accept and what we learn from each situation. Therefore two children in the same family, in exactly the same conditions, among the same people, could learn quite different qualities from their home experience. Or even accept for themselves none of the personal traits they see at home. It is very easy to influence some people, but it could be totally impossible to influence others.

Why do some things influence us easily, while others are unable to move us no matter how hard others try to force these things upon us? That depends on our soul's desires. If you came to this world to experience, for example, how to *be a victim* then you would attract to yourself people who make this possible for you, the kind of people who would *be a tormentor* to you.

I am not talking here about extreme situations where one person cruelly mistreats another person. I am referring to, simple, daily, routine matters, where we are constantly expecting or awaiting some punishment because of a deep rooted belief or feeling of guilt. That is exactly how we attract the proverbial „tormentor". Someone who would do the „dirty job" so that we could feel sorry for ourselves as much as we want to later on. That way we would fully experience what it is like to be the „poor" victim. We feel sorry for ourselves, but the tormentor also suffers as a consequence not understanding how all of this could had happened.

As you can see, dear reader, the victim is not a product of what happens to him, but the cause, the source of it. The victim forces the „tormentor" to torment him, which in the human reasoning of guilt and punishment makes him equally „guilty" for what happens to him. A given event would never occur if the tormentor and victim both didn't want the same thing. I am not writing this in order to bring victims to account. That would only increase their sense of *being a victim*. I want each person who has experienced obscenity to admit to himself that he was not a victim of that situation, but the creator of it so as to experience what it would be like to *be a victim*. And the story could be completely different. Since you cause yourself to be tormented then you can also change that. First, you would have to decide that you don't want to be a victim anymore. This affirmation would help you in that regard: „I... (your name here) free myself from the need to be a victim". Write that down and say it until everything starts to change around you (remember that almost each one of us has something of a victim inside of us). Simultaneously, you have to change your approach to you. A victim is a victim, because he doesn't love or accept himself. In order to change that, you should repeat the affirmation: „I... (your name here) love and accept myself". Write that down and say it in your thoughts, say it aloud and also sing it out. Make it a habit that when you walk every other step is a step to greater self-acceptance and self-love. Furthermore, a victim also has a need to feel sorry for himself. Therefore say to yourself: „I... (your name here) free myself from the need to feel sorry for myself". When you change your desire, your experiences would also change. From being a slave to your desires, you would become the master of them.

The first time I understood that no one else, but me, creates my unpleasant experiences, I obviously got very mad at myself. „How could someone be so stupid and injudicious to complicate their life like this!" – I demanded of myself. I then started to forgive myself. When my emotions had subsided, I understood that since I had the power to mess up my life I was also capable of repairing everything and giving new direction to my life. This completely changed the way I experienced things. Now, whenever something happens to me that I don't like, I check myself to determine what emotions and thoughts lead to it. I then change my desire to what is appropriate for me. Each person who perseveres and follows this path would see how his life becomes much easier and more ordered. He would also be surprised by his achievements and the positive changes to his life.

The most difficult thing is waiting to see changes for the first time. We would be impatiently anticipating the effect of these changes. You have to ensure that you don't allow doubts to enter your mind. Doubts could eliminate everything, because consciously we might want changes very much, but subconsciously we may not believe that these changes could happen at all. The best solution would be to give this entire matter over to God for safekeeping, stop worrying about it and the results would come. And, after the first time, it would be a lot easier thereafter, because you would be conscious that you succeeded once there is no reason you would not succeed again.

It often happens that when we begin to desire wealth, we lose a wallet or get laid off. Or we desire recovery and a pain becomes even stronger or an additional sickness appears. Most people say to themselves – „I tried, but this is absolute nonsense, this doesn't work on me, because the problem intensified even more". However, this is *proof* that change for the *better* is taking place.

Simply put our new *desires* starts to sprout and before they bear fruit in the material world, they must first grow on a spiritual plane. Despite desiring something else, a considerable amount of old desires and thoughts that were growing before we decided to change would still surround us. And, we would be harvesting the crops born of those desires. You can't get rid of these desires and thoughts other than to let them materialize so that they can burn themselves out completely. Only then would you be rid of them forever. This is somewhat like a contractor who has an old building falling on his head while he is trying to build a new one. You need plenty of courage, trust and determination not to mistake that ostensible fall. Certainly, this is a fall, but a fall of the old and used. Ultimately each one of us would learn to create new desires and thoughts and to await the results with happiness while at the same time not giving in to fears that are really the foundation of the old building. These fears need to come to the surface, and like the contractor, you are not allowed to give in to them. If the contractor gave into them, he would return to the old and wallow in his unhappiness. But if he tries and keeps trying, ultimately he would be successful.

I also go through experiences that I don't want to go through. At first they seem to be hurtful, humiliating, and unfair sometimes they even make me cry. However, a short while after I have calmed down from my first, unpleasant sensation I reflect and realize a truth – since they are incompatible with my present desires, I am dealing with something that I created in the past, before I decided on changes. When this truth reaches me, I discover that I don't have to do anything anymore, and the unpleasant experiences go away. They eventually become slightly irritating and almost unnoticeable with time.

Many people wonder how long it would take to wait for changes to start appearing. Ultimately, nobody wants to delude themselves and wait in vain. Everything depends of how quickly you allow for changes in yourself and whether there aren't in you contrary thoughts or fears about that change. You might ask how could I possibly not want to be healthy or prosperous? Many people however, don't want this for a variety of reasons. Some people punish themselves for alleged faults; others claim that they just don't deserve happiness. The list of reasons is actually endless.

Would you ever think that reflecting on pleasant moments from the past could destructively influence the present and lead to bankruptcy? Let me explain. Once someone who couldn't manage his personal life (let's call him Mark) reached out to me for help. He was one of the best specialists in his area of business. At issue were his finances, or constant lack of it.

Despite having a very high income, a company car, per diems, frequent trips abroad which brought additional income and his wife's high paying job, he couldn't make ends meet. He was at risk of personal bankruptcy. Wherever possible he had taken loans and now debt collectors were threatening to seize and auction his belongings. His wife was helpless because her husband was a decent, tender and loving man. He wasn't wasting money on any „entertainment", he didn't drink, he didn't smoke, he didn't have a mistress and he didn't gamble. His income alone would be enough for a luxurious life, not to mention his wife's quite good income from which she maintained the house and paid the bills. She often mentioned over the phone that she couldn't give him her money, because it would „disappear" right away. This was a weird issue for my assistant, because there were no ghosts around them as was often the case with financial problems.

We tried unsuccessfully in various ways to find out what was the cause of this state of affairs. Mark came to one of my lectures. He came up to me during a break and we began talking to each other. More often than not I see a person's entire problem immediately. Usually I ask the person many questions and also encourage them to share their first thoughts with me. Even if these thoughts seem very stupid or absurd. That is about letting the subconscious mind express itself next to the conscious mind.

Finally we reached a conclusion. It turned out that Mark knew his wife since they were very young. When they were still teenagers they started to see each other and he would often sneak into her small room where they would spend nights together. They were so happy together, as though they were in heaven. This unspeakable happiness lasted a short time, because she got pregnant and her parents, the court and the school got involved. Their early parenthood didn't stop them from finishing school and graduating from good universities. Later, they also had three more children. Mark had a loving family, a good job at which he was successful, and a beautiful home with a huge garden. In other words, he had everything that people dream of. However, he didn't feel happy deep down in his heart, because he missed those beautiful moments from his teenage years. He was convinced that striving for prosperity and stability resulted in him losing something very precious. He didn't know, however, what it was. I asked whether he would give away his current life for the life that he missed. He said yes right away. After, I asked whether he regretted having a wife and children. He said no. He said that he loved his wife and children very much. „OK" – I said – „you miss that small room, but would you be able to live again in those conditions, not to mention that there isn't enough room there for the six of you? Would you be as happy in conditions similar to when only the two of you were there?" He didn't answer. He was devastated. For me the cause of his problem was very clear. I saw in front of me not a man who managed a huge company, but a young boy who was trying to lose everything in order to recreate a past in the present moment. My task was to make him realize his subconscious pursuit in order for him to consciously work on it and simultaneously not be scared of it. His subconscious mind thought – why have a large home that must be kept warm and clean. And, on top of that why pay taxes and other bills, constantly fix or renovate this large home when in that little room nothing needed to be done and I experienced many wonderful moments?

I asked him whether he thought that by losing everything he would be able to recreate those moments. I also asked whether his wife and children would be as happy as he would be. And whether he really wanted that, not to mention whether he had the moral right to deprive his family of possessions and have them deal with a situation they were not used to? „If we lived based on that thinking, we would all still be living in mud huts" – I said. „I don't want to make my loved ones unhappy, but don't I have the right to be happy?" – He said as he burst into tears. „I don't cheat, I don't drink, I don't look for company to have fun. I simply recall beautiful moments in solitude. Is that so wrong? A person cannot even do that?" – He sobbed.

When he calmed down, I explained to him what the problem was– „Life is a like a large river, it's constantly flowing and moving forward. Whether you want it to or not, life keeps flowing forward. You cannot stop it or turn it back. If you live in the past then you drag the past everywhere and simultaneously destroy whatever you are trying to build in the present (life happens to be helpful in that regard). You desired to live in a small room, but you didn't consciously take a hammer and destroy your current home, because everyone would think that you had lost your mind. Therefore your subconscious mind looked for other ways to get rid of your home. You could have lost it if you made less money, but that would be in conflict with your subconscious mind's desire to receive a good salary. While you were earning money, you felt fulfilled, but on another level, in contradiction to that your desire to live in a small room also has to be realized. Therefore your subconscious looked for ways for your earnings to be imperceptibly wasted so that you needed loans to manage your life. As a result, the debt collectors did what you would in effect be doing if you had taken a rotary hammer to your own hand. From the outside it looked as though you have nothing to do with what was happening to you. You even suffered, and looked for a solution; you didn't know that it was really a goal that you subconsciously chose that needed to be achieved through your actions or someone else's".

„I think I understand my problem now and I want to change, but the future terrifies me so much. How would I be able to stop thinking about those pleasant moments which I miss so much compared to my numerous daily responsibilities?" – He asked. „I always considered these memories my capital, something that gave me power. Now I have absolutely no idea how to make my life more than just about responsibilities. How do I stop thinking about the past and still live and go about my life".

„Despite what you might think this is quite simple. Please think about or write down on a piece of paper all your assets. Next, focus your attention on the things that could make you happy. Write them down one by one. Now, you have to put both your head and heart into this process, so that, your true feelings can be captured. Please don't take the fact you are almost bankrupt into consideration. I assume you don't even realize what great „capital" you have. Even the poorest person has something that he can be happy about with all his heart, please focus only on that."

He focused and I noticed how his face began to brighten up, he felt really happy. He told me how wonderful he felt. He was surprised how quickly the old memories started to fade away and lose their power. He felt a complete turnaround in his life as though he had turned on an invisible switch. When he returned home, everything changed for the better. Actually, he didn't have to do anything as everything, one after the other started to change and fix itself. This was happening almost autonomously; and, at the same time, as if someone had touched Mark with a magic stick, he stopped losing money.

WHAT IS LIFE ON EARTH

Have you ever asked yourself any of the following questions: What is the reason for my being on Earth? Is there a higher order to all of this? And if the answer is yes, then what is this higher order? And since I am here what role do I play? What purpose does what I do play in the Great Plan? Am I fulfilling my „responsibilities" well? And for whom is it being performed well? Is it for me or for others? Do I have a responsibility to think solely of others or could I think about myself?

When you think that only others are important, and you have to meet their expectations, you go through life very frustrated. You constantly wonder – „When is it going to be my turn?" By giving of yourself in this way you don't bring value to your own or other's lives, because you are not giving from you heart with love, but rather you are giving with constraint.

This is very much like the story of the roll and the role it played in a marriage. This is how the story went. She always loved the top part of the roll. During her childhood she fought a lot with her siblings to get it. When she got it, she was happy for the rest of the day. This made her believe that everyone liked that part of the roll. On the other hand, he liked the bottom part of the roll. When they met, they were so smitten with each other that they gave to each other things that they liked the most for themselves. He gave her his favorite part of the roll and she gave him her favorite part. At the beginning, they were doing this to endear themselves to each other. Later it became a habit. They treated each other the same way with many other things. Each spouse carried a hidden anger towards their partner because they „had to" give away something that they liked very much themselves. This ultimately led to their separation. During the court hearings one of them screamed out loud – „I gave you what I liked the most and you couldn't appreciate that!" The other spouse answered – „It's me who gave away my half of the roll and had to eat the portion that I hated!" Suddenly they came to their senses. They realized that they had wasted a big part of their life. They mistakenly thought that what was good for one person, had to be good for the other person.

Only when you take care of yourself and your happiness would you be able to similarly care for other people. If you are not happy while giving to someone else then you are not actually giving anything, because what you are giving doesn't have even the smallest value. If you think that your sacrifice and submission would enrich the other person and he would get to like or love you, you are mistaken. Your task is to like, love and care for yourself. Then the entire world would like, love and care for you.

Life could be compared to a great restaurant where you order the dish you are really in the mood for. The chef gets it ready in the kitchen, and the waiter brings it to your table. You order it, you don't make it yourself. The chefs are the spiritual energy, which „ prepares" various dishes for you. However, you decide which dishes you want and when they are to put it in front of you. If you don't go to a restaurant or while being there you don't find the courage to order your favorite dish, you won't receive it. When you do order it, you are responsible for it and have to pay for it.

Life is like a great, wonderful restaurant. Learn to order from Life what you desire, exactly as you do in a restaurant. Trust that since you ordered your favorite dish, a waiter (spiritual energy) would put it right in front of you. When you go to a restaurant, you don't worry about each dish and you don't think about how it would be prepared. Sometimes you say to yourself – „I don't deserve this, this cost too much", and as a result you pick something which costs less, but which also provides less satisfaction.

The way you behave in a restaurant perfectly illustrates how you behave in life. When you order something, you say – „This is what I want" – and you trust that you would receive it. But perhaps you still worry (like in life) that they would ignore you and you won't receive exactly what you want. In a restaurant however, you don't run to the kitchen to check whether the chef has the ingredients for the meal you ordered. You don't worry about whether it was cooked, fried or baked right. You trust that you would receive everything, exactly as it should be and you wait peacefully. When the waiter (spiritual energy) puts the dish you ordered in front of you, you say – „thank you", and if you desire something else you ask for it.

Look at your life, the lessons you have learned and your experiences, as you look at meals when you order at a restaurant. Make a decision about what you want, order it and you would receive it. Trust that you would receive it. You are a product of your thoughts. You are on earth, because a soul while in heaven began to think about being on earth. This still very much applies. Each one of your thoughts creates a new experience. Why don't you give yourself a gift and start thinking about yourself in such terms as uniqueness, wonderfulness and sublimity. You are already like this deep down; you just need to recall this so that it would be constantly applied in your life. You would make great progress when you understand that this is a rule, not only for your reality, but also for that of other people.

Very often lack of self-awareness makes us think that everything is alright, even though it is not. It was like that with me. While writing my first book on a computer I was correcting mistakes for myself so the computer wouldn't have to do it. I was doing everything myself. When you have a lot of text there is a lot of correction work involved. One day things piled up and I didn't have the strength to do anything. I gave up... Only then I realized that I was relating to the computer just as I do with people around me. I was taking everything on my shoulders, and when I was falling under the weight of life's challenges, I was mad at the people. In spite of it all, I was still doing everything by myself. At that moment I decided to put a stop to that and even though I was tired and disappointed I let the computer do the work... I knew how computers worked, what functions it had, yet my inner program was telling me that I couldn't rely on others, that I had to do everything myself. I didn't fully use my computer. I was doing everything possible so as not to have to use it fully. I know that this is very funny, but it's not about the computer, but my inner program. Knowing something and actually doing it are two very different things. After a while I forgot about it and I started to do everything as I did before, because the old program was still operating. My habits were deeply rooted. For a long time I had to be very cautious and remind myself about my new resolution. Multiple times while writing I felt discomfort and I realized that was because I let my computer do the work instead of doing it myself. Fortunately, this entire issue dealt with a machine and not a person, because thanks to the computer it was easier for me to recognize my program. So as you can see, our teacher could be anything that we meet on our path, not only people, animals or plants, but also lifeless things. If you have a problem, know that the problem is not in people or your surroundings, but in you and only you can solve it.

You on Earth

Since you decided to learn through experiencing, you need to use a body as a tool. This body feels both pain and pleasure. A physical body is material therefore you can only own it on the Earth's material plane. It's built from the same elements as the Earth and has these very elements, in exactly the same proportion as the Earth. We are dependent on the Earth and the Earth is dependent on us. We need each other, however many of us forget that. By destroying the Earth, we are destroying ourselves.

We don't have a chance to learn where we came from as we do on Earth. Pain, which we appointed as a teacher, doesn't exist there. Obviously, in the Heavens as well as on Earth we can learn without experiencing pain, but for most people that is difficult. Pain is one of the best teachers, because it is only when something hurts us or we lose something we depended on, that we start working on ourselves. But, if we had paid attention earlier to potential solutions to a problem we would not suffer. There are also people who do not do anything with their lives and tell themselves and others that suffering is ennobling. The approach we choose depends on us. We have free will and we can do anything we decide. People who run away from challenges should be told that sooner or later their suffering will reach a very high level and they won't be able to suffer anymore or continue living as they had up to that point. They would happily decide to embrace changes then.

Nobody can force you to do anything against your will. Is it worth it though to resist until the worst is almost upon you? Isn't it better to learn in a more pleasant way? I hope the example below makes this obvious to you.

Mary, a very warm and loving person reached out to me. She had been living in England for twenty years and had a young son named Jack who had lay in bed like a vegetable from the moment he was born. The mother was taking care of her son herself, because some time before, her husband had abandoned them after realizing that caring for the child was beyond his psychological ability. Mary loved her son very much and didn't want give him over to social care. She was having a very tough time, because care for her son required round the clock supervision. I thought to myself, as I have never done before – „How does she handle all of this? Jack is getting older and bigger, even turning him on his side is demanding…" I thought about how I could help her and whether it was even possible to help her. Often such illnesses are the result of karma and I am not allowed to get involved. I decided to check whether there were any ghosts around Jack and I did find a few of them. I felt great relief, and was even elated, because I really wanted to help Mary. However I immediately chastised myself, thinking – „How is cleansing Jack of ghosts going to help, given that he doesn't even get up from his bed? At most, he would have more energy…" I was mad that God gave me such tough cases, but I worked on him until the ghosts went away. When they were gone, this child started to invigorate and return to health. „Oh well, how far would this return to health reach?" – I wondered. However, Jack became stronger every day until one day he wanted to try to get up from his bed by himself. We were so happy… I didn't expect this. I had to make Mary realize that Jack shouldn't be treated according to his age as documented on his birth certificate, but like a baby, because he wouldn't be able to do anything on his own yet. He had to be taught everything, but slowly so as not to discourage him. Jack had to learn so many things at the same time, not only the basics with regards to hygiene, speech and walking, but also many other things which we adults may already take for granted. Even though this might seem obvious, not all parents understand this and as a result many become impatient. Parents understand that a child is unable to do anything when the child is sick. When the child returns to health, parents suddenly think that the child is capable of doing everything right away and more so by himself. Children in such situations are often easily discouraged. Often they would rather return to their illness or even resign from life and die, rather than face such a tough reality alone. This happens most often when they are confronted with their peers too early.

It's the same with autistic children. A return to health and normality requires a lot of attention and effort; the child shouldn't have to paddle his own canoe. If a child sees that he is not equal to other children and as a result thinks that perhaps he would never be like his peers, he might develop an inferiority complex. Often he's afraid to even try and catch up to them. I have taken care of such families for many years and I understand these problems. Many former autistic children have

graduated from school and now have successful careers. A few
of them are in college and one even has a PhD, even though for
many years he was a child with very advanced autism.

Such children learn very quickly however. When they
are well guided, these children master material in a few weeks
that take a small child months or even years. Sometimes the
ghosts return and everything needs to be repeated from the
beginning. But, as time passes by there are less and less ghosts
until the child completely frees himself of them.

In Jack's case it was his grandmother's ghost, Mary's
mother in law. During the latter's lifetime they hated each other
very much and when Mary found out that she was the cause of
her son's illness, her feelings of rage were revived and intensified even more. In order to help her son whom she loved very
much and for whom she had sacrificed her entire life, she most
of all had to forgive her mother in law. Even though this choice
would have been very simple and straightforward for any other
person, for Mary it took a lot more effort than just caring for her
son. She started to forgive her mother in law however. When she
finished the forgiving process, her mother in law went away and
there were no other ghosts. However illnesses returned once in a
while when her mother in law returned from time to time. „Does
she return for Jack or for some other reason?" – I wondered. It
turned out that when Mary was still in middle school she attended a religious retreat. A priest from a big world, meaning city,
came to their tiny parish in a small village. He preached beautifully about the beneficial impact of suffering. He expounded
from the pulpit that only suffering ennobles a person, and
without suffering we are nothing. In Mary's life there was no
suffering so she felt empty and bad, because she wanted to be
good and noble. From that moment on for many weeks she
thought about what she had to do for her life to have greater

meaning, in the sense that the priest spoke about. Years passed by and she had forgotten about it. She got married, gave birth to her son... and here we return to the beginning of this story because at that moment suffering entered her life. Only when she started to work on herself she recalled that event. She understood that nobody but her attracted her son's illness. She had done this in order to demonstrate to herself that she was a noble person. Obviously, she didn't realize the original cause. When Jack was returning to health she always began to miss something. However, she didn't know what and she couldn't describe it in words. She didn't want Jack to be sick again, but she felt it wasn't alright for him to return to health. She felt torn inside and she couldn't handle that feeling. It was only when she recalled the priest's story did she understand that when Jack was returning to health, she felt less noble and unique. When her son was falling sick again, she felt alright again, even though consciously she wanted very much for him to be healthy. It was a vicious circle.

The program was still stronger than Mary and was boomeranging on her. Unfortunately, she needed to work on that issue herself, because nobody else could do that for her. Mary needed to first accept the situation that she had found herself in and think about what she wanted more. Only then would she receive what she desired. Mary up to that point desired two completely contrary things at the same time.

Perhaps, dear reader, you are asking yourself – „What about Jack? Doesn't Mary hurt him with her desire?" I don't think that she does. Jack certainly has a similar problem (program). Most likely he wanted to suffer. Such a timid, suffering soul doesn't know anything besides pain which it needs for growth. Perhaps it also had a strong desire to experience new forms of and increased suffering as well. Jack could also be a great soul that came to this world to help his mother get rid of an unhealthy desire which was based on a false premise. Perhaps that desire had already been impacting her for many incarnations. And each incarnation was harder and brought more suffering which was amplified by circumstances and family, in order to finally awaken her soul. Mary had a hard time accepting that all souls were beautiful and good. She did not understand that there were already many souls conscious of this and internally they were carrying, with dignity, a vision of beauty, good and perfection. Most people don't use what was initially given to them and instead they accept suffering or confusion voluntarily.

Where does this belief come from – the belief that there is nobility in suffering, and a need for suffering in general? In most people it comes from a mistaken interpretation of Jesus Christ's suffering and death. This need arose centuries ago. People who sympathized with Jesus' suffering only took into consideration the latter period of His life which ended with pain and His death on the cross. They completely forget that Jesus spent most of his life *after* Resurrection not before it. His death wasn't supposed to illustrate or glorify suffering. It's quite the opposite. Resurrection or in other words victory over death and therefore happiness, not suffering were the images that Jesus wanted to communicate.

Mary needed to understand that she came into this world to be a happy person – not a person who suffered, or was only happy through suffering. Another reason people suffer is that they are punishing themselves for „bad" deeds. This is a state the soul imposes on itself. More often than not this results from a lack of forgiveness. Sometimes people don't forgive themselves and others because they don't feel worthy of forgiveness. Ultimately many people hit themselves in the chest and say –

"Lord, I am not worthy to receive you" or „Through my fault, through my fault, through my most grievous fault". Feelings of guilt only strengthen the feelings of unworthiness. Many people can't forgive because they mistakenly think that this entails reconciliation or interaction with the person who hurt them. That is not true. We forgive not to free the person who hurt us from fault, but to free ourselves and at the same time the person who hurt us gains freedom as well. Would Jesus be able to rise from the dead if He couldn't forgive his torturers? Did He do this from generosity like many people think? Most of all, He was aware that without forgiveness He couldn't go any further, that He would be stuck in the world of dead.

Think dear reader. If you were in jail and had a chance to leave the prison would you resign from this chance just to hurt an enemy who also sits in there with you? Wouldn't it be better for both of you to take the chance to be free?

On another subject now... Many people resign from spiritual growth because they mistakenly belief that they would have to put aside the life they are currently leading. However you can improve yourself in spite of the situation you are currently in. You don't have to isolate yourself, wear special clothing or sit in a lotus position nonstop. That is what posers do because they think it would bring positive changes to their lives. In reality they are showing off to the world, emphasizing their distinctness, for better or even for worse, as they run away from life into so-called „meditation". I am not talking here about India where such behavior and clothing is a tradition, although even there many people do this not from heart, but to show off.

When you start having appropriate thoughts, many unnecessary things would automatically disappear from your life. You would resign from many things by yourself, because you won't need them anymore. This takes place in the same, painless way as occurs when you outgrow various toys. When you abandoned rattles, you started to play with cars or dolls. You entered the period from infancy to childhood with happiness, without losing anything. Together with this change different things started to interest you. However many people abhor change. They prefer to remain immature or sick forever (because they resist too much) rather than to change. When they give in, this process happens by itself and it's neither unpleasant nor painful. Basically, it's not the change that scares us, but the FEAR of what it brings. When we begin to take a closer look at it, the fear starts to disappear by itself. You just have to find the courage to do it.

THE GOAL OF LIFE

Have you ever wondered, dear reader, what is the true goal of your existence here on Earth? Sometimes people ask me to help them discover why they came to this world. It is then that I see how much misunderstanding and mistaken beliefs there are about this. They want me to help them discover the special mission they came to Earth to accomplish. In reality, the answer is very simple and moreover the same for everyone. The goal of your existence is to take care of matters related to your behavior and emotions with regards to people, places, things and situations. We came here, to start something, finish other things, clean up, eliminate and harmonize. We incorporate into life „something" that is connected to people, places and matters from the past, present and future. All of this is connected to your understanding of God.

Before I write more about this, I would like to remind you, that as souls you came here to learn, to experience, what it is like to BE, for example, stupid, jealous, naïve, heroic, a victim, a coward, a strong person, a big head, lazy-boned etc. In other words, you came to know various qualities, understand all the positives and negatives and experience the results of each your own.

One soul incarnated as a human may experience only one quality and then recognizing how tough is to live and *not be love*, return immediately to God. Other souls experience many of these qualities at the same time. Often they fall under the weight of all these qualities but, they still don't resign from further experiences (like Jack's mother who wanted to be noble at all costs).

However many people there are in this world (or, however many souls there are in human bodies in this world), that is how many people are experiencing different qualities in various configurations. We get so lost in our own experiences that we forget, *Who We Are in Essence*, we forget about our divine roots.

Therefore, our primary goal on Earth is to remind ourselves, *Who We Are in Essence* and not to identify with what we seem to be. We are not the experiences that we came here for, nor are we the thoughts, emotions, deeds or even the body we inhabit while we are here. Who are we then? We are our self, the divine spark, God's particle which lives deep inside each of us. That is exactly what we have to discover inside of us, on our own. Nobody, even the brightest priest, therapist, doctor, parent, friend or guru can do this for us. They won't achieve this for us.

I wrote before that the soul while leaving heaven, on the way to physicality puts on a few bodies like overalls, one on top of the other. A diver going under the water after putting on a diving suit doesn't stop being a human. It's the same with a soul coming down to Earth, after putting on a physical body. The soul doesn't stop being its Self, the Divine part in a human.

When we finally know, *Who We Are in Essence,* we would willingly return to God. That doesn't mean that we first have to die and leave Earth. It's about living here and now, with God and in God – consciously. When we begin to live according to this knowledge, we will discover that we are constantly connected to Him, and it's impossible to live without Him.

Deep inside we never forgot about it, all of us without exception, know that God is Almighty, All-Embracing, All-Pervading, and therefore that He is everywhere. There isn't a place where He wouldn't be. For some reason – maybe because of fear, laziness or the preference for the easy way out, we allowed ourselves to be convinced that He sits somewhere on a cloud in Heaven and watches us from there. That point of view is unreasonable because it assumes that God is separated from what He created.

It is like having our eyes closed while standing on a highway with many speeding cars and convincing ourselves that the cars are not there, because we can't see them. And we believe that because someone „smart" told us so.

You belong to God whether you realize it or not; and you depend on Him. You can pretend that is not the case. However, then you would be just like the person on the highway, at risk of unexpected accidents. When you come to understand this, you would open your eyes (it is what each person standing on the highway should do) and would no longer be faced with a multitude of adversities. You would know how to manage your fate.

If you drive, you know that while driving a car, most importantly, you need to know where you want to go and firmly keep your hands on the steering wheel. Otherwise, you won't get to your destination; instead you might get into an accident or have to pull over to the side of the road. Many people do exactly the opposite. They race through life with their eyes closed, without a goal, or they might even pass the steering wheel over to someone else because it's more comfortable for them that way. Then, they complain to God that they got lost, that they collided with something they didn't want to collide with. And, this collision with fate could be very painful.

We don't have to go through life alone, there is always someone to accompany us, someone who would help us to understand, and guide us in the right direction. You should be aware that simultaneously, each one of us has our own path to travel. You have yours, and your loved ones have theirs. By deluding yourself into thinking that anyone can do anything for you, you become helpless, until the moment you wake up and realize that you are losing your focus on your path.

It may seem that all people, without regard to skin color, desire the same thing – love, appreciation, security, and fulfillment. Why don't they strive for it in the same way? Why don't they achieve what they desire? Why are some people as poor as a church mouse while others live in the lap of luxury? Why are some people who have everything unhappy, grumpy, resigned and unable to enjoy their possessions while other people who have nothing are fulfilled and happy?

We fear spiritual growth, because we mistakenly belief that all we have, we will have to give up and live in poverty. We have many mistaken associations. If God wanted us to have nothing, use nothing, and abuse ourselves, why would He create all these beautiful things in the world? That would be unreasonable. Simultaneously, we can have all things beautiful and luxurious while developing personally. We just have to fix our mistaken thinking.

Many people claim that the world is unfair and only death is fair. If this were true then a person who lived impeccably, went to church, prayed, fasted and was a good father or mother would depart the world to so-called heaven. However, quite often this doesn't happen. Why wonder around in despair, not knowing what to do with yourself? The problem lies in our mistaken thinking, in our perceptions. I write more about this later.

In order to better illustrate this I would use the example of a student, a very sick person whose father asked me to help her. She was physically sick, but she also had a few ghosts. In my practice, quite often the people who ask for help for someone else want to „protect" that person from the knowledge I presented in the book *Possessed by Ghosts* – knowledge which could heal them immediately. This was one such instance. When a game of Chinese whispers exhausted both my assistant, who was assigned to this case and I, we told the girl's father if his daughter didn't call for herself he shouldn't call us anymore, because it was a waste of our time and his money. We could tell from the tone of his voice that something inside him was boiling up. However, perhaps after he had given it some thought, his daughter called a few days later. My intuition suggested I should talk to her personally although that rarely happens. She prepared in advance for our conversation, as though for an exam. She talked a lot; she didn't give me a chance to say anything. At the onset she said that she knew she had ghosts, she had read my book and thanks to it she now knew why her sister had committed suicide. She claimed that she was very sick and the doctors didn't think she would live much longer. She talked about how many doctors treated her without success and how many therapy sessions led by the best psychologists, and psychiatrists, she had gone through. When I was finally able to interrupt her, I told her that I would lead the ghosts away, but in order for the therapy to be successful she needed to cooperate with my assistant and I.

At the same time, I wanted to ask her a few questions. „Of course, I have already gone through many therapy sessions so I know what this is like" – she said cheerfully. First I suggested she think about what benefits she derives from being sick and list them. „What do you mean by benefits, Mrs. Pratnicka. I am sick for real, many tests have confirmed that" – she said. „But I don't negate this at all. I would like to find the cause of your sickness and it's necessary to look at what benefits this sickness brings you and what disadvantages it causes you. We can take care of the disadvantages later. But for now, what, benefits do you get? Is it your parents' attention and love, the opportunity to feel sorry for yourself, your friends' sympathy, what is it?" – I asked. She understood what I meant and she started to list the benefits. Together we counted twenty seven benefits. Here are some of them: she was pursuing a major which her parents forced her to and which she didn't like. She could attend lectures when she wanted, or sleep in as much as she wanted, even when her parents knew that she would be late. When she had a problem with any of her professors, she just explained to them that she didn't feel well. Even for exams she enjoyed advantages over other students. And, she was permitted to take time off from school without any problems. She had already taken time off a few times and nobody held it against her.

Other benefits were that she didn't have to get married, have kids or work. In considering her advanced age, the appropriate time for that had already passed a long time ago. She also didn't have to help with household chores and in general didn't do much in her surroundings. She could hang out with her friends as much as she wanted and if she wasn't in the mood for that she could cancel without notice. She was listing them out for a few more minutes and when she was finished she was very proud that she had found so many benefits and expected me to praise her. However, I told her that until the benefits from being sick were exceeded by the disadvantages of being sick, I wouldn't be able to do anything for her. „You have to want the change in your life. I can only support you in that" – I said. „You have to understand one thing. Nobody can live your life for you. Not me, not your parents, not anyone else. You claim that your life in this world is slowly coming to an end. Do you want to continue senselessly wasting your time, especially knowing that the ghosts that are with you certainly won't let you pass to the other side after your death?"

„Subconsciously you told yourself that you had benefits from being sick. However, each one of us, including you, comes to this world to act, experience, learn, and not to play games and „wisely" slink away from what we came to do in this world. If you don't want to study, then don't study. The world would not come to the end as a result. Or study what you like, what you would be passionate about. If you don't want to get married and have kids, then don't do it. You can live however you like, and nobody, including your parents, can forbid you from doing that. This is your life and only you are responsible for it. You have the right to constantly try new things, change or create, and yet what do you do? Instead of standing up to your parents, you escape into sickness and it seems you see this as the easy way. However, your „wisdom" would end at the moment of death. If you die now, you would go to the other world empty handed and without any achievements. Is this what your soul desires? In the face of death, everything you find attractive now, you would have to leave, otherwise this thing would keep you among the living and you would suffer. The fact that ghosts are next to you isn't an accident. They come only to people who they are similar to. When we change, we stop being „attractive" to them. When they have no chance for existence next to us they leave us much easier. And, after I lead them away, they won't return. The cause is not in the ghosts, but in you. Whatever the cause, it attracts them like a magnet, keeps them attached to you and they won't let go. I lead ghosts away every day, but they have the right to want to stay. They have free will and they could take advantage of that. You also have free will, and your task is to ensure that you do not attract them again after they have been led away. Even if the ghosts don't want to leave you still have a responsibility to object to their desire – to possess you".

As she hung up she was lost in thought, absent. Honestly, I was resigned. Even if I cleansed her nonstop, day and night there was little I could do if she didn't desire good health. A moment later her father called asking, what I had found out because his daughter didn't want to tell him anything. I said that I heard what I had already known, and we had told him about it multiple times in the past – not only the ghosts were responsible for her sickness, but also his daughter as well. The girl never called me again.

After some time her father called me again. He claimed that his daughter had changed dramatically. I said that lately besides checking in on her, I didn't do much work with her, because there were already no more ghosts around her. The change could have resulted from his daughter finding the courage to change as I had guided her to. He couldn't believe it was possible for one conversation to cause so many positive changes, since she was treated by many specialists before and nothing had helped. „Apparently, she finally grew up to face her life" – I said. When a person is ready, big changes could appear in their life, even after hearing only one sentence.

It may seem that this case was very unique, perhaps too extreme. However, it's enough to have one or two benefits to fall seriously ill. Most sick people want to be sick and take full advantage of it, but simultaneously they want to be healthy and not suffer. However one preempts the other, there is no intermediate state. In order to be healthy, one has to find the benefits that sickness brings and think about how to achieve those benefits while being healthy.

Many people may think that each case is different, that it doesn't work that way in their life. That is mistaken thinking however. The faster we wake up, the faster we would be able to change what we don't like, and we could change absolutely anything.

BROADENING YOUR PERSPECTIVE

When you look at yourself from the perspective of your physical body and that is the only reality that you know, it is as if you were looking at the world around you through the window of a ground floor apartment in the building you live in. The reality that you picture is always what your ego perceives it to be, it is completely related to your personal perceptions and beliefs. Your understanding of life is limited by how your ego perceives and interprets the world.

A consciousness looking out a window from the lowest floor has a different view to that available on higher floors. It believes only what it sees and it doesn't arise in its consciousness the thought that something more, beyond the reality which it looks at every day could exist. It disbelieves people living on the higher floors could see more than it does. You are in a better situation. The fact that you are reading this book proves that.

There are many people who completely „board up" their

windows thinking that they don't need any knowledge or they place a television set where the window should be, mistakenly thinking that with the help of television set they would gain knowledge. But knowledge, as I wrote previously, is not everything. Knowledge needs to turn into wisdom, and this can only be gained by experiencing – our own experiencing, not other people's. Furthermore, theoretical knowledge, no matter how advanced, is never sufficient. For each gained aspect of knowledge you need to use it in practice and learn from the mistakes you make, sometimes during numerous experiences. You can certainly gain knowledge otherwise, but you would still lack wisdom. And wisdom you gain slowly. Sometimes easily gained mental knowledge has to be transferred to the emotional sphere, so that it could reach the subconscious mind. Only then would it be consolidated forever. At that point you would have achieved wisdom with a big W. In spite of appearances, on the physical plane there is currently a great lack of wisdom, even though humanity as a whole has a lot of knowledge.

Some people may say that they have free will and thus the right not see and hear. They are so sure about the reality of their world that they won't consider the possibility of the existence of something greater than their own „I" in terms of their physical body. That is why you often don't understand other people, sometimes you don't even understand yourself, because you only look from the perspective which you see, which you are aware of. You feel you are the best among people who live on the same floors as you, (who are on the same level of consciousness as you) and you only hang out with people like that.

Don't condemn yourself, because you could always climb higher and see whatever people living on higher floors see. You only have to want that. Who knows, maybe you would find it breathtaking? You would wonder why you didn't want to see all of that before. And on each higher floor you would see more and more. However, even while living on a higher floor you could have a distorted view. It all depends on how clean your windows are. If your windows are clean then your view would be unrestricted. However, glass is often tainted by mistaken beliefs. While moving on to a higher level you often carry over your beliefs from the previous floor and replicate the mistakes you make in perceptions. You have to be ready to revise any beliefs, to sanitize them. On each higher floor your range of perceptions would broaden. You would be more conscious of broader and broader perspectives – in addition to what you had seen before there would be a new range added. The main goal is lucidity of perception – clean windows, not covered by cultural, family or other beliefs.

In the past, people commonly believed that the Earth was flat. This belief was adopted by people who had knowledge, in other words the „omniscient" priests. They did this to keep the uneducated society in submission. I write more about that in the chapter „Fall of Civilization". People were afraid to walk too far from their homes because they believed that they could fall into an abyss, to hell. It was the same with boats. People claimed that if boats drifted too far, they would fall off the edge of the world or be eaten by dragons. This type of deceptive belief limited people so much that they didn't see the need to search for greater knowledge or understanding. This was created by only one idea, overblown to an extortionate level. That idea was the image of the devil. It created great ignorance and superstition which filled people with fear and paralyzed their actions. Next were the tricks of priests' about an angry, punishing God. Fearful, simple people fell for this. In the past such attitudes and beliefs filled people with fear and worry. It's no different today, except for the subject of fear changing. However, even now for many people the idea of the devil is still alive and influences their attitudes.

A few years ago I was invited on a catholic television program to participate in an on-air group discussion. During the discussion someone said something to the effect that the devil is the main reason for every evil. I said that it's very easy to blame the devil for everything, just as it was done in a past with scapegoats. I added that the devil didn't exist, and really only lived in people's consciousness. Several people on the panel strongly disagreed with me. So I quoted Pope John Paul II's words to validate this position. During his visit to the United States in 1999 Pope John Paul II clearly said that hell and the devil were only metaphors expressing a state of existence without God. The participants in the discussion jumped on me then, incensed, pointing to the Bible and its inspired writings.

As you can see, dear reader, even today during these „enlightened" times people who desire the maintenance of the status quo at all costs hold on to their old beliefs even after the Pope himself denies them. What they built their life on is not sustainable and realizing that appalls them. Many people have the mistaken belief that they are better, unique. That is why they have an illusion that they would go to Heaven, to God as a reward. Since there is no hell, and everyone has an equal chance then what is their uniqueness based on? Such people have to manage their overblown spiritual ego which despises other humans. This type of ego is a lot harder to tame than the small, self-focused ego, which you deal with on a daily basis and which is mostly displayed through selfishness and indifference to others.

As I mentioned before, education is just knowledge – obtained and taught. It only gains value when it's turned into wisdom. Without wisdom, knowledge leads people to nonsense.

Knowledge is needed but knowledge alone is not enough. By relying solely on knowledge we would only reach a certain level of growth after which we would hit our heads against the ceiling and we would be unable to go beyond that level. That is why there is so much rubbish in the media and there is no one to correct it. And if people do come forward to correct it, most likely they would be publically mocked (the same as occurred in my case with hell). This makes it harder to promulgate the truth. People who run media companies haven't grown to deal with the truth yet, and they mistakenly belief in old patterns. They resemble the former priests who wanted to rule over the ignorant masses.

What great courage heroes and visionaries like Columbus, Magellan and other discoverers had. Despite talk of the devil and superstitions people, they were brave enough to change basic beliefs during their times (for example: that the earth was flat). They led humanity in its entirety to change its beliefs with their relentless faith. Certainly, they also learned from their mistakes, but thanks to those mistakes their horizons were broadened, and through them the horizons of other people as well. Ultimately, they and others crossed the borders of the world of illusion, borders of our own beliefs. They proved that the truth was different and that the idea of the sun ostensibly circling the Earth was an illusion. There were many such great people. Each of them acted with a Higher Consciousness. It is this Higher Consciousness that leads people to understand that no set of beliefs or attitudes could be fixed. If a person is to grow and live successfully then he has to change his views and beliefs. And when it is time for serious changes (as applies now), then the existing worldview would also have to change. There is no other path.

People who don't find the courage to change would

suffer unnecessarily. However, it's sufficient for each person to create large groups which would accept specific ideas and others would then follow them, not even knowing why they were taking that course.

THE PROJECTOR

Even one person in a million doesn't feel free enough to live in the way he perceives to be appropriate on the inside. That is because when a man entered physicality he gave in to the opinion of the external world, and consequently he gave in to the beliefs of the people closest to him (his parents, family, neighbors, etc.). And, even long after attaining adulthood, a man would still listen to the external world instead of pursing and finding his own true, inner being and acting solely according to its suggestions. He ignores the senses or feelings he receives from the inside, not believing that these suggestions are his truths. And when he doesn't listen to his inner being, that is, *Who He Is in Essence*, he perceives that he is only what he notices with his own eyes that constantly prove to him that he is only a physical human being that exists only in a material world. He gives in to the crippling power of illusion (hypnosis) to the point that he doesn't even suspect its existence and the power with which it influences his life.

Such a person suffers as a result and things don't work out for him. But he doesn't do anything about it. He claims that his experiences are preordained, by fate, that it is all inevitable. This is why he surrenders to such reality. And, in order to sweeten his tragic life he deludes himself that at some point death will rescue him from this captivity, that he will leave this world and enter that hazy place which is commonly referred to as heaven.

However dear reader, this is not the kind of destiny that is written in man's life plan. The difficulties that we experience, which we can't manage, result from not listening to our own inner being. Most people don't know that they have that inner being, they don't listen to the Higher I. The lives of many people are too turbulent for them to be quiet for a moment and hear their quiet voice that comes from within. However, in order for life to change for the better, we have to find our true self that dwells within. Otherwise, you will always feel bad. And if you are feeling bad now, after death you will feel the same, if not a lot worse.

Know that by obeying your inner being, your Self, and expressing life in a way that you instinctively, intuitively feel, is fundamentally the only way to build the foundation for your life. If everyone knew this then everyone's life would change dia-metrically. Most people blame the world instead, because it doesn't work as it should, from their perspective. The problem is not rooted in a „bad", cruel world however; rather it is due to your constantly looking to the outside. You are not ready to listen to your inner nature. Most people think that mistaken beliefs and distorted ideas all come from the outside world. They are wrong. They are rooted inside of them, but they don't realize that because they don't have access to their inside. That is caused by irrational, unadvised knowledge gained in this life or from previous incarnations. This unadvised knowledge confronts the soul's truth and the soul forgets *Who It Is in Essence*. This is what prevents the soul from further growth. This is how people drift further and further away from God, the universe and from functioning correctly. I write more about that in the chapter „Fall of the Lost Civilization".

Because you don't look far enough into your inner being, your thoughts become obsessive, unhealthy, and your soul gradually more disturbed. If you think (feared) that you would lose something, become sick, get into an accident, get robbed, or wouldn't succeed in some endeavor then your failure is guaranteed. You always achieve success in realizing your reality, in this case; your „success" is expressed through your failure. First the thought appears. Your experience is always secondary. A thought that comes, for example about an accident, would be the umpteenth such thought, and not an original thought that causes the accident. You feared it multiple times, often thought about it and as a result you experienced it. Do you understand how this works now? The universe always ensures your success, but you pick whether you would achieve „success" through success or through failure.

Many people think that the problems they deal with originate from relations with other people. They mistakenly think that they could free themselves from the problem (and be happier) if their husband, daughter, wife, boss, or neighbor changed. Other people only push the button on a problem they are ready to overcome, but they don't accept that it exists in themselves.

I would now try to explain to you how this works, dear reader. All of your beliefs and habits lie inside of you and whether they are good or bad qualities, you project them unto others. „How is that possible?" – You may ask. Well, God knew that you wouldn't be able to and wouldn't want to look at them, on the inside. To make this possible or easier, God created the world such that each quality you have inside of you, you see in others. If you have „kindness" in whatever form inside of you, then you would see it in everyone. Moreover, people give you (pay you back) this kindness, proving to you that you have it inside you. This also works the other way around. If you have „evil" inside of you, something that you don't accept, then you would see it in others, and they would show you (pay you back) „evil", thereby proving its existence. It's not hard to validate this rule. Notice how a person, who is not aware of his „bad" deeds, would never be punished. If he is punished, it means he carried a feeling of guilt inside him. That feeling of guilt demanded punishment.

Overall, this works like a mirror. You reflect in the other person, as in a mirror, but more often than not, you are not aware of that happening. You only see in the other person what you have deep inside of you. You would feel this inside, because you are constantly comparing yourself to others. But two identical people don't exist. How could you compare something that doesn't have an equivalent? That is similar to comparing finger prints and studying which one is prettier while each is simply different from the other. Perhaps, you won't agree with me. However, answer for yourself how often you rely on others rather than trust in yourself? You would obviously claim that it's not the same, but in reality you don't respect yourself, because you don't like yourself and constantly blame yourself for things that happen in your life. How often are you dishonest with yourself? And then people around you pay you back with the same treatment, because they are your mirror.

It would be a lot easier for you to understand this principle, the functioning of this basic law, with the example of a projector in a movie theater. The picture and the source of the picture are located in two different places. The projector is located on the back of a room, and the picture is shown to you in front. You also have such an inner projector. You project unto others what you have inside of you. Often you do not like what you see when you look at the images that your soul's camera displays. You become resentful, sometimes angry and full of blame and determine it is best to change what you see. You would develop the misplaced desire to make changes on the outside, and start to fight and attack. Sometimes you don't feel strong enough to let others see this. Instead, you hold a grudge on the inside, resulting in resentfulness and dejection.

Both ways are painful. You feel that way because you don't realize what is bothering you are the qualities which don't work for you anymore. These are qualities which you can't identify with any longer. Hence you can't handle it anymore and want to change it at all costs. What happens to people who you direct your blame towards? They react in various ways. They may react with puzzlement, sometimes with agitation or they may even feel offended. They may also be unaware of what you mean exactly, because what you don't like is inside of you, and not in them. Often your complaints play on the other person's feelings of guilt, and as a result that person struggles with that challenge.

Even if others want to help you, it doesn't matter how hard they try, there is nothing they can do because it is not their responsibility. Besides that, people who you blame have their own experiences (sometimes painful) to address. Therefore, it's hard for them to notice what you need if you don't openly speak about it. Do you remember what I wrote about basic needs? Everyone has the same basic needs, but not everyone realizes that. This gives rise to grudges. In order to change that you would have to take a deep look inside, a closer look at the foundations of your resentment towards yourself and discover the cause. Only then would you stop projecting them unto others.

If you want to change what you don't like in yourself, you have made a good decision because it demonstrates that you have matured and you are ready for changes. However if you want to make changes in someone else it would be like wiping clean, fixing, or restructuring a picture that is showing on a screen in a movie theater. You would fix and fix again, you would fight with the picture, and the picture just wouldn't change. The source of the picture doesn't come from the screen you are looking at, but from the projector inside of you. In order to make the changes you want to see, you have to change the film in the projector. Understand that the conflict is in you, in your soul, and not in the other person.

After one of my lectures, a large group of people came up to me, asking me to help them impact positive change on their boss. The list of his vices was very long. He cared only for the company and not for the needs of his employees. They didn't complain about poor conditions because they had gotten used to them. They were most bothered by their boss' erratic, cold-hearted behavior. „We have to provide for our families" – they said in unison – „without regard for conditions, we have to work there. We can't look for other jobs because this is the only company in that area and our boss takes advantage of that".

First, I talked to them in a group and later with each person individually. I convinced them that from that moment on, no matter what the situation and their boss' behavior, they needed to forgive him and think about him as a good, caring person who looked after their needs. Some of them understood that and right away started to follow that advice. It turned out that by acting together with a change in attitude, their boss changed dramatically. He started to transform into the new image they had of him. He offered them many benefits and they even received salary increases. And, the change in their boss' behavior only impacted the group of people who started to view him positively. Those who „didn't believe in such nonsense" were doing much worse in the workplace. It seemed, as much as the first group of people were doing much better, the second group of people who „didn't believe in such nonsense" were doing worse. They felt that not only their boss, but also the entire world was conspiring against them. Even though they had clear proof of this wonderful law of the universe at work, they didn't do anything aligned to it. They preferred that I „cast a spell on their boss". They didn't want to do anything themselves. After some time (around a year) I was in that area again and everyone showed up. One group showed up to thank me, and the second group to complain that they were on the edge of a breakdown. And, it would be like that until they woke up and came to understand that by changing their state of mind they would automatically change their own life.

Dear reader, if you are in a similar situation maybe you should try this for yourself and see how it works for you? If you are not ready yet, then try to observe your loved ones when one resents the other. Take a look at the person who is more embittered and blames the other. Don't his words almost entirely pertain to his own vices and not necessarily to that of the person to whom these words are directed? Perhaps, that person doesn't fight, but gossips, judges and/ or points out the mistakes of others. That is also a sign that he has on the very top of his psyche a quality which he doesn't accept. He is ready for a change, but first he has to overcome in himself that which „eats" away at him from the inside.

When you get to know and understand how this process works, you would be grateful to others. Every time someone gets you upset instead of being angry at that person, you would think about what the situation has conveyed to you. Ask yourself this question – „What do I have to process inside me (accept, understand, forgive, etc.) so that something like this would stop affecting me negatively". Instead of enemies, you would only have friends around you. You would come to understand that people who stir up anger have a very important role to play in your life. You met them so that you could understand your own lesson.

Everyone should be open to new information and knowledge, even when it threatens their current beliefs and consequently their identity. Unfortunately, in today's society only a few people recognize this. If most people did, there wouldn't be as many wars and varied disputes, whether on an individual, family, national or global level. I think that this happens because people are afraid of change and are precondi- tioned for a static identity. Instead of thinking through a given issue, they usually react with insult and fear. They incorrectly assume discovering that they are mistaken means they have suffered defeat. But, recognizing their own mistake should be celebrated as though it were the greatest possible gift, because it would lift them to a new, higher level of understanding and consciousness. And that is something everyone should strive for deeply in their soul.

Too often we hide ourselves away from the world, in- dulge in complacency and in the illusion that we are better, greater or smarter than others. Jesus from Nazareth said: „Woe to you you who are full". Not because being happy and enjoying life is wrong, but because complacency closes us in like a shell.

It stops the growth of our soul. When we are doing well or quite well, then we stop growing. We think – „Why should I bend over backwards to change things. Things are good the way they are now". However the universe is like a river where everything is in constant motion. When we are stagnant life starts looking for opportunities to awaken us, sometimes in painful ways. That is why people go bankrupt, get into accidents and go through other tragedies. It is supposed to remind them that they stopped being constructive and they stopped growing.

On the other hand, some people fear that they are worse, less intelligent or are worth less than others. If they looked inside, into their Self, they would notice or sense that as souls we are all the same, that we are all in the same school. (I write more about this later). We all came here to experience, and each experience whatever it might be, is only a lesson for us. And is one lesson better than the other? It could be asked – „Is mathematics better than physics or chemistry?" Understand, dear reader, souls don't have a sex or skin color.

Most of all people are a soul (and not a body that has a soul). Unfortunately, we don't always realize that. Otherwise, we would know that our soul is the essence of our life; it's the main participant in our daily life. It is present at our most trivial and our loftiest thoughts, it stores all that we think about and feel. It carries this record with it at all times. It doesn't only take this to the other world with it, but it also brings it back (in future lives) to earth. You don't believe in a power of your soul? Do you realize, dear reader, that without a soul your body has nothing to keep it alive? A body only functions when it has a soul, a body is a soul's servant, making it possible for the soul to have experiences. A soul can experience, even when it doesn't have a body, the same cannot be said about a body. This doesn't mean that a body is not important. However you must always remember the soul. Perhaps you don't understand this fully, because you forgot *Who You Are in Essence*. Hence you mainly identify with your body, and this causes the soul to forget who is it and as a result it falls lower and lower. It becomes a home for urges, desires and obsessive thoughts. As a result you become like a volcano, boiling with various (most often contradictory) feelings, emotions and reactions. These stay in hiding waiting to erupt under pressure. This all causes you to be tense and feel trapped. You can't find focus and you are unable to determine whether what you are doing is right or not. When you identify with your Higher Self, your soul finds a direction, knows where it came from and where it is going. Your thoughts and feelings become clear, calm, and life becomes straight-forward.

No matter how your body currently looks (maybe it is old, sick, stoop-shouldered or paralyzed), your soul is as beautiful and as powerful as any other soul in the universe. Always remember this and don't be misled by the physical appearance of other people. When you understand this fully, you would start to see and feel the difference. You would no longer feel worse or better than others. You would get rid of the burden caused by the desire to keep up with others or exalting yourself over others. This would also free you of the belief that you should own people or things. This knowledge would strengthen you.

But, how could you strengthen yourself if you are not in the habit of taking a deep look inside your soul? It is only when you do that would you be able to change your beliefs and views, which in turn would change your future. If the world around you, your present reality, doesn't give you an inner sense of happiness and satisfaction then the solution is obvious. Make a decision to change. A conscious decision to change your beliefs would move you to higher levels of consciousness where you would recognize what is real and what is an illusion. Know, however, that for some people this is a very difficult task, a very hard lesson, which they may be unable to appreciate at that moment. This doesn't mean that you have to be stuck in one place and be in the same situation they are in. Find the courage and get started today. When you do, things in your life would change for the better and others would follow in your footsteps.

YOUR BELIEFS

You came to this world with set perceptions gained through your soul's evolution and experiences from previous incarnations. Therefore, you were born with your own built-in program, akin to what applies with computers (your unconscious mind stores and runs this program). It consists of your basic system of beliefs by which your mind works.

You interpret everything based on that program – every phenomenon. And from the moment you appear in this world you continue to build on that set of beliefs. It would include any and all messages that were ever directed at you. All your childhood experiences, for example: the way your parents treated you, you carry over to your adulthood. You grew up relying on what your parents and you also learned from the other people around you. They were the ones who taught you to repeat the same mistakes that were passed down to them by their parents and before them by their grandparents, and before them great grandparents, etc. You may hold this against them, but you need to realize that each experience is filtered through the pre-existing, set program that you came to this world with. It's built on a solid foundation, because it's based on all of your previous experiences.

It doesn't matter who, where and how you got confused and imbued false truths about yourself and the world. It is important to recognize that you have been continuously making the same cardinal and compulsive mistakes that were passed down from generation to generation. I describe how this occurs in the chapter „Fall of the Lost Civilization".

Do you intend to teach the next generation the same mistakes you were taught? Maybe you are ready to change things for the better? There has to exist a better way of life. And one does exist. When you read the chapter „Life in the Lost Civilization" you would be convinced that in the past, at a very early age, people were taught how to successfully harness and take full advantage of the capabilities of the human mind. This point is particularly emphasized because people claim that if you lived without this you could get lost. They studied how each individual feels and whether they have the correct perception of reality. They did this because they knew that this would define how people reacted to reality when presented with it. Happiness, success, love, peace of mind or anything else that captures the ideal of the greatest good is felt deep in your being, as a continuous increasing flow of life's energy. When you feel the emotions of happiness, faith in yourself and success, you would feel like you are being flooded with life's happiness.

Today, just as in ancient times, everyone desires the best possible Life. However, false programs often slow you down and you are unable to take full advantage of the gifts you encounter along your path. You destroy God given abilities and allow yourself to suffer – through concern, fear, self-condemnation, and even self-hatred. By the same token you divest yourself of life's force and fail to notice, or rather don't want to receive gifts, which constantly pour in from God, our Creator. The fact that you turn down these gifts is not the worst thing. If you want to suffer, please suffer, that is your choice. However, when you turn down the gift of life from God, you also embrace the seeds of death. The seeds of death are perfectly masked, in the same way a swamp or quicksand is camouflaged. When you find yourself near them, they initially seem insignificant, but they suck you in more and more intensively with each passing moment, and ultimately consume you, claiming you completely. As I have already mentioned, suffering doesn't benefit you at all. If you suffer here on earth, then you would also suffer in the netherworld, in other words, after the death of your physical body you would suffer, and the force of the suffering would be intensified. When you decide on a happy life here, this in turn would lead to great happiness after the shedding of your physical body.

Everything entering your life is the result of your thoughts and beliefs. If you think that the world is bad then you would experience such in the world. Someone who lives in the same conditions as you are may feel and experience something absolutely different. External experiences are nothing but a true reflection (a mirror) of what is happening inside of you. Recall how the workers were able to change their working conditions by changing their attitude towards their boss. And, those workers who kept to their old beliefs had no influence over anything in the workplace. A deep understanding of this truth could lead you to change. When you take full responsibility for the effects of your actions you gain complete power over your life.

Therefore, I hope that when you are not doing well, you

stop blaming others for that state of affairs and know that you, and nobody else, made the decision for things to be like that. You are the only person who can hurt or cheat you. If you don't like what you are experiencing then work on your beliefs.

In a critical situation, you would be under the impression that you were a poor, passive victim. However it's not like that. On a deeper level of consciousness you attract everything that you experience to yourself, good as well as bad. „How is this possible?" – You may ask – „ Nobody would consciously want something bad to happen to themselves". That's true – consciously no. But your subconscious beliefs push you in that direction. I meet many people who don't want to accept that they attracted to themselves, through their own wishes, the negative events they are going through. I suppose that many readers won't agree with me on this either. How could someone possibly want to be robbed, hurt or raped; more so, since unpleasant events occur regularly for quite a few people. While seeing how such persons suffer you may find it difficult to understand why they would want to suffer even more. It turns out that they would. When I speak to such persons for the first time and I try to find out what brings them all these misfortunes, I am met with disbelief. However, after a few glimpses into themselves, these people are amazed and happy at the same time when they discover that they attracted the unpleasant events to themselves. Obviously, it was never brought on by conscious thoughts, but rather by deeply hidden feelings of guilt. In my practice I have met tons of cases like this. Sometimes people who are involved in the same accident reach out to me. Two persons unknown to each other get into accident at an intersection. An accident? Misfortune? Could you have influence over that as well? What influence could you have? It turns out that you do have influence over an accident. An accident is a form of punishment you attract to yourself. Feelings of guilt could certainly have various sources, but most frequently they are – feeling of guilt due to betrayals, lies and all sorts of fraud – often tax related. In such situations, ghosts are attracted to such the feelings of guilt and ... misery is ready to step in. I wrote about this before, but I would reiterate here – feelings of guilt always attract punishment.

Until you stop holding on to these destructive beliefs and heal these tendencies, you would be constantly attracting difficult or sometimes even tragic situations. More often than not, with certainty, you would blame an unjust fate, God and your surroundings, but when you learn that you are the cause, you would discover with happiness that you are not the victim of the situation but rather its perpetrator. And as the perpetrator you have a choice. You could decide to change the beliefs you hold which aren't useful anymore. Because, if you know that you create „evil", then you have the same power to create „goodness", of every kind.

With every misfortune there exists an individual reason that satisfies an internal need. Even if you have a need to punish yourself for some act, that is your choice, and it is not punishment for sins. You have to realize that. I could already hear outraged voices – „What about punishment for our sins?" From a higher perspective, in other words, from the soul's perspective, sin in your current understanding doesn't exist. That which you call a sin, is merely human inability to recognize what causes mistaken concepts to take root within us, in other words, beliefs that lead to misfortunes.

All beliefs I would call hidden desires. And desires should be fulfilled, as I describe in the example below. Note though, there are also other reasons why they should be realized. You would find out why this is very important when we cover, in detail, life in the causal world. From a higher perspective, fulfillment of your desires, no matter what they are (even the innermost desires which are disgraceful or unacceptable in other people's eyes) means taking off your blinkers. As long as you desire something you are unable to understand the nature of it, because your desire obscures your vision. Only the fulfillment of your desire leads you to understanding,… because most often (in the case of false desires) it brings disenchantment. The word disenchantment is interesting and contains a very positive aspect. To disenchant is like turning down enchantment or an illusion involving another matter. Therefore, the realization of a desire ultimately offers you self-discovery and your soul's positive growth. Each earthly desire has such great power because it's a reflection (pale, but still a reflection) of what you were experiencing in the higher worlds, in other words, a reflection of divine desires.

So many people on earth suffer by divesting themselves of any desires, and if they already have desires they don't fulfill them because they think that their desires are bad. It's true that you should free yourself from earthly desires for divine desires. This is not about mortifying yourself however; rather it is about experiencing and understanding desires, so that they fade away by themselves, because you don't need them anymore.

One day I met my old friend Brian who had been obsessed with sex for quite some time. He had a very strong desire to participate in an orgy. This thought haunted him. He couldn't sleep, work or enjoy his family. Sometimes when he couldn't handle it anymore, he escaped into alcohol, but he knew that didn't resolve the issue, it only postponed his suffering. When we met, he was on the edge of a breakdown. I advised him that for therapeutic purposes he should fulfill his desire by using an escort agency's services. I didn't persuade him to engage in laxity or lasciviousness, I meant for him to see whether his desire was worth losing his wife and separation from his children... I hit home, because he jumped when he heard that. „Are you crazy" – he screamed – „I have a loving wife and children. I would have to be a rascal to fulfill such a capricious desire". „Perhaps you would be a rascal" – I said – „but you would free yourself from your suffering, from the obsession which has taken over your entire life. Who knows, maybe you would once again be a normal husband, father and boss. Presently, you are unable to fulfill any of these roles, because a compulsion controls you, without fulfilling that compulsion you are unable to function. Maybe when you see what this is really like, you would return to normalcy." We said goodbye to each other. He didn't call me for a long time. Finally he called and at the beginning he asked – „How did you know that this would so radically help me?" „From ghosts, who like you, didn't fulfill their earthly dreams" – I said. „As you know I deal with ghosts on a daily basis. If you were a rascal by nature, then without a doubt you would visit prostitutes every day and nothing would stop you from doing that. Since you never made a decision to do so, because you are a decent guy, then one visit won't demoralize you. You needed to find the courage to fulfill your desire, to stop influencing you so strongly"

Here is the story about his experiences – „When you advised me about what to do, I thought that you were nuts. It was unreal to me. However I found the courage to try it. I guess I expected a miracle after visiting a prostitute. I thought I would receive from her, something wonderful; however, I can't even describe what happened. It was as though I was making love to a corpse, without even the slightest bit of sensation. She was just waiting for me to be done and pay her. I was so disgusted that I wanted to shoot myself. Imagine dreaming about something for years and later this vision is transformed into a debacle. I came to the conclusion that I probably got the wrong girl and I should try one more time. I went to a different escort agency. This time I got 2 girls at the same time. The second time it was even worse. Everything was the same, except this time it was multiplied by two. This healed me. Perhaps I expected the girls would awaken love, inspiration and passion in me. I understand now that all of that was already inside of me, and not on the outside. Now I appreciate my wife and believe me, I am really happy. Thank you from the bottom of my heart. Do you think I should tell my wife about it?" „I don't know if that is a good idea. Perhaps you can tell her, but only if your wife would be able to understand this. Otherwise, you would hurt her feelings" – I said. „Do whatever you like, but you won't gain anything from this confession and you could lose a lot. If you are feeling guilty a „confession" like this won't free you from it. If you don't forgive yourself and tell your wife, she could suffer to the end of her life. This is a very sensitive matter and everything depends on her level of understanding".

Many people think that a debasing life is something good and worthy, for which they would receive a reward in heaven one day. However, when their physical body dies, they notice that their further existence consists of yet escalated debasement, and there is no „reward". They feel greatly deceived then. This causes, among other things, a great number of ghosts not to go to the other side. Some want to tell their loved ones on earth about it. „Change your life, don't be fooled like I was" – they scream, most often unheard by their loved ones. Others want to take revenge for their naivety, on the basis that others should suffer because they suffer. Yet others seek revenge on those persons from who they acquired these beliefs.

Most such problems involve unfulfilled sexual desires

(this is the number one reason ghosts remain among the living), but it could also pertain to any other, unrealized desire. Know, dear reader, your desires don't go away with the death of your physical body. Many people hide their desires and when they die, their desires demand fulfilment with such force, they are unable to resist them. They then possess someone (most often someone with similar unfulfilled desires) and rape them day and night (if the desire is sex) until the desire dissipates completely. Due to unfulfilled desires many souls are haunted by acts of violence and sexual invasions, on this side and on the other side. Like a damaged record, again and again, they repeat their experiences, until they take a different exit out of the situation, similar to what obtained with Brian and his unfulfilled sexual dreams.

This happens with all people, even with some monks and priests who believe in and teach one thing, but experience something else after death. They, more so than other people feel disappointed. I am writing here about unfulfilled sexual desires, but the same applies to other desires, even those that seem to be innocent or trivial desires. This includes any addiction. Many people don't fulfill their desires because they made a conscious decision to suffer. They deceptively believe that they would receive a reward in Heaven for their suffering. That is why people self-inflict pain. They don't understand that their learning is not the suffering (and drawing happiness from it), but growing beyond it. Only life without pain is a pleasure. The purpose of suffering is growth on earth and the fact that it prevents you from being stagnated. It indicates a call to life, to action and not to backtracking from life. When I explain this to people, most often they are embittered, they feel disappointed, because reality turns out to be different to what they had believed up to that point. Quite often they initially can't accept that „Heaven" is the fulfilment of desires, in other words a fulfilled life, and not a lack of it. The main principle of the universe (I write more about that later) is as follows – „As in Heaven so it is on Earth". Turning that sentence around – when we have a fulfilled life on earth, then you would feel like you are already in heaven and after death you could attain the continuation of that, in other words Heaven. However a person who turned his life into hell, constantly suffering and with unfulfilled personal desires, would also experience suffering. Often that suffering is much more intense than on earth, after the death of his physical body. Most ghosts tell me – „Throughout my entire life I didn't think about myself, I put others first. Now, when I was expecting a reward I received punishment instead".

Perhaps, you are surprised that this is possible. On a deeper level, other people are just like you, as we are all connected, and as humanity we comprise one body. If you think only about others, and never about yourself, you hurt this greater body. You are part of it, and by neglecting yourself, you are neglecting the whole. It is like caring for most of your needs – giving your body food, sleep etc. – but most importantly forgetting to drink water. Water is one of the things needed to live, without it we die. Do you ever think this way? If you particularly forget about yourself a call for life would appear, coming in the form of sickness or misfortune and it would say – stop! You can't do that anymore. Often we don't listen to our body and instead we reach for a pill which would relieve the symptoms (and obscure the body's suggestions). We would be pleased and return to our old habits. And if we don't get rid of the cause of the illness we could end up in the hospital for years and still be sick. But, all that is needed is for us to think about our desires and what we are doing wrong in our life and what we should change.

Old habits could be deeply rooted however and it's not enough to think once and afterwards forget about a new direction. We have to constantly remain alert and not allow old habits to return. Many people have tried, but they didn't have enough perseverance and commitment to ensure they didn't return to their old habits. Therefore they decided to acknowledge that this method doesn't work for them.

Sometimes we suffer because we do not want to give anything of ourselves, or receive anything, good or bad from life. We do this because we don't understand deep inside that to give and to take is one and the same thing. By giving we already receive a reward because we open ourselves for taking. But, only by receiving would we be able to give something from ourselves. By giving you are opening your hand through which you can take something. If a hand is clenched then you can neither give nor receive.

When a soul is clean then the world that is watched through its eyes is clean. If a soul forgets *Who It Is in Essence* it would be uncertain and filled with fear. The entire world would look disgusting and dreary to it, and you as a human would suffer. Look around you and see how many people are suffering because they are consumed with unfulfilled desires. Take note that it doesn't matter whether these people are wealthy or poor, healthy or sick, beautiful or ugly, big or small, educated or illiterate. Some people suffer because they don't have what they desire or have too little of it (no matter how much they have, it still wouldn't be enough). And even though others have that „something" they desire, they are not happy about it, because they suffer while thinking – „How can I enjoy my wealth (health, love etc.) even as others don't have enough". They watch the world from the perspective of their own beliefs, biases and superstitions. They make their happiness dependent on the happiness of others. But other people may have a different approach or perspective on how they should live their life. You mistakenly think that poverty is something bad. However, many people came to this world to learn something by experiencing poverty. Poverty would never exist in the world if it wasn't needed for the growth of someone's soul. Because of the fear of personal poverty very few people admire the inner beauty of the mendicant, lost soul in a homeless person. But, in spite of appearance, each person has their own purpose and meaning. Therefore, let others experience their own life (meaning their own desires). You never know what a given soul has to learn in its life. If your path intersects often with such „poor, lost" souls certainly do not take pity on these souls, or feel sorry for them, rather think about what you have to learn from such meetings. Each soul (as well as yours) is responsible and obligated to extend kindness towards all other souls, also towards poor and lost souls. Everyone, without exception, is obligated to help in the developmental process of every other soul. Both sides benefit (learn) from each meetings, because as you already know, giving is synonymous with receiving.

There are many ways to understand that reality exists. However, how you interpret your own position on the stage called life depends on what you decided to believe in. You are the way you are and in the place you are in, because you hold certain beliefs. If you believed in something else, then you would certainly be in a completely different place now. You built your world by yourself, and the bricks and foundation of this building, the result of present and future experiences, are individual (small or strong) beliefs. Beliefs are based on your own decisions and confidence in your experienced and per-ceived reality. Tell a person who doesn't believe in himself that he is smart, beautiful, kind and hardworking, and he would immediately reject such a statement. He would think that that is not true, that you were making fun of him. Another person who lacks in confidence would rejoice when told the same thing. He would take it as a compliment, because it would boost his self-esteem. As you could see, everything depends on your beliefs. Over the years, your beliefs created a powerful, consistently growing, invisible inner force. With its help you build a concept of yourself. It determines how you perceive your place at home, work, school, and even in the entire Network of Existence. Beliefs are the programs on which you base every life experience. Often you are blindly guided by them. Usually these are unintended thought forms which arise in your imagination.

Each one of us carries great set of beliefs that come from many sources. It doesn't matter whether it comes from this incarnation or from countless sensations carried over from previous incarnations. All of them influence us in the same way. Most often we are not aware of them, even though they determine all of our experiences during life on earth and life that follows. We store our beliefs with great care, like diamonds in a bank, in the subconscious memory. They determine your experiences in both exterior and interior world and program you for success or failure. You will experience life happily or ecstatically with the positive approach to the world and everything will work out for you. If you view the world pessimistically and interpret the reality negatively, then the feeling of helplessness or even despair will accompany with your every physical or spiritual experience.

SELF-IMAGE

As you can see, dear reader, you carry within yourself a complete, mental self-image picture. It is filled with even the smallest details about your person. It doesn't matter whether you realize this or not. You may not recognize it consciously; it may be undefined and indistinguishable. However everyone has one, and there are no exceptions to this. Your inner image could be very different from how people perceive you. Look around you and see how many beautiful people are ashamed to show themselves to others. They hide themselves under increasingly thicker layers of powder or bronzer, a beard, or glasses. For them glasses are like a wall, behind which they could peacefully watch and simultaneously not be seen.

Certainly, dear reader, you already fully realize that your self-image is not imposed on you in advance, but is built from your *own* beliefs. Therefore, you are the author of *what kind of person you are*. Beliefs were formed (often unconsciously) based on your numerous experiences. They could consist of successes, triumphs, small failures, great defeats, friendships and humiliation. People who you meet along your life's path play a huge role in terms of what you accept from them and recognize as yours. The people you met in your early childhood influenced you the most. From those experiences you assembled your personality and set the image of your lower self. Presently, you react differently to different situations. Everything depends on your self-image. If some new perception or belief about yourself enters this *image* and it is compatible with an earlier, developed image, it then immediately becomes a truth to you. If it's contrary to earlier images it would be immediately rejected. This process is not often subjected to reflection, conscious assessment or decision making, it happens automatically. You very rarely mull over this process to decide what is right. You don't question the things which are stored in your bank of information that describe your personality.

You were born with an endless amount of capabilities and talents and you would be a true master if you would expand on them. However, over time some beliefs inhibit you instead of supporting and developing you. When you don't observe this process in a timely fashion, at a very early age these so called talents and innate capabilities become a blur. Your sense of self-worth would be lowered even more, sometimes to the point where you have a complete lack of self-worth and instead of benefiting from your innate powers, more and more you would feel powerless.

Consequently, behavior, actions, feelings and even capabilities result from the image which you carry within you. Regardless of your efforts, you are unable to act or create above the image anchored in your belief system. For example, a person who thinks of herself as a down on her luck, a loser, who doesn't deserve anything or is afraid of loss, always, finds a way to fail. Consciously she may even have the best intentions, a strong will and the most favorable circumstances, but at the end of the day she would fail anyway. People, who consider themselves resourceful, often create for themselves unpleasant circumstances in order to harness their resourcefulness to action and overcome negative situations they created. A person who thinks of herself as a victim (in various circumstances) would find adequate opportunities to confirm that belief. For such a person it would seem, and incorrectly so, that her experiences describe or create beliefs which she holds as truths in herself. This in turn would strengthen her image and a vicious circle would be engaged – „Why did they hurt me?_They hurt me because I am a victim. And why am I a victim? I am a victim because they hurt me." Or – „Why does nothing work out for me? Nothing works out for me because I have bad-luck. And why do I have bad-luck? I have bad-luck because nothing works out for me". She could easily include every quality or opinion about herself here.

Dear reader, know that you always receive what you expect, and not necessarily what you desire. If you dream about love, and expect to be rejected (because you are afraid of love) then you would always be rejected. If you want to be happy, but you don't believe that it is possible then you would always experience concern, misery, and worry. Start to expect happiness, fortune and success, but simultaneously don't be afraid to receive these things, and they would all spontaneously appear in your life.

A self-image could always be changed. It is never too late for that; you are never too old or too young. One of the reasons you do not effectively achieve personality change is the fact, that in general you usually focus all of your efforts on the surface of your Self. Very few people try to reach their interior. You may think positively, in other words, use positive affirmations – I would quit smoking (or drinking), meet the love of my life, get a job or adopt a healthy lifestyle, but still never receive these things. But you have to put enough effort into reaching to the interior levels of your Self which would enable you to realize these changes. When you achieve this and convince your inner self about the righteousness of changes, your thinking would change by itself to so-called positive thinking. This never happens the other way around. When the Self's perception about itself undergoes a change then everything else automatically changes. In line with your new perception, the things which earlier caused you great difficulties you would suddenly start to achieve simply, easily and pleasantly, in other words, in a way that doesn't require any effort.

The first step in the process of change is to replenish your entire reality with conscious attention. You cannot change anything if you are not completely conscious of it. A personality is made up of a uniform, connected system of ideas, beliefs, convictions and all of them have to be in a state of mutual agreement. As you already know, all ideas incompatible with your system of beliefs are automatically rejected. Hence, your careful attention is required. While wanting to change things, you should, with courage, introduce new models and carefully control them so that they are not rejected by your subconscious. To achieve this you have to make contact with your subconscious, which could be difficult at first. Actually, most of us have never done this before. However there is no other way as your subconscious comprises your central management system, the base upon which everything that makes up your self-image is built.

For your life to be satisfying, and I am not yet talking

about being happy, you must be comfortable with your self-image. Often a false image effectively prevents a satisfying existence. Notice how many people are unable to look in a mirror at their face or body. They suffer even though many of them are really beautiful. And that is certainly the opinion people have about them, but they do not feel that way about themselves. I write about the outside appearance because this is easier to evaluate. However there are a great number of people carrying huge emotional wounds that are very hard to live with. No matter what problem you are dealing with, what opinion you have of yourself, only you could change it.

Your sense of self, as a whole, has to be such that you are fully able to accept who you are. You won't have respect or trust yourself without this acceptance. And trust is the basis for normal and effective (that benefits you and others) functioning in the physical world. You not only have to believe in your self, but you also must not be ashamed to show it on the outside, because you don't want to hide it. Many people think – „I won't show myself to people, because I have a pimple, dark circles under my eyes, I am too fat/skinny". But, the definition of things is constantly undergoing change. During my youth, women hid and squeezed their breasts, and now they want to make them bigger – the trend has changed. The definition of beauty is formed by leading fashion designers. Currently, everyone is getting tattoos, and in a few years they would be spending great amounts of money to remove them. That is understandable, because how many years would you look at the same faded, distorted picture, after the idea of putting tattoos on your skin has long passed. And it could turn out to be impossible to fully remove because it may leave scars. So, while other people tell you what to do with your body, it is up to you whether you accept those thought forms and recognize them as yours.

It would be a lot easier to control this process if your lower self had an image compatible with truth (you would have to be paying attention to your emotional-thought processes and looking after it for this to be the case). Your lower self's image of you (qualities which you are sure that you have) has to be closely equal to your real image, not bigger, not smaller. If that is the case and you accept this, and you feel satisfied with it, you would then feel self-confident; you could then be you and express yourself. You would then function optimally. Your every quality (even a huge scar on your face) would increase your self-esteem and your faith in your personal growth.

If your self-image (for example: an imaginary or real, proverbial pimple on your nose) is a cause of shame, you would try at all costs to hide it from other people. Being afraid to show yourself to the outside world, you would close yourself off, as though hidden away in a shell. Your self-esteem would diminish and sometimes you would even have zero self-esteem. If your self-image lowers your self-esteem, then a loss of freedom and self-confidence would follow. You would not only feel unhappy, but also completely lost. You would feel lost because you wouldn't be able to function creatively.

Respect and trust for yourself comes from an encoded image of the world in your mind, and this respect and trust for yourself would determine your level of happiness, which in turn would dictate your state of health. When you send signals of suffering to your body, your cells shrink under the influence of fear which causes numerous illnesses. When you send signals of happiness, your cells would generate good health. Also, low self-esteem blocks creative expression. You get stuck in one place and at the same time you would complain about others moving forward in life. You would become more and more biased against everyone and everything, and life, along with the environment in which you live would become increasing more difficult for you to manage.

Many people think they can improve their self-esteem by changing life on the outside, for example: changing their outside appearance. They think that this would improve the quality of their experiences. However in such situations even plastic surgery performed by the best plastic surgeons won't help. Internally, there would still be an image of your own ugliness or low self-worth. Proof of this is the large number of people who continue to experience disappointments because each progressive cosmetic surgery (even the surgeries that went very well) didn't change anything in their life. However, a change of beliefs about you, immediately changes your life, and then any „outside" action, in this case surgery, becomes unnecessary because you would feel confident in any situation.

CHANGE OF BELIEFS

Do you remember how I compared a person's soul to the clearest diamond? In each person you could find such a precious jewel. Imagine that you are such a diamond. It has thousands of facets, but many of them are covered with dust, dirt or mud. Where is this dirt from? It consists of your beliefs and the warped image you have of yourself that was created in this incarnation, and perhaps also in previous ones. The task for the physical person and the soul is to clean up each facet of its perfect surface to allow the light which is inside you to shine through.

Some people work persistently on themselves and cleaned up many dirty facets. These people are doing well and shine bright. Others also try, but only manage to clean up a few facets. Perhaps along the way they resigned themselves from cleaning or had doubts. They constantly stumble upon various difficult situations, because they barely shine, and it's hard to go through life blindly. Others don't shine at all, because they never started the process of changing their beliefs. For them life never falls into place and they fall under the weight of life. It doesn't matter how thick the layer of dirt is and from how many incarnations it came. Everyone, including the person who behaves in the most horrible way, has in their heart this precious, perfect, diamond. When a person who is considered bad gets around to cleaning his interior his diamond will shine again with the same white light as it initially did. And what can be said about his previous bad deeds? Those were only experiences, through which to learn what it is like, not to be love.

All souls are powerful, strong and much more complicated than most people could imagine. The basic function of a soul is to cultivate truth about itself, in other words reminding itself, *Who It Is in Essence,* and not get stuck in imaginary perceptions, that is, false beliefs about itself. For a soul to be able to read out a given truth, it must have the will to cleanse itself. As you know, dear reader, everything in the universe functions on the basis of vibrations. By cleaning itself from mistaken beliefs, vibrations constantly grow and you start to shine more and more. Therefore, each soul should build into its existence a program of climbing to the level of truth's vibrations, for the purpose of reminding itself *Who We Are In Essence.* It is true that **you are already perfect,** exactly the way you are right now, and not that *you will become* perfect one day when you attain certain requirements. You bring to yourself what you believe in, and what you believe in, you project on the outside. By believing in God, the Truth, the Light and Angels, you attract consciousness of the existence of God (because you live in God), the Truth, the Light and Angels.

When you continuously remind yourself, *Who You Are in Essence*, you would become a part of the universal flow of energy where light, protection and healing come to you on its own and flow through you. On the other hand, confusion, corrupted knowledge, negligence towards your own life and the direction that leads to, bring on sadness, and sadness with time causes suffering. A soul through careless or corrupted knowledge separates from the truth about its existence and would suffer more and more. And when even one soul suffers, we all suffer, because we are all one.

BELIEFS AND YOUR BODY

Perhaps during your life (for example: maybe through watching commercials) you learned to fear for your body. It was instilled in you the view that your body could break down on its own, without any clear reason. And if it could break down any day, almost without a cause, then you grew to believe its actions are unpredictable so you couldn't rely on it, you couldn't trust it. This is downright nonsense however. A body is a self-regenerating intelligence. The above-mentioned way of thinking is caused by limited beliefs and this is what blocks the flow of life energy through your body. Each sickness, and it is different for each person without exception, serves to inform one part of I, through the second part, that something in your life isn't working as it should. This applies to your emotional reactions towards life which in turn are based on your beliefs. In order to understand messages that come from inside of your body, it is first essential to have your body's complete acceptance and respect, and its inner intelligence. When you understand what your body has to tell you, you would have no reason to be sick, and each sickness would go away by itself before it manifests itself on the physical plane.

As you already know, a body consists of individual cells, molecules, atoms and subatomic particles. Every one of them leads a separate, intelligent life. When connected as one, in a great union (your body), these cells enable you to become visible in the three-dimensional physical world and utilize them for experiencing. You probably saw one of the shows during the Olympics' opening ceremony where hundreds of individuals form a group in the stadium, coming together in unison to represent beautiful scenes. It is the same with individual cells, molecules etc. They group together in great formations to create your liver, eyes, hands etc. All of this happens so that the soul would be able to have experiences in the three-dimensional world, in order for you to see for yourself and function in it. Your body is an unimaginable miracle of nature. It is the world's greatest laboratory. Your organs, blood and bones all work according to a Higher Intelligence and that Higher Intelligence directs this great mass of cells and also perfectly and efficiently controls your individual organs. You don't consciously instruct your individual organs about what they should do. Your Higher Intelligence does that for you. Your cells communicate with each other, but they don't work arbitrarily, rather they obediently react to the Higher Intelligence's (meaning your) commands. You wouldn't be able to consciously direct such a great mass of individual cells. Therefore, this happens beyond your consciousness which makes it seem as though it were happening on its own. Nobody but you, give commands to make this communication process easier. Such commands are your beliefs. Thanks to these beliefs, your body's individual cells, as well as its organs know how to maintain a functioning body.

I would explain this to you a bit differently now. Your body is similar to the organizational structure of a country or even the entire world. Its success depends on compatibility, integrity and the appropriate functioning of all of its residents; in terms of what they believe and how they behave. If one group of people go off on their own and, for example, pour waste water into rivers and lakes then all residents in that area would be affected. Some actions are only felt by people in a specific area while other actions would have effects on the national or possibly even the global level. Therefore, the functioning of a country depends not only of the head of state (in the case of the body your soul), but also on every individual resident (every individual cell). This analogy can be aptly applied to your body. Every day, a large number of cells are fully utilized and die. They are replaced by new, beautiful and healthy cells that ensure the body continues to function perfectly.

As you know, dear reader, this great collection of cells make up your body, but it is not you (however many people identify with it). You, in the sense of the essence of you, are not a body, but a being that inhabits its interior. This powerful collection of cells just enables you to see, feel and experience things for yourself.

Constant fear, worrying about every detail, doubts, and self-pity all send signals to the body's cells informing them about your insecurity, helplessness, powerlessness and hopelessness. Your cells immediately absorb every such signal (coming from your beliefs) and submit to them. And not just your cells alone. Also, your life's situations confirm to you, affirm to you that you are right based on the rule – „That must be right, you are the boss here and you and only you govern your world". This is why I repeat again – if you change your beliefs you would change your life. If you decide differently and trust your intuition, then a new conscious choice would automatically recode the old models that are directing your every action. From those new models a new you would sprout. I repeat – only you lead your life and only you have the power to change anything that is undesirable. Feelings of love, appreciation and respect for yourself (and others), along with the need to share, care, kindness, honesty, forgiveness and acceptance would not only rebuild your health, but would also improve your character and usher into your life and mind, harmony and peace. Your body doesn't work against you, but for you. You have to learn to listen to it intently. If something doesn't work the way you want it to, you just have to change the mistaken code which you once introduced in the form of a mistaken belief.

Everything you believe in automatically becomes a program which in turn creates your reality. Such programs, as I have mentioned before, define the functioning of your physical body's cells. Even though your body is a wonderful self-healing system, these programs have a greater priority over your body thus they define the direction your body follows – health, well-being, longevity or failure. Therefore, take care of your body because it's a reservoir of power, and disharmonic beliefs stop its natural flow.

When you don't listen to your body you act only halfway. You fear a full, open life, because deep inside you believe in pain and automatically expect it. Thereafter almost every experience becomes the creator of new (bigger or smaller) pains. You don't act spontaneously because you have a program that is supposed to help you avoid painful situations. Every new signal, pleasant or painful, instead of being an ally, becomes an enemy, and you approach all circumstances with suspicion. Your body creates a self-defense mechanism to avoid pain whereby your body starts to shut down. You constantly hear the command in your mind „avoid pain at all costs", and this command would usually be accompanied by turbulent emotions, such as: paralyzing fear. You unconsciously give in to that process and simultaneously neglect your body's natural intelligence which creates a blockage in your cell's communication field. Sooner or later this blockage would lead to an illness in that part of your body. But such a signal very clearly points to the existence of a false belief. That is confirmed by the strong emotions which created the painful problem. They result from some unfulfilled desire. As I mentioned before in a previous volume, all people have the same desires. If you don't fulfill them, you suffer and simultaneously prevent yourself from acknowledging what that desire is. You suffer and you would still not fulfill your desires, which create a vicious circle.

As you see, dear reader, every illness and the pain that accompanies it always has some important message for you. That is its goal. It arose in your life only to awaken you. If pain, suffering and illness appear then it's not so that you could lie in bed, rest, withdraw from life or stop working on yourself, but the complete opposite. It is supposed to revive you. Perhaps you didn't want to work on yourself when you were well, young, healthy, and everything functioned as it should. You have to find the courage now when you are not doing well or when everything is falling down all around you. Definitely take the following into consideration– if you lack the willingness and courage now, as later (in this or a future life) it would be even more difficult for you (for example: the circumstances that you live in would worsen). Any unsolved issues need to be resolved. This is not an option, but a must. Why is that so important? If you reject the chance for growth then it appears bitterness, anger, hatred, or in other words smaller or bigger emotional wounds. They become a trauma you would carry over from your physical life to life after death, and later all the way through to your next incarnation. You would get a better understanding of this when we discuss life after death and reincarnation. Reincarnation is obviously not a necessity, but it becomes necessary when you avoid solving unresolved issues. That is why you have to return to earth (I write more about that later). That is how you enchain yourself to the wheel of life.

Remember, dear reader that your body is your greatest friend; a friend who loyally reveals to you the consequences of your own beliefs. If you didn't listen to your intuition up to this point, boycotted or criticized yourself, belittled an image of yourself, then your body was just obeying you and now you are receiving the results of that. Perhaps you are weak, sick, abandoned, and angry. Don't be upset with your body. Your body was only obeying the strongest demands contained in your beliefs. To turn all of this around now and change your life for the better, you have to find the courage to, most of all, change your beliefs and trust yourself. When you trust and start to listen to your intuition, your new beliefs would give you (your body, circumstances, etc.) a completely new form. When you accept these beliefs which would begin to support you, your body would start to radiate with great vitality, and you would feel the inflow of energy. A happy, cheerful and enthusiastic mind would make you more receptive and open to inflows of divine, cosmic energy.

Grace was the owner of a huge company. She was the only woman there and she forgot about herself long ago. Life often let her know she needed to slow down in the form of heart attacks. However when the pain went away she would always return to work immediately. She was very active professionally;

she took care of her huge home and did her gardening for herself, even though she had a husband and three grown up sons. She never asked for their help, because she claimed that she liked to work. At some point she got a very difficult to identify illness. She developed contorted limbs, which she couldn't move and had to be confined to a wheel chair. The pain was unbearable. Even the doctors didn't know what was happening to her. Besides a large dose of painkillers she didn't receive any other medications. When I met her, she said to me: „Mrs. Pratnicka I could tell you this, because you would understand me. I am in this condition, because I never wanted to listen to what my inner self was telling me. I had hunches constantly, but I ignored them. If I had slowed down, even for a moment, and paid attention to what the hunches were telling me, I would certainly still be healthy. Now I listen to myself and I could boldly say that I am happier now than back when I was healthy. Maybe my body would never recover, but I certainly know that I have regained myself. Perhaps this is hard to believe by looking at me, but I finally feel free and happy like never before. I am even afraid to desire good health, because I am not sure if I wouldn't immerse myself in life again and forgot about myself. Everybody told me that I am very strong mentally, but being a workaholic was my way to run away from myself. I don't know if I would hold on to what I learned while ill once I am healthy. I won myself and this is more precious to me than my physical function".

Dear reader, you could also become free if you start listening to yourself. And if you do that you would begin having influence over everything in your life. But of course, everything depends of you, although right now, not being conscious of that and being consumed with mistaken beliefs, you may feel enslaved by these beliefs. When you create the correct beliefs to support your development, you would feel full creative freedom. You would be aware that from now everything depends on you solely. Your lessons would begin to be based on safe, honest, respectful and pleasurable life experiences. And that's not only as relates to a specific area, but in everything, whatever you desire to experience. You don't believe that? Let you explain how that is possible in another way.

As you already know, your cells are subject to constant exchange. Every day new cells are born and the old ones die, although your consciousness doesn't actively participate in that process. New cells that are full of life obediently focus attention on accomplishing your commands, which in turn are based on your beliefs. If your beliefs are mistaken, then despite your constantly new, beautiful and healthy cells being born, they would replicate the limited version of you – the lonely, poor, lost, ugly, sick, incompetent, and defeated you. New cells by relying on mistaken beliefs, receive old commands that put you into a state that you may not be happy with. Therefore your body is a loyal reflection of your beliefs, effectively – your experiences. The body carries in it every experienced fear, hurt, pain, trauma, belief and also knowledge of how bad you were hurt as a consequence. If a given experience is accompanied by strong emotions, a mixture (similar to an explosive combination) which accelerates the process of similar experiences appearing in your life will be created. This would be directly related to your beliefs. How long could this last? Sometimes it lasts to the end of your life, and even longer. This process only stops functioning when you fully appreciate that you attracted certain experiences to your life because your soul needed them for its lesson. Your beliefs coupled with your emotions to that point, would act against you. If you retain your old beliefs you won't be able to forgive yourself, which coupled with a lack of understanding would only confirm your mistaken beliefs. That is the next vicious cycle.

From a broader perspective, any return to good health in life is due to an exchange of beliefs, from those that don't serve you anymore, to those that agree with your soul's direction; that is, what your soul desires to experience.

As I write these words Grace is already a healthy woman. And, she also has enough strength not to forget about herself anymore, in other words to constantly listen to what her inner being and body has to tell her.

DEALING WITH DEATH

As far as I can recall we never talked about death in my home. It was the same in my friends' homes as well. I wondered whether people weren't comfortable talking about death in front of their children or whether they just thought that by not talking about death at all it would pass them by. But death didn't want to be forgotten. This was right after the war and death was often a guest in our area. Every time that it reached somebody from my area it struck like a bolt of lightning. I often heard, no matter, the age of the person who died, comments such as: „What do we get out of life, he has hardly lived and already he is being put into the ground". Moments later, elders would comfort each other by saying: „Death is the only justice in this world. It comes no matter your status, qualities or even good or bad deeds. It touches everyone – the rich and the poor, the good and the bad, the healthy and the sick."

How many times have I also heard: „Oh well, you only

live once, why deny yourself anything". Consequently, many people around me indulged themselves. They needed to blow off steam, drink alcohol, take drugs, get as much out of life as they could, so as to benefit as much as possible. I assumed that people were behaving like this because they are abreacting horrible thoughts from the recent war. Although it had ended it was still taking its toll. Houses were demolished and walls had collapsed, and there were missiles in the rubble which led to the demise of many people. Today, I see that I was mistaken. I am an adult now, but many people still think and behave in the very same way.

Times have changed, but people still live in constant fear for their life. There isn't much positive information in the news. The events reported are primarily negative – accidents, catastrophes threatening us daily, global warming (the subtext being Earth's impending doom), AIDS, other serious illnesses, terrorism, and many other dangers. Many young people being fed this information every day don't believe they would reach twenty years of age. The number of suicides and unsuccessful attempts to end life is constantly growing. This reflects the many stresses experienced globally in today's society. In such circumstances contemplations about death seem beyond the strength of most people. Understand however, that you don't live in a peaceful world where death only comes at an old age after you have lived with dignity. Just the opposite – death seems to be around every corner. But shouldn't that be why you want to know more about it?

Just think about it dear reader. If you actually only live once, as some people claim, shouldn't each one of us respect our lives even more? Why don't people do this? The answer only came to me when I started dealing with exorcisms. By studying ghosts that possessed people, I realized that most people treat this inadequately because of their lack of knowledge. Because they don't know anything about death, people are frightened by the thought that it may happen to them or even worse, surprise them. And, not only do they not want to know anything about death, they also don't want to know what happens to them after death and how to prepare for that circumstance. They wonder if it makes sense to think about death and contaminate their short period of life here, on Earth. And because they don't know what death is, they also don't know the basic laws of life. This is the source of their thoughtlessness, carelessness and stupidity.

How could you not want to know about something which is a basic fact of life and which it seems nobody can avoid? Ultimately, this is as important as, for example, daily hygiene. With full confidence I can state that knowledge of death is much more essential. As you read further in this book you would see that there are serious consequences to a lack of knowledge in this area.

How Children Perceive Death

In many families – as it once was in my family when I was growing up –death is a taboo subject. Sometimes death is only mentioned when someone close to you passes away. If you did discuss it, then God forbid you did so in front of children. We think, quite wrongly, that they have enough time for such matters and until such time they should enjoy life.

However, children are the ones most keenly interested in their (and your) existence. Children, not adults, most often ask: „How was I born?", „What would I do when I grow up?" And just as they ask about life, so too they ask about death: „How do we die" „What would happen to me when I die?" Such questions are not only appropriate, but natural; it is just that adults don't like to bring up these topics. They fool themselves into thinking that talking about death brings it on and that by avoiding the topic they could somehow escape death. They put off their children so that they don't have to deal with this matter. If they did answer though, what would they say? They themselves know very little or nothing on this topic. However, when children are deeply bothered by something they are not easily satisfied with unclear answers. They start looking for answers themselves to cope with the emotions triggered by their concerns about death. The first answers they arrive at would dictate the nature of their future enquires on this topic.

If the answer satisfies them, they stop searching based on what they have heard. Other children though, keep searching, and where this would take them only God knows. I know of instances where young people were so fascinated by death they had a desire to try it to see what it was like. The history of those who unfortunately succeeded, I often only find out about from their telling me (as ghosts) while I am performing exorcisms. Many other cases I find out from the letters of potential juvenile suicide victims or from their school friends asking me to help them.

It is heart breaking when an eight year-old, nine year-old or ten year-old writes for help for himself or a friend. Why don't parents teach children about death? The answer I received from a little girl: „My parents don't know anything about death; they don't even want to read your book Mrs. Pratnicka" „Did you read my book?" – I asked surprised. „Everyone in my class read it" – she answered proudly. On the one hand her answer stunned me. I didn't address my book to such young readers (otherwise I would have written it differently). On the other hand however, I noticed how much this knowledge is needed.

Sometimes outraged parents call me because they caught their children reading my book. „Did I give it to him? Did I force him to read it?" – I ask. Only then do they calm down. When I ask the respective parents whether they had already read the book, I always get the same answer. „No? Then please do it together with your child and help him understand it." – I advise. They then back off. I think that when a child expresses an interest, something must be done about it, especially when it comes to very sensitive topics. At the same time you could tell them about love and responsibility and answer other questions. Children don't give up on a desire to know more about what interests them, especially when it is perceived to be forbidden. Therefore when parents don't care to educate their children about these matters, their older friends would do it and, quite often in a vulgar and questionable manner. Is that what you want for your children?

Adults must realize that the fascination with death cannot be suppressed in any age group. It is only by understanding death would you grasp the essence of life and respect it. Some time ago, a mother called me asking for help for her only daughter. Three of her daughter's school friends had committed suicide within a few months of each other. The mother claimed that her daughter was behaving erratically and she was concerned that her daughter might harm herself. I cleansed the daughter of ghosts and thereafter she unilaterally threw away all her black clothing and metal and hard rock music. After many conversations with her mom, death stopped fascinating the daughter. This time the intervention was timely. Parents, please be observant and notice similar conditions in your children in a timely manner!

Other parents were less fortunate. The parents of a boy a few years old called and asked me to assist in finding their son. He had written a goodbye letter and run away from home. I asked his soul if it was alive, and he continually answered: „Of course, I am alive". Even after his body was pulled out of a lake, he continued telling me: „But I am alive!" For many days his soul was continually repeating to me in despair: „Tell my parents where I am. Tell them to take me home. I don't want to sit here. Why are they not coming? I wrote a letter saying that I want to kill myself. It is so horribly cold here". On and on he went. My remonstrations that it was too late, that he had drowned, that he didn't have a physical body anymore weren't working. He was screaming over and over: „But I only wanted to scare them and force them to love me more. I didn't want to kill myself". When I told his parents about these messages, they were horrified. They continually asked themselves: „Was it necessary for this tragedy to occur for us to finally understand this?"

Dear parents, these are not unique cases. I have had many such cases in my practice. Similar cases were also high-lighted in the media. These were a few front page headlines in newspapers: „Polish teenagers are fascinated by death", „Death is trendy. It solves all problems", „Since 2001 the rate of teen-age suicides has quadrupled", „In 2005, there was a six fold increase in the number of student suicides", „Suicides are no longer an adult issue", „Children from the same grade commitsuicide", „In 2009, there was an eight fold increase in the number of suicides in middle schools", „This is the 39th suicide in the same town. Priests don't react". Children and teenagers often have psychological problems (which are primarily caused by ghosts), but they also want to know more about death at all costs.

The reason people attempt suicide is possession by ghosts, and it is significant to note that ghosts are attracted to people with existing problems. On both sides of the equation, suicide could be effectively prevented. Would suicides occur on such a scale if we spoke about death in our homes? I am sure they wouldn't. I hope that by reading this book you change your point of view on these matters. I return later to the subject of suicides.

I will quote here from a letter a reader sent me. This reader completely changed her point of view on her own and a loved one's death. I receive many letters like that. This is what Mrs. Johnson wrote: „Mrs. Pratnicka, when my mother fell sick and we found out that nothing could be done for her, we took her (similar to what you did with your mom) to our home (before that we lived separately) so that she could end her life with dignity with us. Mom was dying and the entire family was there for her. She was dying for over a year, losing and gaining consciousness. All of that was happening in a multi-generational home where my young children's bedroom was next to her bedroom. Downstairs there was a kitchen – always noisy, full of people and smelling of food. In this extremely strange circumstance of life and death I noticed the symbolism of human existence – evanescence, the inevitable end written in our every step, gestures, and feelings. My departing mom in a beautiful way got mixed in with our every-day reality. On their own initiative my children sat down next to their beloved grandma and read her favorite books to her; they even did that when she wasn't aware. When the painkillers worked we familiarized her with the matters of death. Obviously, we didn't just talk about that. We also brought up other issues, even those unpleasant topics. We were also able to recall the old days and even joke. In that way the children were also learning about interacting with death. We allowed for that, because we didn't want them to think that at some age they would simply dematerialize, they needed to be prepared for the inevitable – because the end is written for all of us, just as the sorrow, sadness or despair of losing a loved one is also written. Obviously we cried when my mom and their grandma passed away. Even to this day we haven't touched anything in her room. Perhaps this is how it would be until the end of the mourning period. Mrs. Pratnicka, thank you for this wonderful book. If it wasn't for that book, I don't know how we would have survived that tough period. Regards, Mrs. Johnson"

CONTEMPLATING DEATH

Conversations about death are appropriate at any age and you should return to it from time to time and all the more so with people who are nearing death (for example persons who are elderly or bedridden). It has nothing to do with a lack of decency. On the contrary, it's proof of how much you care for those persons. You display great ignorance and a lack of respect for that person's greatest need when you don't address that subject. I am writing about this because when you know enough about death your departure proceeds smoothly and painlessly. When you resist this knowledge and leave things up to fate, the transformation from your material to immaterial body, in other words from physical life to death, is very traumatic for your soul, because it would be born out of great fear.

There certainly are cases of people who, being old, bedridden or moribund, don't want to know about death. There are others who lose their loved ones and don't want to talk about it.

The reason for this is ignorance born of an immense fear of the unknown. We should be able to overcome this obstacle in helping others to relieve this immense (and completely useless, as you will learn while reading this book) fear.

Most people don't realize the importance of being prepared for death. They don't do anything until the last moment or neglect the preparations altogether. People often ask me if they should tell their loved ones the truth about their serious illness and that they could die soon. When I confirm that they should, they panic. It turns out most people don't talk about the final case at all.

We should talk to the diseased with love in our heart. We should ask them how they would react if their disease was incurable or terminal. We should ask if they're afraid to die, if they have prepared themselves to pass away and have thought of what would happen next. On hearing that we are seriously ill or that our dear ones are ill, we often panic because we don't know what to do. We dread to even think that something terrible could happen to us. We are usually frightened of death.

Most people deny obvious facts and pretend everything is okay, even when the end is near. They say there's no reason to worry, that the diseased is going to be cured soon and everything will be as it was. I know about cases and these are not exceptions of families lying to the patient until the end, persuading him that the medicine he is taking serves just to strengthen his body. This is what the diseased say about it: ,,They convinced me that these are just vitamins. I am strong but it would be easier for me if they helped and told the truth me instead of making it harder." And ,,Why do they visit me at all? Do they think this is funny?" Such people want to talk about death, their suffering, and fear of dying very much.

Christina was 28 when she became a widow. Her husband died of cancer. She wrote me a letter:

„Mrs. Pratnicka,

The time of my husband's malady was so hard on me that only a thought of my three children being left alone stopped me from crashing my car into a tree. I couldn't eat nor sleep, I didn't want to talk to the kids, my spirit dried up, and my heart shrank. I was on the verge of despair when I coincidentally saw your book, Possessed by Ghosts. Although I was very weak I read it in one sitting. I understood what death was, or rather, I understood that there is no death. I trustingly turned to God, asking Him to help George go through it. I calmed down and noticed that my husband was more serene and that he had come to terms with his tragedy. He told me he had straightened everything out for himself and had said goodbye to us. He said that death didn't terrify him anymore and that he was ready to go away. He also asked me to stop despairing because it made it harder for him. I started to talk to the people in the hospice. They said dying people who suffer a lot ask for simple things such as being there for them, a delicate touch, a smile, or some warmth. And then I understood that instead of crying I should tell George how much I loved him. I realized that love was the only thing I could offer him in this difficult moment and that if I didn't tell him about my feelings this would be the only thing I would ever regret. This realization made his death, his passing away, our parting, became bearable. And when George died, I let him go immediately. It didn't hurt as much as I imagined it would when I thought death was the end of everything. I wonder how hard it would be if it wasn't for your book. I would probably be unable to let my husband go and force him to suffer in a vegetative state. Thank you for such a tranquilizing lecture.

Grateful,

Christina"

The ones leaving the physical dimension not only feel that they are dying, they also see it. A few days before their expected death their dead relatives gather around them. Spiritual guides come to cleanse the surroundings to make it easier for the soul to transform. This happens a little bit before death at any place or time, not only when we are lying on our deathbed.

Most people think that sudden death is something that happens just like that, something that the dying are not aware of. This is not true. The majority of people who have died suddenly informed their loved ones about the premonitions they had months before their passing. People mostly don't want to listen to such things, saying, „Oh, don't talk nonsense. You're imagining things."

Such was the case of my uncle, a strong and healthy man of forty, who had premonitions of his death half a year before it came. It was not long after the death of my mother, his beloved sister with whom he had a close relationship, so everybody thought he was oversensitive on the subject of death. Therefore, nobody wanted to hear about his premonitions. They waved him away as if he were a bothersome fly. At first he feared those premonitions. I tried to calm him down many times saying there was nothing to worry about and reminding him that his beloved sister was waiting for him. In time he became tame with the thought and got rid of his fear. Half a year passed. A day before his death he came to me and I suddenly felt that this was the last time we would be seeing each other. This was not only my feeling, we talked about it at length. We even joked that he was going to die because he was in a hurry to see his sister. I told him that I wouldn't try to persuade him to stay. He entrusted me with his unfinished business (nobody else wanted to listen) and we said farewell to each other as if it was our last talk. He died at night. Later I talked to many people including his wife, children, and friends. At the beginning none of them realized that he was constantly talking of his death. All of them were rejecting it from their consciousness. It was only after some time that they came to terms with his passing away and started to recollect their conversations. They felt guilty. They realized that if they had listened to his premonitions their last months together would have been different.

I have analyzed many cases of sudden death since then. Most of them confirmed the tendency for people to avoid discussions of coming death and that long before the date of his passing away a man knows what will happen, no matter if he is going to die suddenly or become ill.

You probably wonder why people don't or can't support their loved ones with feelings of peace and hope. This is because they don't understand death and are afraid of it. This problem, however, affects only those who treat life shallowly. They don't perceive it the way it really is. Under other circumstances they would understand and internalize that death, as a transformation from one state to the other, is a natural part of life. They would become more patient (without an effort) and learn how to spontaneously share love and compassion, too. If you know anybody who suffers from fear or loss of a loved one, take care of him but don't send him vibrations of sadness so that you don't overburden him with additional weight and pain that these vibrations carry. Send him your understanding and love instead.

After my Mom died, many people who knew they were going to die soon or who lost their loved ones turned to me for help. Many of them were not ready to hear about life after death. There were not many books on the subject at this time. Yet although they lacked preparation I felt that I could help them. I spoke to them in a sensitive tone, had a cordial attitude, and tried my best to see and understand their fears and feelings.

Often it was enough for me to look, touch their hand, and say a good word. I could tell more about death and dying to those who were ready to accept it. It touched them deeply and moved some invisible string. Sometimes the reaction was unusual. They felt spiritually strengthened and although some of them suffered from pain they felt new hope being born in them. They got new spiritual energy, remembered intuition, and saw things I was telling them about for themselves. They were not frightened anymore and I could see blissful smiles on their faces when they acknowledged their fate. In most cases the diseased knows that his end is near and he is left alone with this important and difficult problem. But it doesn't have to be that way.

In a sense children, even the smallest ones, are harder to deceive. They know perfectly well what medicine they get and why. Persuading them that everything is going to be okay makes the situation worse and causes their fear to grow. They need to hear an explanation of what will happen to them on the other side. But to be able to tell them anything we have to know something about it first.

That's why I suggest that every therapist, doctor, and nurse should consider the possibility that there is life after death and should include this subject in their counselling programs. They should stay open minded to sharing their knowledge with their patients and not belittling their experiences. It would be enough for these people to know that we don't die, ever, that we still live after death, we never part with each other, and that we are always together. Those who don't believe it will see it soon for themselves.

I know how painful it is to say good bye to a loved one. It is equally difficult or maybe even worse for people ending their lives to have to face the unfamiliar state of transition called death. If both sides knew more about death they would definitely accept the fact definitely more calmly. We would still grieve but we wouldn't suffer so much. It would be more like a departure of a loved one going to a distant country. He or she would be apart from us but we would know they still exist. Maybe we could even realize that we never truly part (it is impossible) and that a dying person just passes to another classroom. For the soul who is leaving the physical body the education continues on higher levels that are essentially higher planes of consciousness. The dead one has left the physical realm but we stay eternally connected to them in the spiritual plane. We can contact them through the love that is in our hearts. Love is eternal and if a person has ever truly loved someone he can use this love to keep in contact after death.

Nothing can be more wrong than the belief that death is a process you don't need to know about and that everything will go its way. It is true that they will put your body in a coffin and bury it or burn it in a crematorium, but these treatments consider just a body. So what will happen to the real human? He is still alive and feels much better than he did during his physical life. He is not limited by thick matter anymore. It is as if he took off a heavy, uncomfortable outfit. Is it wise to lie down in such a situation as you do with your physical body and to wait for merciful fate? The situation reminds me of a cork drifting in the water. Is it worth flowing where we wouldn't (and most probably won't) like it at all, but where we are being taken by a blind fate? Fortune helps those who can steer it and work on it.

That's why I reckon that we can't talk about death enough. It seems that most of us need to get used to the thought first. We need to realize once and for all that what we fear so much doesn't exist. Death doesn't exist. A real human lives eternally. This is the only reason you dared to come to this world. God promised you that and He is always true to His word. The state that seems to be death is just throwing away the old, used body we don't need any more so we can travel further in its identical copy. This copy is an exact reflection of a physical body with one difference: it is not visible to physical eyes. Where are we going? It is one hundred percent up to us. But to make a choice we need to know at least what the situation looks like. Jesus of Nazareth exhorted continually: „Know the truth and it will make you free." Free from what? From limitations we put on ourselves thinking that our senses tell us the truth but they don't. How do I know this? From thousands of cases I used to work with during many years, multiplied by the quantities of spirits that possessed a single man, which equals an enormous number of beings.

This is the letter I received from a man, after he had read *Possessed by Ghosts* and had stopped fearing death:

„Mrs. Pratnicka,

At first, I didn't realize that I had changed and when it came to me I didn't know why it happened. I could see that I was calmer and more patient with my wife and children. My friends asked me why I was looking more relaxed and joyous, as if I had won the lottery. When I started to think about it, I came to the conclusion that I don't fear death any more. I also stopped fearing my nonexistence and all of this is thanks to your book. I'm also not that afraid of losing my loved ones (this used to be my greatest worry.) I realize that I would still grieve a lot but wouldn't be in despair. Since I know that death isn't the end of life I am aware of the fact people don't really die, they just pass onto another state of being. Why would I despair knowing they are right here? Mrs. Pratnicka, you don't even know how much this realization changed my life. I can finally create,

enjoy, and live. Thank you again. Sending my regards and
wishing you all the best.
    Mark Robinson"

    Oh, how powerful and universal is the fear of death! It is
because of this fear that people behave so strangely. First of all,
they try to keep life as long as possible. When they realize it
runs through their fingers, they usually experience a deep
internal crisis they don't know how to deal with. This is the
reason people search for new relationships all the time, get
obsessed with their looks, fitness, fortunes, procreation, and
other things that are usually completely useless. This stuff helps
them forget the real purpose of their lives.
    And what do you think of death, dear reader? Do you
sometimes wonder what would happen if you met it? You
probably ask yourself sometimes what would happen if a person
close to you died (your Dad, Mom, or husband) and you were
suddenly left alone. I doubt, however, that you think about your
own death. Don't you see that it's time to change that? Death is
inevitable to us all; do you think it won't happen to you?
    Maybe you think, „Why would I deal with such an un-
pleasant subject? What will be, will be. I can deal with nicer
things." You are wrong. After you come to terms with death, it
won't appear so terrible and cruel. It is only then that you start
to live fully. You probably squirm now and say: „I live now and
this is not a bad life". True, but this life is filled with anxiety.
You don't necessarily see it; maybe you've pushed it deep into
your subconscious. But this fear shows itself during every day,
hour, and second.
    We should all think not only of life but also of this inevi-
table thing that is death of a physical body. This body disinte-
grates but we never die. We leave the body the same way we

take off our clothes. Some people know it for sure, others sense it vaguely, and others haven't the slightest idea what will happen after the death of their physical body. There are people who tell themselves that by rejecting death from their awareness they push it away for good. This last group is quite numerous—they deny death even when it is around the corner.

Please understand, dear reader! Death doesn't apply to a real human (the one that resides in us all). It is not the end of life, nor is it the beginning of another one. It is a continuation. I will explain it fully in the chapter called *The School of Life*. Passing on to the next plane of growth is a natural process. Translating it to physicality: does a chrysalis in the cocoon die or does it transform into a butterfly? The butterfly only comes out of the cocoon. Now it is able to fly to the sky whereas before it could only crawl on one or a few leaves. When a man truly understands the principle of death, he doesn't fear the transition phase anymore. He doesn't despair when his loved ones pass on to the next phase, not because he is indifferent but because he understands. He knows that, although death came to him so many times before, he and his loved ones are still alive and well. What's more—instead of loss he sees an advantage for himself and his loved ones. He greets death calmly and without mutiny even when it is his beloved dying. He grieves over the parting of course, but it is as if this person were going somewhere far away. Such a man knows that those who have left are as close as they were while they were alive and that you can throw off your physical body during sleep to reach them.

But note: the closeness I am writing about is something completely different than the closeness you feel while being possessed. In this case both sides are free and independent, while in possession the ghost becomes an invader, a parasite on a living person and drawing their energy.

When we don't understand death and our loved one passes away we feel immense pain and grief. It is a natural human reaction. But if you considered this grief more deeply you would soon see (and probably be greatly astonished to know) that you don't bemoan the person but yourself. You grieve because your loved one passed away and left you. You wonder how you will manage without him or her. First of all, however much you dread the thought of inevitable death, it will eventually happen to you in the unpredictable future. You fear it much. But before you finish reading this book you will probably understand that your life can change completely. If that is not the case I suggest you read it again, think about it more deeply, and meditate on it.. Do it for as long as you need to become a new, stronger being and for the positive changes to start in your life.

MOURNING

Your ignorance keeps you from deeply understanding what death (or any other loss), is causing you to suffer. When a person dies it is absolutely necessary to pass through a period of mourning, letting a person come back to life again. Although you're experiencing a difficult time, don't let others persuade you that you shouldn't despair. Let yourself cry, despair, rage, and grieve as deeply as you can express. Let yourself ignore life that is going on around you. When the time of your mourning is over you will raise your head and come back to the living. The deeper you experience it, the quicker you will regain mental balance. Suppressing despair, anger, and sadness changes you and makes you a different person than the one you used to be. There's a deep wound inside you that is very difficult to heal.

It is not easy to imagine but everybody will experience this one day. The loss of our loved ones is a part of life. The mourning doesn't apply to death only but to every other loss like treachery, abandonment, even theft, fire, and flood. The more attached we are to someone or something, the more deeply we suffer.

I experienced it once, too. When we are going through a personal tragedy we need a lot of time to understand that the whole world can go on as if nothing had happened. We wonder why we are surrounded by smiling, jolly people. Their happiness irritates us and even a sunny day seems like a punishment to us. The sun, colors, and greenery burden us instead of lifting us up. It is difficult to bear people's laughter, happiness, common noise, and music. Why does all of this exist if we are so unhappy? Why didn't the world die, why didn't I die together with my beloved one? In such situations reality loses its meaning. There is only pain, negation, anger at fate, God, ourselves, or our loves ones. And then comes the deepest despair, the whole days, weeks, and months spent crying. But eventually the day comes when something unimaginable until this moment becomes possible—coming back to life.

I'm writing about mourning because most of us don't understand how important it is to the people who don't understand death. I'll repeat once more that mourning applies to every loss—not only death but every parting we experience. Grieving isn't an easy task in our culture that tends to pretend we are all tough. We don't usually try to understand the person in pain and instead of supporting him we say, „Get a hold of yourself, you have to be strong, don't show your weakness." Or we offer him drugs or alcohol to calm him down or put him into a stupor. Loss is the most difficult experience for those who clam up. They fear their heart will break and they need to live it through somehow. Send such people your understanding and love mentally; this will lift them up and help them get through this difficult time.

It was easier in the older days, when the families gathered around a dying one, wanting to be close to each other. His family, friends, neighbors—everyone lit candles, prayed a lot, put heavy curtains on the windows, and covered mirrors with sheets. Everybody showed compassion and understanding. And today? I've heard hundreds of people left alone with their pain claim that nobody was with them. And all they need is one person. They don't even have to say anything because their presence alone is what is important. People can take turns in order to give the suffering one good care and support. Such service can include listening to a long soliloquy or lamentation. It shouldn't bother anyone. The caretaker should hug the suffering one and let him cry loudly if necessary. Suppressing pain is the worst thing in the time of mourning. The effects will stay with him or her for the rest of their lives.

Passing through a mourning phase is necessary to living again. There is no other way; modern psychological ideas are useless here. They serve psychologists only. They take advantage of the visits of the suffering people who come to them for years, sometimes for the rest of their lives. I often get calls from people who suffered a loss of their loved ones long ago, even decades prior, and they still can't come to terms with it because nobody let them cry it over.

I think that religious people have it easier than nonbelievers. They believe in God so they experience some spiritual relief in time, no matter what they go through. It is more difficult for someone who has been convinced that death is the end of everything, that there is only emptiness, void, nothingness. This fear often stays until the end of their life, making living intolerable.

Most of us avoid mourning people. We do it out of fear

because we don't know how to behave when we see someone suffering. We think it is better not to disturb them. Quite the opposite is true, however. Every man's duty is to care about other people, keeping them from living alone in great despair.

THE DEATH AND WHAT HAPPENS AFTERWARDS

Dear reader, if you read my last book you know by now that, at least in theory, there is no death. What you refer to as death is simply putting away your physical body like taking off your clothes. However, it is not only getting rid of this uncomfortable and bothersome shell, it is the soul becoming liberated so that it can feel free at last. It reminds me of a caterpillar transforming into a butterfly after having released itself from a cocoon. The caterpillar exists through the whole process as the soul released of its physical body still exists in its astral body. It is free, however, and can travel anywhere like a butterfly.

What we commonly call death isn't the end of life in this world and the beginning of another. It is the continuation of a process we are dealing with. A dying man who wants to break free after leaving the body and fly like a butterfly has to gain the special knowledge while living and remember to apply it at the moment he leaves his body. A butterfly that leaves the cocoon has to have this knowledge too, otherwise it would consider staying in the cocoon forever, wouldn't it? Nature equipped a butterfly with an instinct, which is the source of its knowledge. People are mostly blind and deaf to what intuition tells them.

Dear reader, you probably don't realize how many people haven't the slightest idea about these matters. They rely on fate completely and blindly. They don't realize how cruel the consequences they expose themselves to can be. Lack of knowledge doesn't make us free from the effects of such „carelessness". It is too late to learn after we die because this is the time of harvest for our longstanding preparations. It is not the time to regret, nor to explain or excuse. There is not even anybody you can complain to. And what would you complain about, anyway? That nobody told you, that you didn't want to listen, or thought that God or some other force would do everything for you? As you know already, dear reader, the Laws of the Universe are immutable and consequential during our physical existence and afterwards. Did lack of knowledge protect anyone from any laws? The knowledge of visible and invisible forces acting on us is a necessity. Can you protect yourself from electric shock if you don't know about electricity in a wire? It is the same with life and a state that we used to call death.

The example of a butterfly and its cocoon is deliberate. Many people let themselves become closed in such cocoons after death. That's why we should discuss it day and night. We will come back to it soon.

ALIVE AND ALIVE

Judging from the tens of thousands cases I've gathered during all the years of my practice, I can definitely conclude that a man is as much alive after so-called death when he leaves his physical body as during his life when he still possessed the body. You may believe that first we are alive here, in the physical realm, and also later, in the astral world. The truth is, however, that we are alive simultaneously in both worlds. We are both alive and Alive. This doesn't mean that we live in both places at the same time. We possess two states of consciousness and should be aware of them both. The problem is that while living in the physical body we usually are not aware of the other state. That's why, while leaving the body, we don't realize that we have already entered the other state, that we have been there always, and that nothing changed. This is the basic reason why so many

people don't notice their death and they wrongly think they
still live in their physical bodies.

TRANSFORMATION CALLED DEATH

First of all, you need to realize that neither at the moment of death, nor after it, is there any change as far as a man is concerned. He remains the same person he was before. Of course, he doesn't have his physical body anymore, but the rest remains the same. He's got his mind, his character with its virtues and vices, and his addictions, if he has any. Taking off clothes doesn't change a man into a different person, after all. Many people think that if the deceased has transitioned to non-physicality, he has almost automatically turned into a saint that can do anything for them. They pray not really for him, but to him, asking for help, support, or advice concerning matters that are beyond the scope of his control. How could such a man answer specific questions if he didn't know about the subject while being alive? Nevertheless, many people demand it from the deceased. Instead of getting help they become possessed by either the ghost they pray to or another one that happens to be around.

The same is true concerning the conditions the deceased finds himself in after death. He doesn't start a new life but continues the old one, exactly the same as it was while he was living in the physical world, although in slightly different conditions. These are fundamentals, the most important facts we need to realize. Otherwise, we are in danger of not noticing our death like so many other people passing away from this world.

There is no need to be afraid of life after physical death. There is no prize awaiting us (such as heaven), punishment of hell, or purgatory sent to us by a stern God. What we will meet after death is solely the effect of what we believed in, what we thought, felt, did, or said while living in our physical bodies. Nobody imposes anything, neither rewards nor punishments. We live on as we did before when we had the physical bodies.

A man wakes up after death to the awareness of the astral world and sees literally everything he was accustomed to in the physical world. Until that moment he didn't realize that the astral world was an exact copy of the physical world and presently, he cannot understand what really happened to him. He thinks that the fact of being self-conscious is the proof that he didn't die but still lives in the physical world.

In order to understand it well, imagine that this very moment the physical world ceases to exist for some reason. Although you would lose the physical reality, nothing else would change. You would still do exactly the same thing you are doing now with one difference: you wouldn't reside in the physical reality anymore. Most likely, you wouldn't realize it at all. You would still see the walls of your flat, the same trees outside, the streets, the people, everything you were used to seeing. That's why so many people have difficulties believing in their own death. They can still hear, see, and feel yet in their imagination death means turning into a stiff corpse unable to feel and move.

One of the advantages of living in the astral world is lack of tiredness and an absolute freedom from many necessary things in the physical world such as eating and drinking. These needs impose many tiresome activities like shopping, cooking, cleaning, excretion, etc. In the astral world man is truly free, he can do whatever he wants to do whenever he wants to do it and spends his time as he pleases.

The astral matter reacts to man's thoughts and wishes much more freely and quickly than the physical world does. The effect is the immediate materialization of worries, fears, cares, desires, and feelings the instant man calls on them. Imagine a person that gets frightened. The thing he is afraid of materializes in front of him at once. If he desires something it appears instantly. So whatever man wanted, was afraid of, or cared about in the physical world determines his life in the astral world, whether it is a happy life or not. The astral world is similar to the physical except for the fact that here we must wait a while to have the thing we desire materialized. In the astral world it is materialized at once. Man's life in the astral world depends on what he got used to. Let's say he thinks, „Oh, will I be able to deal with it?" and suddenly at the very second, he faces the challenges he can't deal with. He thinks, „What if someone attacks, kills, or robs me?" and then he is immediately attacked, robbed, or killed. He thinks, „What a beautiful place" and the wonderful world surrounds him or, „How wonderful and easy is to live" and he immediately lives exactly like that. I am sure you understand, dear reader, what this is about.

After putting away their physical bodies many people fail to understand the principles of the astral world and don't take advantage of its specifics. That's why it often happens that people, although they are free from the necessities of earning a living, eating, sleeping, etc., still cook, eat, and work. They cultivate their gardens, start building houses, and do many other things they used to do. If, for example, they build a house, they put an effort into carrying the bricks and mortar, although they could build it (materialize it) in an instant. While working they could make the bricks and the mortar weightless and they wouldn't have to climb the stairs or use the door to pass from one room to the other. Instead of walking they could flow freely in the air. But they are used to hardships and it is difficult for them to acknowledge that it could be different. Even if they see that things are possible that were not possible in the physical world, they immediately think it is just an illusion or a dream.

Time passes and a man slowly comes to notice that something changed although he doesn't understand it. First of all, he realizes that he can't communicate with this friends residing in the physical world He sees that when he talks to them they don't listen and when he touches them it doesn't make any impression on them. But even then he thinks that what he sees and feels is a kind of a dream or that he somehow offended his friends. That is because such a man needs to believe at all costs that he is not dead and that he still lives in the physical world. He wonders how it could be otherwise if he is still conscious of himself. If he knew more about life after death while living in the physical body, he would have a guidepost, a sort of a map that would help him to move around the new territory of the astral world. Instead he's got many wrong concepts creating some kind of a false „map" that deceives him. He was taught all his life to believe things that make no sense in the astral world. Because of these wrong beliefs (I will write about them in a moment), instead of living their new life in peace and tranquility, as God meant for them, many people experience true *hell* built on their beliefs. Instead of living in the truth they start to live in illusions they had created for themselves while living in the physical world.

After spending some time in the astral world man gradually starts to notice the difference between his present reality and the physical world. He begins to understand it better. At last he sees that he never gets tired, doesn't feel any pain, that he is younger, more fit, and uninhibited. It is only now that he realizes that he doesn't really see the physical bodies of his loved ones or friends but their astral counterparts. Although he can't closely observe the facts of the physical world (as he did living physically) he nevertheless is immediately aware of what they feel—love, hatred, jealousy, envy—because it is these feelings people express in their astral bodies.

The living are convinced that they lost their loved one forever, but it has never occurred to them that they had lost the ones who stayed in their physical bodies. A note of caution is due here. The deceased in the astral body experiences all the feelings and emotions in an easier and deeper way, especially the emotions and feelings of loved ones. The deceased doesn't have a physical body anymore, which until that time suppressed his sensitivity to these sensations. That is why we should always keep in mind and consider the fact that the feelings of the physically living very strongly affect the dead ones, especially if there is a strong bond between them. You can't just stop loving someone in an instant. If you love truly, you love eternally because love is eternal in both this and the other world.

If the physically living despair and miss their loved ones, the deceased suffer even more than the living.. I think that after reading this book, dear reader, you'll become more aware of the essence of death and you won't expose your beloved deceased to such additional and unnecessary tortures in the future.

When the moment comes for the man to finally and fully realize that he no longer lives physically and he hasn't got his material body anymore, at first he may feel confounded, restless, and even panicked (as was the case of Lucy's grandpa as you'll read about below). It is caused by various thought forms. These were usually created by man himself or by people similar to him. They can accumulate even through ages or incarnations. These are concepts from Satan, the angry and cruel god of eternal condemnation, hell, and purgatory.

When a man is confronted with such a thought form (which he believed until that moment) he gets frightened and suffers deeply. This suffering can last very long, until the moment a man realizes that he himself is the cause of the problem and liberates himself from the fatal influence of such concepts. Although they are false and delusional, they have a powerful impact on the panicking senses. If some other man who didn't believe in such things while living physically faces the same thought form, it doesn't impress him much, nor does it frighten him. It dissipates like a fog before his eyes. You can see now what the difference is. Belief and fear or their lack in our created concepts determine if a thought form in the astral world will make us suffer enormously sometimes.

I discovered it many times while helping in such cases. Every time I managed to wake the ghost up to get into contact with it, the change was instant. It is not an easy task because it is in a state similar to physical shock. A man in the physical world can be awakened by a shake, slap, or pinch. You can't apply it to the ghost. It is absolutely convinced that its delusions are reality that it has deserved it, and nothing can change its mind. It falls into it head over heels because he wants it, not because he is forced to. And this is a big difference.

The Protestants are in a particularly difficult situation here. Catholics have it easier because they believe in purgatory and they know that no matter how long they would have to endure the tortures (I repeat: tortures made of their own beliefs), it will pass. I don't have to stress that their suffering is absolutely unnecessary. While we deal with delusion it is entirely real and painful for the beings tied up with it.

In most cases, religions don't teach their believers how to act in the astral world. It comes from the fact that the priests of these religions don't acknowledge it. I met dozens of priests and nuns (of all creeds in my practice, who (already as ghosts) had serious problems with further existence. That's how I know for sure that learning what will happen after so called physical death while we're alive can protect us from unnecessary fears, stress, and suffering. If you agree then you will benefit greatly from reading further.

BEFORE YOU DIE

We don't realize how little we know about our earthly existence while passing through it. Only death (and looking beyond it) can explain to us what life is. We need to confront this knowledge, however, and bring it into our lives. Many things reveal themselves to us in a broader view. Until now, death seemed to be the end of everything. In reality, it is a continuation of our previous life. In order to pass from one level to the other undisturbed we should know as much as possible about the process. When we know everything about death we can start to treat life differently.

Life truly comes down to a very simple formula. The primary reason we come to the physical world is to take care of each other and the Earth. Before and during our earthly journey we get everything we need to work on our soul's growth—these are our gifts. When a soul touches the Earth, it can't leave it until the moment all of its commitments are fulfilled. While living on the physical earth we take on many tasks and all of them should be accomplished before we end our lives. If, for some reason, someone isn't sure that he will live long enough to accomplish his task, he shouldn't take it on in the first place or he must find the right person to accomplish it for them. Nobody can die leaving his tasks unfinished. We would otherwise leave a part of ourselves on Earth and wouldn't be able to pass away in peace. You will know that the time has come to leave this world when you can't accomplish anything more in this incarnation.

If any one of us discovers or intuitively feels that a moment of death will come for the physical body, he must perform a „ceremony" in which he passes his unfinished tasks on to another who agrees to accomplish them. Every person leaving this world has to settle his temporal life like this. He ought to apologize, give and receive love and gratitude for the time spent with his loved ones, and cede his social and familial responsibilities. We should all do it on a daily basis. But how many people do it? If a person falls behind with it, if he didn't do it before, he would have to take care of his matters at least mentally, in a symbolic way. Our modern society that lives in constant fear would never let it happen. A person wanting to sort his affairs out will definitely hear, „Don't be silly, you are going to live long, etc." It is nevertheless their business how they react. The task of the dying one is to liberate himself of everything that could bind him in his further journey. It concerns ceding all his possessions, even personal items to his loved ones. He can do it symbolically while he's alive, of course. It would be wonderful if people granted acknowledgment of the gifts (even if only symbolically) to release them from their duties. The point is that his spirit's job has been accomplished. It is only then that a man can leave this world in peace. His energy is absolutely clean then. His soul can continue the journey along the individual path.

The dying one is often unable to perform such a ceremony because his loved ones don't let him do it. The alternative is writing (even secretly) his will. People leaving this world should be aware that even the poorest man has something that can be of use to others. If we all knew this, life would be easier. We would face death differently, in peace and understanding. Remember that the ultimate purpose of humans is extending freedom through cultivating the sense of one's own dignity, self-love, kindness, and self-esteem – they are all the same. No sooner than you accomplish this task will you gain love, respect, knowledge, kindness and understanding in relation to others, even all of humanity. If you try to gain it in the wrong order and you first think of others and not of yourself, you will never accomplish the goal you were born to accomplish. You will die unfulfilled.

It is important to know that the date of any death is not coincidental (even when it seems sudden and unexpected for the physically living). When the personal obligations of a man get fulfilled by the stream of the universe—the forces that make possible the continuation of the individual lifeline from one incarnation to the other—they need to be rightly placed. There must come the right moment of passing, as it was with birth.

Although every soul has its own obligations, it is closely related to all Life in the universe. Every existence that touches the Earth has its own schedule. No soul can leave as it pleases. Its departure needs to be synchronized with other souls because there is a basic plan concerning all the streams of the universe.

This plan concerns not only those who leave this world but also people who stay. When a soul leaves its body, many forces such as angels and spiritual guides help to re-establish the energy balance of everyone that was somehow connected with the deceased. It is not easy to leave a material body, because everything that this soul undertook on the Earth must be fulfilled.

"DEATH"

Death is the putting away of a physical body. It means as much to the soul as a living man taking off his clothes. Death doesn't exist in the soul's understanding. I repeat it over and over again to embed it in your subconscious. It is like memorizing a poem. When you read it once you don't remember anything, but repeated reading makes you learn it by heart. When you die one day, you won't get confused because you will have a map of consciousness in your head that will guide you. Seeing a disturbing phenomenon won't frighten you because you will remember the cause of its creation. The understanding of its essence dissipates it in front of your eyes like a bad dream.

In the chapter called *The School of Life* I will explain that physical human life is as short as a blink of the eye. Man often takes off his physical clothes and comes back Home. I don't mean the existence of a ghost hooked to the physical world, but a being that lives eternally.

Do you remember how, as a youngster, you welcomed the last day of school and enjoyed the beginning of vacations? In exactly the same way your soul, putting away its physical body welcomes the longed vacation time and returns Home. Only someone totally ignorant and afraid of the subject of death holds on to life and doesn't know what to do with himself. Talking about death serves its goal because man comes to terms with the passing away that we generally call death but that is the further journey after life.

It is but a huge dumbing down because this journey is divided to many phases (stations). Each one is set in a different world, on a different plane. As you will see in a moment, each plane and or world has many levels in addition. If I was to tell you in short what life is after putting away the physical body, I would say: every soul, the immortal part of a human being, puts away its many external covers, that is, bodies. Do you recall, dear reader, the descending of a soul to the physical body? It put certain bodies on it. Now it takes them off one by one. First it is the cover it put on as the last one. To understand it right, imagine that you put on different clothes, one after the other. That's what the soul did when it descended to Earth. Now, to take them all off, you need to do it one by one until you are completely naked.

So the soul first takes off the physical and etheric layers. The process goes on before our eyes in the physical world. Both layers, the physical and etheric, are physically real although the second layer is invisible to us. Next, after quite a long life in the astral world (much longer than the physical), the soul takes off the astral layer. Then it takes off the mental layer and returns to the causal body, proverbial Home or Paradise. I won't describe the journey further. As you will soon see, most people don't ever get higher than this level because they are eager to come back to Earth.

Individual bodies serve the soul as tools helping it to grow and „vessels" at the same time. Coming back home, the character of the soul's stay in certain planes or worlds is determined by what it has gathered from the subtle bodies and whatever it carries in these „vessels". When a soul liberates itself from the physical and etheric bodies, it lives in its astral body. It is nothing new to it, though. The soul passes to the same body and to the same world it spent its nights in and which it moved freely through wherever it wanted.

How long does a soul stay in the astral world? Until all the energy created by human feelings, emotions, and passions we allow ourselves to keep during our physical, earthly living dissipates. The essence of the astral life is all the emotions and feelings that contain personal elements.

If thoughts and feelings of a physical man are mainly egotistical they create a tough life, especially tough sometimes for the astral man. If a person was good and kind to others, such thoughts provide them a relatively pleasant astral life. There are certain limits, though, because much depends on the way a man reacts to his death, especially if he is aware of it and accepts it.

If feelings and passions of a man in the physical life are strong, his astral body will be quite vigorous and his stay in the astral world will be quite long (several dozen or even several hundred earthly years). If his former earthly life was characterized by intellectual work and purity instead of passion, the stay in the astral world will be relatively short (about fifty years) in comparison to the length of life on Earth. Isn't it worth considering how we live today, then, while we can still have direct influence on our future? The characteristics of the astral body are created during the physical life by our present passions, desires, emotions, and indirectly by our thoughts and physical habits such as nutrition, alcohol use, hygiene, abstinence, etc. It doesn't mean, of course, that our aim is to mortify one's body or refrain from physical pleasures. It only means that we should understand what it is all about and not to get too attached to earthly matters. We should use the knowledge presented here in order to be well on every plane.

After a long or a short stay in the astral world there comes the second death when the soul or a real human gets rid of his astral body. The soul liberated from the astral body is still alive, though it lives in the mental body, and, more specifically, in the lower mental world.

How long will the soul stay there? It is determined by the nature of one's thoughts during his physical and astral lives. Analogically, the stay will be as long as the energy created by these thoughts doesn't wear down. As you will see in a moment, altruistic thoughts and feelings influence our life deeply in the mental sphere. The life of such a person is blessed and untroubled. I will write more about this issue in the chapter *Mental Life*.

When all the mental energy or energy of thoughts wears down, there comes the third death, the death of a mental body, when a soul liberates itself from this body. This is when a real human passes to his causal body, his real body in the causal world called Heaven by many. A soul having journeyed far returns Home, to God.

As you can see, dear reader, the way our future life looks (and that concerns all the phases of life after the death of a physical body) depends exclusively on our life on Earth. Life in the physical reality has the most powerful influence on our fate, both present and future. The sages, prophets, and Masters have emphasized this since ancient history. Although our astral life is usually longer than the physical one, it is only a transitional stage in the cycle of life and death, preparing a soul to live in the mental world, which in turn prepares it to live in a causal world.

Death, according to earthly understanding, doesn't exist. These are only subsequent levels of one's life in successive worlds. As you will learn from the chapter *The School of Life,* certain phases are the equivalent of a day (incarnation) in a greater educational program. They are only small pieces in the endless soul's life.

The duration of stay in various planes is different for individual people because it depends on many factors. Suggesting any length of time could unnecessarily mislead you, dear reader. In order to illustrate the life I am talking about I will use an example of an ordinary man running a small business. His life in the astral world will last about forty or fifty years and his life in the mental world about two hundred years. A spiritual and cultured man can spend about twenty years in the astral world and about a thousand years in the mental/causal world. A man of an unusual level of growth can stay in the astral world for just a few minutes, hours, or days and about fifteen hundred in so-called heaven.

The souls that belong to the lowest levels of growth have unusually strong physical bodies yet their other bodies are underdeveloped. This is the reason why they come back to the earth shortly after death. This example shows that without a well-developed subtle body we cannot possibly stay in the corresponding world; for example, an underdeveloped mental body cannot last long in the mental world. We stay there but we are not aware of it so we desire to return to earth.

A soul of a man whose life was filled with evil (both deliberate and intentional) throws away his astral and mental body instantly after his death in order to set itself free. Without these bodies it cannot exist in higher worlds, which is why it has to come back to earth at once. We sometimes draw precipitate conclusions that there are more „bad" people on earth than good ones. The truth is that the members of, let's call it, a „negative group"—just pass away more often by either being killed or killing themselves and return. They don't have proper bodies to live in the netherworld after the death of a physical body.

Not only does the time spent in higher worlds differ for different people, but the conditions of the soul's stay are different. The length of time certainly changes while man grows spiritually. A vulgar man lives in the physical world only, as I explained above. The less developed one lives in a near-physical world, spending only some time in the astral world. He is completely unaware of the higher worlds' existence.

The more we grow emotionally, the longer our astral life becomes. If he grows intellectually and cognitively a man can also spend more time in the mental world. A so-called cultural, grown, civilized man stays longer in the mental than in the astral or physical worlds. The more advanced his growth is, the longer his mental life and the shorter his astral life. How long is it? It all depends on the power of feelings and passions and the thoughts connected to them gathered during their physical life. Its quantity and quality depends on when it gets used up. The more power, the longer stay in a certain world.

As we have said before, the quality of life on different planes depends exclusively on a man himself, on his thoughts and feelings. The death of the physical body changes nothing materially. Life in the higher bodies will be just a continuation (precedence) of present emotional and mental conditions. If we wanted to explain it in terms of religious beliefs, the astral life is equal to purgatory while mental life is equal to heaven. These are, however, subjective states of consciousness and not specific objective places.

Hell is also a state of consciousness, not a specific place. I have already written that this notion was confirmed by Pope John Paul II during his visit to the United States in 1999. A man that believes in hell or purgatory creates all of his (sometimes extremely) unpleasant experiences himself. Staying in a proverbial self-created purgatory or hell can cause much suffering. But even such a misperception of reality will end sometime. I will write about this later.

The state of consciousness that creates our reality, meaning a very deep knowledge or certainty of a specific subject, begins in the physical life. If that state we find ourselves in after we die is a continuation of a physical life, meaning it depends on us only, isn't it sufficient enough reason to revise and change our way of thinking on life and death? How are we to achieve it? We should change our unfavorable thoughts and the emotions will follow. We should abandon our negative attitudes based on fear and change them into more perfect ones filled with love and beauty. It is extremely important. When a physical body dies it goes in the direction of its thoughts. If we are frightened, bitter, or full of hatred or anger we will find ourselves in a place that corresponds with the vibrations of these thoughts and emotions. These will be equivalents of hell or a purgatory, if we are to speak in religious terms. If our thoughts are noble, peaceful, filled with gratitude, love, and forgiveness, we will find ourselves close to God in the equivalent of heaven. This is a lot although it is not Heaven written with a capital letter.

THE MOMENT OF DEATH

At the moment of death the real human with his etheric body leaves his physical body and drifts over it. However, he doesn't completely break the bond with it and remains connected with a silver thread. One can observe it as a gradually thickening purple fog, taking the shape of the dying person. This is the same mute figure that is apparent to some people, most often those connected to the deceased in life. Such a phenomena occurs sometimes long before death. The shape is glittering and similar to sparklers. It is by that glittering that you can recognize that the silver thread is not broken yet.

Also, people remaining in a state of clinical death remain connected to their physical bodies by a silver thread. That is how they're able to return to their bodies any time. Such a person wanders where they please and the thread remains unbroken. We can talk to them as though we were talking to a living person, no matter if we're sitting at their bedside or living on another continent. They cannot only hear everything we say but read our thoughts and feel our emotions. If we say one thing and feel another they will know it in an instant. Let me prove it by example.

I was asked to help a businessman who fell into clinical death after being severely beaten. He was in critical care and the doctors said there wasn't any chance of him surviving. The family was despairing. I made a connection to this man (let's call him Ron). I had a hunch he would live for some time yet. My assistant passed this message on to his family by phone. She urged them to talk to him, stand by him, and encourage him to come back to life by giving him the reasons his life was worth returning to. They did what we asked them to do. The doctors were surprised to see him get much better. He woke up after a month and after several more days he returned home. Everyone interested in the matter thought it was an exceptional phenomenon. Many people talked about it. One of them was his daughter's cousin, my good friend. I would get information from three sources: Ron's soul (mentally), his family, and my friend. Ron's story was as follows:

He was attacked and beaten by his two associates, with whom he had been running a prosperous business. After beating him they took him into the woods and left him there to be found by hunters with a dog a few days later. He was cut badly, frozen stiff, and had lost a lot of blood. His other associates thought Ron was dead and managed to defraud their handsome assets. When Ron was recovering at the hospital he told his daughter about it. He forbade her, however, to talk to anyone about it because he worried about the safety of his family. He knew his former partners were capable of anything. „How did this happen and where is justice?", his daughter exclaimed. „They must be judged and sentenced, maybe even to death." Ron answered her:

„It's true. You can't violently take anyone's life because he
hasn't lived through his karma yet. I haven't lived through mine
and that's why I needed to return. You are right. Many people
kill others even though they don't have the right to. They act out
of ignorance. They think man lives only once on this earth. If
they knew what I know now they would never dare to do such a
thing. They would know that you not only have to pay for
everything you do in the future but you will also suffer deeply
after having passed into another dimension. And when they
come back to Earth they are going to have a tough life. They
will have to compensate all the people they treated wrongfully,
too. So don't worry about justice and revenge, leave these things
to God." He was so convincing that she understood and promised that she wouldn't tell anybody. He told me the same thing
he told his daughter and asked me to watch over her in case she
forgot. It was only the two of us who knew about this incident:
me mentally, and his daughter physically.

Ron complained that he didn't have a purpose in life anymore. He was disappointed in everyone with no exception.
While in a coma he noticed that he had somehow incapacitated
his family. He gave them everything they needed so they didn't
feel the need to do anything with their lives. He told me one day,
„I don't feel connected to them. My family used to tell me 'Ron
(or Daddy), come back to life. Get well, we will walk along the
beach, go for vacation, and buy this or that.' Nobody (neither my
kids nor wife) told me that they loved me, missed me, and
wanted me to live for them because they needed me." I told my
friend then, „Talk to your family. May your cousin take care of
her father and your aunt of her husband. Make them talk to him
deep from their hearts, with love. If they don't they are going to
lose him." „Why will they lose him?" she asked with surprise.
„He is perfectly well now, even the bruises have disappeared. I

know what I'm saying, please do what I ask you to." None of them, however, were able to find love within their hearts. They had been without it for a long time. One day I heard Ron say: „Time to leave this world. I sorted everything out and I can still not see any sense in living." He died on the next day. My intuition told me that would happen from the beginning.

As you can see, dear reader, if a soul is convinced that it cannot gain anything more in its physical existence, it will pass to the spiritual dimension regardless of modern medical successes. And vice versa. If a soul must learn something more, even if it is in critical care, it will come back to the body if only for a few moments or days like in Ron's case.

I talked to many people who had been in a coma, at death's gates, and returned to their bodies. They mostly drifted over their body observing how people resuscitated and rescued them. I was in this situation myself. When I awoke after almost three weeks in a coma I remembered everything that happened during and after my surgery. It wasn't an ordinary day at the hospital. It was midnight on New Year's Eve. Even though I was in critical care, they opened a bottle of champagne and raised their glasses. Everyone held a grudge against me. They complained that instead of enjoying themselves or spending time with their families and friends they had to stay in the hospital and operate on me. Some said it aloud while others just thought about it, but I could feel everything with all my senses because I didn't have a physical body to cushion the flow. I felt guilty. When I said to the doctor who had operated me that I was sorry he almost fainted. (There were very few publications about life after death or coma in those days.) He staggered, leaned against the wall, and couldn't move. Somebody called for help and he was finally led out of the room. Later, he would come visit me every day, sometimes even a few times a day. He apologized and offered to operate on me once more to repair what he and his colleagues „made a hash of." He meant the big scar that was left after the surgery. I didn't agree, though.

You may be wondering, dear reader, if it is possible for a sleeping patient to remain conscious. I can confirm that he can hear, see, and feel.

The mind is still conscious of what is going on. Many people cannot calm down for hours after the surgery because they had heard something during the operation that frightened them. Surgeons often talk while working and they discuss many things not necessarily connected to the surgery itself. They treat their patients routinely, exchanging jokes, laughing, and even getting angry and cursing loudly. Much of this reaches the patient's subconscious and influences their thoughts and feelings. Such commentaries can have a strong influence—either positive or negative—on the patient's recovery period. It's normal for a patient to give up and die on the operational table after having heard a negative prognosis. I'm writing this so that doctors may be more cautious of what they say, think, and feel. Their patients know it all although they cannot always be aware of the fact. Nevertheless, the message rests in the subconscious and influences the man in a positive or negative way.

While experiencing the clinical death, almost every one of my interlocutors saw light or a „spiritual" being of light standing at the end of a tunnel. During this time none of them felt any pain even though some were suffering from severe wounds. When they realized that their tasks on Earth were not finished yet they immediately returned to their bodies and felt pain and other sensations again. They could return because of the silver thread connecting them to their physical bodies.

I performed many sessions of regression (coming back to former incarnations) with various people. When passing from one life to another they often reported how the process of leaving the body went. These are their words:

„I left my body" „I can see a wonderful light" „I am drawn to a wonderful light, the source of the light's energy" „Wonderful people come close to me. I am not afraid. They came to help me" „I feel so light" „I feel at peace" „I rest after the hardship of life. I left all my ailments behind" „I am peaceful and joyous" „This is a wonderful feeling... splendid, as if the sun was always shining here" „This light is so radiant" „The source of strength is light. Everything comes from light" „This energy comes from light" „I am drawn by the magnetic force and my soul follows" „I am among friends. I can see many people. Some are close to me, others are not. We all wait for something"

Many people said this but all of them thought in more or less the same way. Those who feared death were frightened of what was happening, others were surprised, and some of them were delighted.

If a soul decided to leave the physical world, the funeral itself, embalming, cremation, and other special rituals connected with death are of no meaning to it. They are important to the living but not to the soul passing away. It doesn't need such preparations. Its leaving reminds me of passing through an open door or curtain. Sometimes the living want me to ask the soul if the body is to be buried in a coffin or cremated, what clothes should be put on it. There is plenty of time to decide that before death. A soul that is already passing away is not interested in such things.

There is a large group of people who don't want to die and hold on to dear life even after death. They want to live, not die, so they are not interested in funerals because they are downright frightened of them. The mourners have to decide for themselves then.

At the moment of definite, final passing, the silver thread gets ultimately broken. The net of life, the etheric body, is being put into the causal body. It stays there as long as it gets to build a new physical body. We get to decide to manifest in the physical body one more time but I will talk about that later.

When the etheric body leaves a physical body the cells start to lack *prana*, a life force. Without *prana* there is no welding force that keeps the cells together as a whole. The body of the deceased becomes a gathering of independent cells which results in it breaking apart. The cells of a physical body don't die. Each of them starts living on its own, which until that time had served the organism. Hair and nails still grow although the man as a whole died some time ago. However, even if it was confirmed that he body is dead, it needs three full days before the soul leaves it.

At the moment of death (even if it is unexpected), a man watches his whole life after due rest. Everything he experienced in this incarnation passes before him, even the smallest details. He can see that every second of his existence, even while he was resting, is memorized or retained. He watches everything as a spectator, being the onlooker and the main actor at the same time. He gets to know the causes and effects of his actions. It is only now, in the light of the truth, that he can understand the nature of his being without sugarcoating or lying to himself. He sees all the good and bad moments, all the ups and downs, everything he loved and hated all his achievements and things he could achieve or do better. What he enjoyed and what made him cry. He recognizes what he should have learned but he didn't even though he had many chances yet somehow missed them.

He looks at every one of his relationships individually. He remembers all the talks and analyzes the motives of his behavior. He feels now what the others felt then. He can sense their fear, pain, feeling of being lost, embarrassment, abandonment, etc. that he had been the cause of. He looks at the good and bad moments that had meaning. Even those deeply hidden and shameful moments when he raged and pitied himself but also the times when he was proud and happy. Now he knows that everything, literally everything, every attitude and every view, is the source of positive or negative energy for which he is fully responsible.

During such a check-up of his life Andrew understood that his life was filled with greed, violence, falsity, hatred, and prejudice towards others. It eventually resulted in great violence. He understood why his house was burnt down and his wife was accidentally killed inside of it. After death he realized that love is a consolation in every suffering and that the task of his life was not to punish or judge people, even those who burnt his house down and were indirectly responsible for his wife's death (karma, the divine law, takes care of it). His job was to understand and forgive. Unfortunately, he wasn't able to do that and died in bitterness.

Michael, the manager of a big company, understood that you cannot judge people hastily. We should be honest with everyone. It was only after his death that he saw how many lives he had ruined due to his ill-considered decisions and judgments.

Madeline, a beautiful girl and a successful model, was born to this world in order to believe in herself but she wasn't able to achieve it this time either. She was to trust her feelings and premonitions and stop being influenced by other people, especially men. While dying she saw that they had the upper hand when she didn't believe in herself. She gave them too much power when she bereaved herself. She could feel it all her life but she couldn't put a stop to it because she didn't love and accept herself.

Susan, a housekeeper and mother of three children saw that she had gained more anger and grudges against people instead of getting past it. This was the cause of her lack of control over her life. She wanted to manage it but failed constantly. She understood the deeper cause of her problems—she felt condemned from the very beginning. She didn't look at the world with joy, she didn't have faith, and she constantly doubted herself. She came to this world to learn how to believe but decided to doubt instead of trust. She taught her children to act the same way.

Ryan, a small businessman, felt lost for his entire life. He was supposed to learn trust, too, but it was a difficult task for him. He was to trust people who deserved it but he didn't recognize them which is why he was convinced that everybody wanted to hurt him. He didn't want to trust everyone, so he didn't trust a soul, not even people who were his friends or close to him. He kept a distance from favorable people and situations and chose the ones that were wrong for him.

As you can see, dear reader, everyone must take care of themselves while living on Earth. We should do what concerns and constitutes us directly.

While everyone has to learn many lessons, it always happens one at a time. Only after learning one lesson we can start learning the next. When we learn all of them we will understand what our neighbor needs and what he lacks. Then we establish a harmonious union.

Leaving the physical body is always absolutely free of pain. Even after a long and severe illness the face of the deceased is usually peaceful and conformed, almost smiling. At the moment of dying a real human's consciousness leaves the physical body and stops for a short time in his etheric double.

Most people drag a part of their etheric body while dying. Before they liberate themselves of it they are unconscious, at least for the moment. The etheric body is neither a tool nor a vehicle. A man wrapped in an etheric body in the astral or physical world is unable to act. Those who recognize the substance of death during their lifetimes liberate themselves in an instant, while others need a few hours to throw away the etheric body. People who lack this knowledge altogether need days or even weeks. The less a man is aware of his death, the longer it takes; the more spiritually advanced he is, the shorter the time is, if it takes any time at all.

Next, the real human passes to the astral body. Death can be painful only if the dying is afraid of it and protests against the natural process. In other words: if a person is holding tightly onto life, death needs to pull her out. And where force and resistance are used, there appears to be pain and suffering.

THE DANGERS OF THE PHYSICAL BODY DYING

People aware of the nature of death, those who think about it a lot, are not afraid of it. They meet it trustingly and peacefully. It is possible because they have prepared to die, both physically and mentally. They don't try to keep hold of life but welcome death without fear, resulting from a deep understanding. Thanks to such an attitude they remain conscious of themselves and, more importantly, the moment they experience. They don't give in to anything that could take hold of them; they are the masters of their lives. Consequently, they are protected from very unpleasant experiences.

ENVELOPMENT IN THE ETHERIC BODY

I will explain why it is so important to learn as much as

possible about transitioning from one world to the other while we are still living physically. If we understand life on a deep level, not just superficially, we realize that death is a natural part of it. It is the same as with physical life. To become a child we need to leave the infancy. To become an adolescent we need to abandon childhood, etc. We transition from one stage of life to the next. To achieve spirituality at last we must abandon physicality. Understanding this, we know that during so-called death we don't disperse into nothingness but rather put away our physical bodies and go further as real humans. We understand that death is a natural passing from one stage to the other and we accept it and give in to it without fear. We don't attempt to stay with the physical body any longer. However, to be absolutely sure that we have reached this stage (because only this stage frees us from fear of non-existence), we need to study our subtle bodies while we are physically alive. Although we use this knowledge every day, most people block it out. They prefer to think they are exclusively a physical body because they are afraid to look further beyond into the unknown. When somebody believes he is only ae physical body, losing it causes him to think he was deprived of everything he had possessed until then. He is wrongly convinced that the only alternative is to fight to keep the physical body. This is impossible, however, since it is unnatural. When the etheric body recedes from the physical body, it is left lifeless. The physical body never had its own life. It came from the etheric body that nobody really cares about. It is a facsimile, an identical copy of a physical body. When the physical body dies many people hold their etheric bodies tightly, judging wrongly that it is their physical body. I repeat once more: the physical body had never had a life of its own. Since a physical body is all we had known until that point it is all the same to us if we stay in the etheric or astral body. However, people hold on tightly to their etheric bodies, thinking they're keeping hold of their physical body. This situation has serious consequences.

A dying man who is strongly attached to the physical world and his physical body doesn't let go of his etheric body which is physical as well but invisible. He wants to keep it at all costs. He can succeed for some time but will pay for it with a lot of pain and distress. Such a person doesn't understand that holding tightly to the etheric body excludes him from both the physical and the astral worlds at the same time. He thinks that he still exists physically and doesn't realize that he is surrounded by thick, grey fog which doesn't allow him to see the physical world clearly. Everything seems blurred and barely visible to him because he doesn't want to accept the fact that physicality had left his field of experience. If he wanted to see he would notice that his physical body was absolutely dead. It all comes from fear of nothingness, while a person has left the physical life only.

Although the deceased resides in terrible conditions, fighting excruciatingly, he doesn't let his etheric body go. He regards it as a link connecting him to the only world familiar to him. He wanders lonely and unhappily until exhaustion forces him to leave the etheric body. It is then that he passes into the astral life where he could have gone immediately after his death.

Before it happens, a man distraught at the necessity of leaving the etheric body (which, as we remember, he believes to be physical) often tries to take control over the body of someone else. He is so determined that he often succeeds. I wrote a separate book about possessions and its consequences, *Possessed by Ghosts* and I suggest that you read it. I will come back to this subject later.

COCOON

Many of us are not aware that we possess an astral body even though we all spend some part of our lives in it. We don't notice that we find ourselves in it after the death of the physical body. Many people believe that they will experience a change after physical death but nothing really changes for them. They are not aware when they are entering the astral body just like they were not aware during their physical life.

When we agree to the death of a physical body based on knowledge we gathered during our lives, we are awakened enough to avoid being harmed while leaving physicality. If we fear death we escape into unconsciousness. We behaved in a similar way while living. We escaped into unconsciousness drinking alcohol, smoking cigarettes, taking drugs, working too much, or giving in to many other habits. And it is in this short period of unconsciousness in which we can find ourselves after leaving our physical body that we can experience the rearrangement of the astral body. This means, of course, that the astral body doesn't need to rearrange itself. We cannot let it happen meaning we need to commit to opposing it. For such an option to become possible we should be conscious of ourselves as a whole, not only of our physical part. You can't influence the astral world without realizing that you live in it and knowing its rules. The knowledge most people have is rooted in the physical world because they believe everything that exists is a physical body. Moreover, they escape into unconsciousness out of fear of death.

Everything depends on the state of consciousness, then, which is based on our knowledge of life itself (meaning Life written with a capital letter) and our being prepared to enter its respective stages. Otherwise we mistakenly believe that we can't influence anything and worse, that everything will happen without our consent. It is not reasonable to set out for such a long journey unprepared. Trusting a blind fate after putting away the physical body (and this is a journey too) can bring us an enormously cruel fate. At the moment of transformation called death a battle is going on in which the winner is not a stronger one but the one who is more conscious. If a man doesn't want to take care of his future well-being it will be done by the astral essence at his cost. If a man is fully conscious then both sides win.

The astral body consists of the fundamental essence that is still alive, even after the death of a physical body. At the moment of physical death the astral consciousness instinctually begins to worry that it will have to die one day too. Its lifespan gets limited from this moment on so wants its astral body to live as long as possible. It cannot exist by itself as a separate being. It can reach its goal only by a close relationship with a real human. That's why the astral consciousness instinctively does its best to protect itself and its position as much as it can. It doesn't know about a man whose astral body it temporarily stays in. It only understands that the more astral energy it draws to itself, the longer its astral life will be. It shows an enormous cleverness and incredible ingenuity in fulfilling such desires.

We know from the chapter about the astral body that the astral matter is not as thick as the physical one and that this quality helps it move freely. In a state of pain, the astral consciousness tries to rearrange its particles so they can hold every attack they're exposed to in the future. Such maneuvers can be compared to the strategy of a leader on the battlefield. The astral body arranges its particles putting the stronger one made of thicker matter on the outer layers, creating a sort of embankment or a hard shell similar to a coconut's shell. The remaining weaker cells, more delicate and subtle, are put in concentric layers inside the structure. The subtle particles are being placed closer to the interior since they are useless in defending the body. This composition reminds me of a cocoon in this way. Its goal is gaining resistance to friction for as long as possible. The effect is eliminating the flow of astral matter normally occurring in the astral body.

The cocoon is made in such a way that it can be compared in structure to a coconut (considering its hard shell and delicate interior of milk). On the other hand, this structure reminds me of an onion with it characteristic concentric layers.

The astral body rearranged in that way can be called a body of suffering. The average man experiences many unpleasant sensations because of it and for a bad man the experience is almost unbearable. Moreover, in the second case the shell is also very hard and difficult to break, any help from the outside world is most often impossible because it is ineffectual.

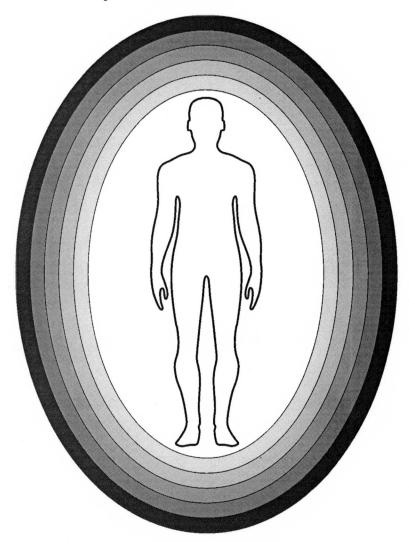

Cocoon – a body regrouped by the elemental of desires

A real human's life, no matter which level it is on, requires maintaining self-consciousness. It is the same in the
physical world as in higher worlds. If we get used to the state of
constant unconsciousness by developing habits,, as we do when
we wander with our thoughts here and there, get drunk, smoke
too much, take drugs or work excessively when we're in fear of
life, etc.), the essential life of our cells gains control over us. We
wouldn't escape life or become addicts if it wasn't true, am I
right? When we're unconscious we don't even notice that there
is something wrong with us. We become accustomed to it
through years spent in the physical body. Due to such a pattern
we are not aware that there is something going on beyond our
control after the death of the physical body so we just let the
rearranging of the astral body take place. An observant man will
eventually notice that different things start to disable him,
though this realization usually comes too late for him to react. If
the cocoon is already made, a real human stays inside it like a
prison or some astral cage. He sees at the same time that everything around him gets worse. Because an outer layer of his
cocoon is spun of the most vulgar emotional human traits, and
therefore the thickest and heaviest, they are the most resistant to
friction.

The law of attraction is present in the astral world—like
attracts like. Since the outer layer of the astral body is made of
the most vulgar particles, it will attract similar forces from the
astral world. Only the most vulgar sensations will reach it from
the outside. If the lowest of a man's traits was hatred, envy, and
fear, these will characterize *all* of his experiences. While living
he sometimes loved, sometimes hated, showed courage, cow-
ered in fear, was tormented by jealousy, but was occasionally
free from these feelings. It all leaves in the astral world except
for hatred, envy, and enormous fear that are felt more strongly

and intensely than they were during life because there is no longer any protection offered by the physical body. Such a man doesn't see the entire astral world but only a small piece of it corresponding with his most vulgar vibrations. It is as if someone was kept in a cell since early childhood and thought the whole world looked like what he saw from inside. Such subjectivity creates a man that lacks self-consciousness. Because he is constantly hating, fearing, and envying, he believes that he lives among equally hateful, fearful, and envious inhabitants of the astral world. He could be surrounded by other people whose astral bodies are normal and not rearranged but he wouldn't be able to feel nor see their higher traits. He would regard them as criminal and anomic.

Also, his former friends and family members don't feel the same as they did when he was physically alive because he's not able to notice their positive traits. He only sees their defects. He believes the astral world is hell under such conditions and you can't blame him. Meanwhile, the cause is not the astral world but his actions. Firstly, he gathered a lot of lower type matter (which he should have gotten rid of while living physically). Secondly, he programmed himself to be unconscious and allow the astral consciousness to control him and rearrange his astral matter in this unfortunate way.

People call me every day asking for help regarding themselves or their loved ones. All is well until they learn that it is their Mom, Dad, husband, wife, child, etc. that is possessing them as a ghost and causing them so much suffering. They can't believe that the person that was so kind to them while living changed into such a monster so suddenly. „What happened to his love?" they ask. I hope they can now understand the cause of it all. If not, I suggest they read this chapter carefully one more time. The following examples

188 IN THE WHEEL OF LIFE, VOLUME II

could also be helpful in gaining an understanding.

Margaret, the mother of two married adult daughters and one bachelor son suddenly got very ill. Despite receiving the best possible care (one of her daughters was a known doctor in the local clinic), she died a few months later. While she was alive they were a wonderful, loving, yielding, cheerful, and caring family. There were no fights among them, nor treachery, alcohol or anything that would suggest any negativity. When Margaret got ill she felt angry, however, at the injustice of life. Now that she could finally enjoy life (her children had grown up) she had to die. The most difficult thing to accept was the fact that her husband could eventually meet another woman after her death and make love to her. She couldn't stop thinking about it. It had become an obsession. She couldn't talk to anyone about it. She couldn't tell her husband. He was so worried about her being ill and she was afraid it would crush him and she never talked to her daughters about such intimate subjects. Besides, everyone assured her that she was going to be well soon. None of them granted permission to think about death. They didn't want to waste time and energy on thinking about the impossible. Although they tried hard, Margaret died unconsciously, stunned, and intoxicated by pain killers.

When they came to me terrible things were happening in their homes. None of the family members were possessed by ghosts but they were all tormented and kept awake at night by them. They were tormented physically and mentally. When I discovered that the ghost was their Mom and wife, they didn't want to believe me. „Why is it Mom?" they asked. „She was a real saint. She wouldn't hurt a fly yet this ghost torments us viciously every day. And even if she had been a beast during her life—she died three years ago and this horror has only been going on for six months. Mrs. Pratnicka must be wrong..." Since

they didn't trust me my assistant suggested they look for someone else who could help, such as a priest. They agreed but called
us again after a few months. „We visited all the priests and lay
exorcists" they cried on the phone. „Nothing helped. That thing
still attacks us with growing rage instead of becoming calmer.
Nobody suggested it was our Mom. When we mentioned her
they laughed at us." My assistant asked them how they explained what was happening. „Some said it was Satan, others
called it black magic or a curse" they said. They always had
organized conferences gathered around a phone. „Do you agree
to work together on my terms?" I asked. „We don't have a
choice. Otherwise we will go crazy". „I will do my thing," I told
them. „Listen to me. First of all, you must forgive your Mom
and yourselves for everything you can think of. Next, you must
ask your Mom's forgiveness. You need to do this until the
ghosts go away." They consented. „The other thing you have to
do is tell your Mom at least a few times a day not only that she
has died but how and when it happened because she thinks she
is still alive," I said. „How anyone fails to realize they're dead?"
they asked doubtingly. I suggested they read my last book
Possessed by Ghosts as many times as necessary to fully understand what I was telling them.

My intuition proved to be correct. Dying and unconscious (stunned by medication) Margaret let herself be wrapped
in a cocoon. Her jealousy, regret, and anger, intensified by a
lonely death, were put in the outer layer of her astral body and
turned into a hard shell. Like most ghosts she didn't realize that
she had died. She thought that she will become cured in some
miraculous way and that everything everybody promised had
come true. According to her, she came back home as a healthy
person without pain. She couldn't understand, though, why her
loved ones had become so negative around her. She could feel

love and kindness on the inside but could only see and feel the outside through the veil of her cocoon. She was convinced, however, that it was her husband and children that changed radically. She talked to them and they ignored her. She asked them questions but they didn't answer. What was worse, they started to move things in her house, rearrange them, have it their way. She couldn't let it happen; they didn't even ask her consent. It was the same in her children's homes. They would ask her advice before and now they treated her as if she didn't exist. „I have brought them up the wrong way. They don't respect me at all. Let me show them! They want war and they will have war" she said. She was craving revenge.

She didn't realize, of course, that it was she who had changed, not her loved ones. Even when I explained it to her she didn't believe me. She finally began to understand and change for the better after I explained it to her for a long time. Her loved ones helped me by telling her that she was dead. Of course they couldn't hear her but she thought they were answering her questions.

I told Margaret to forgive herself for everything she blamed herself for. She was supposed to forgive the others, too. They forgave her and asked her for forgiveness. It seemed to her as though they were talking to each other. The most difficult thing for her was to forgive her husband because he met another woman in the meantime which provoked an avalanche of anger and hatred. When both sides gave and received forgiveness the cocoon shell began to dissipate and finally Margaret liberated herself.

Everything we did during the exorcisms could have been done by the family as a whole while Margaret was still alive. Talking to her while she was ill and not leaving her alone in pain and full of fear would have sufficed. Moreover, if they had understood then what death was they wouldn't have fought so vigorously for her life and would have let her soul go when the time came. Margaret wouldn't have created such evil emotions on her own. She wouldn't have consciously chosen to be wrapped in a cocoon. And even if the cocoon had been formed, it could be delicate and full of good traits such as love and cheerfulness that were present during her life.

Let's take another example. Philip spent his life as an average man, neither exceptionally good nor bad. He sometimes had a glass or two with his friends just for fun but you couldn't call him an alcoholic. He could keep alcohol at home for months without opening it but he wasn't able to say no to his friends when they proposed a few beers. It was like something would get into him when he drank and he became a completely different man. When he drank (and sometimes even when he was sober) he blamed everyone, cursed people and hated them so much he was capable of murder though it would eventually pass. Philip didn't realize what the causes of his emotional outbursts were so he didn't look for a way to stop them. After his sudden death due to a rage-induced heart attack he let his astral body be rearranged. Before that, all of his bodies coexisted and the particles circled freely. After his death they got shut in the concentric zones. The cocoon surface was made of hatred, anger, and fear particles because they were the strongest and most resistant to friction. During his lifetime Philip was mostly a calm and cordial man. He was still like that inside but he started to perceive the world through the vibrations of the outer layer of the cocoon. It was as if he put on colored glasses. He not only perceived the world as being full of hatred, he heard and felt it. He could have been in the most beautiful place with the most reliable friends but he wouldn't have been aware of their existence. The outer sphere of the cocoon was impenetrable and the subtle particles of the astral body were unable to be reached by lighter vibrations. He could sense others only when they felt hatred or anger or when they cursed others. He wasn't aware of his own limits. People seemed like degenerate monsters to him. He would often attack them in self-defense.

While Philip was dying his neighbor Joan was living in Britain. She had a family there and a good job. Her family in Poland asked me to help her. A while ago Joan began beating herself up and covering her body with bruises. The bruises looked as though they were made by a strong man, not a woman with small hands. „In the beginning, we suspected it was her husband" her sister said. „But then we saw that he often protected her from herself. We noticed that she would curse loudly with a low male voice during the attacks."

The assistant asked how long it had lasted and it emerged that it was a few months. At first it was small bruises and sores but it got worse with time. The family was worried that Joan could harm herself severely. I found one very strong ghost around her. I asked her for a list of deceased relatives but the ghost wasn't on it. Then I asked her to supplement the list with friends and neighbors which is when I found Philip's ghost. I contacted him. Firstly, he complained that he was possessed by the ghost of a girl he could not free himself of. Philip thought he was possessed by Joan and that she was responsible for his misery. He was beating her to try to free himself.

When this was clear I began a long and strenuous process of exorcisms. This time, I couldn't lead the ghost away as I did in other cases because the cocoon in which Philip was wrapped made it impossible. We had to wait for the shell to dissolve so he could break free. Joan's task was to recognize what thoughts or emotions drew Philip's ghost to her. The next move was healing her psyche by changing the thoughts and emotions drawing the ghost in. Joan forgave herself as well as Philip. She told him constantly that he was dead and that it was him who was the ghost, not her. Success finally came. Philip left Joan and the beatings ceased.

I hope, dear reader, that you understand now the conditions of staying in the astral world and that you will immediately start working on your future so that you won't let the elemental of your desires rearrange the astral body after you leave your physical body. I trust, above all, that you don't let death frighten you and that you remain conscious. This is critical. Moreover, avoid having addictions. I mean during your physical life, of course. When we let our addictions control us we find ourselves in the claws of the aforementioned elemental which is going to determine our fate from now on. Breaking free of even the biggest of addiction is possible. Addictions and cocoons come from the same source and if you have a problem of that kind, dear reader, I suggest that you reread the chapter about addictions in my previous book, *Possessed by Ghosts*. It is necessary for you to fully understand the nature of addiction and eradicate your addictions now while there is still time. Otherwise you will suffer greatly after leaving your physical body because you won't be able to satisfy your hunger in any way. There is a large group of people that have a problem with their addictions but they won' admit it or consider controlling it. Turning to a rationally thinking friend and asking if we are addicts takes courage but can be of great value.

If a cocoon doesn't form, the astral body particles stay interspersed as they were while a person was living in the physical world. Therefore, the deceased is not shut within one zone (level) of his astral body and can move freely through all the levels depending on its structure. He can move through all the vibrating zones provided by his astral body. If his feelings and emotions vibrated on a high subtle level during his life it would be similar to living in paradise even if he stayed in the astral world. Conversely, if his feelings and emotions were vulgar he would believe he was in hell.. All the levels between proverbial „heaven and hell" correspond with Christian purgatory. Let me remind you that these places do not exist objectively but are rather states of mind. I will write more about this later.

One more note for the future. The fundamental desires that half-consciously worry about fate will try at all costs to project fear onto a man trying to defend himself against the rearrangement of his astral body. It is possible only in the case of a man that fears death. Otherwise, he would immediately recognize that it is not his fear and that it comes from the outside. He would never give in to such feelings.

A man that fears death will think that the fear is his own. The feeling will intensify. This is, of course, a delusion one cannot give in to under any circumstances. The fear is only suggested yet it instigates action. It will disperse into thin air the moment you deny it.

It is worth learning the laws of death and becoming familiar with them while we are living so we will remember them well into the future.

A STAY IN THE ASTRAL WORLD

Nothing lasts forever. A finite cause cannot bring infinite results. It is true for both astral happiness and misery. It is some consolation for those who allow their astral body to be rearranged. To describe the processes going on within the cocoon more precisely, I have to say a few words about the astral world and its various levels first.

This division concerns the astral world as a whole. It encompasses all its inhabitants—the people physically dead—those who can move freely and those who are wrapped in cocoons, attached to one subjective zone of someone's astral body. Other large groups in the astral world are people visiting while dreaming, angels, and spirits of nature.

The astral world is divided into seven zones or seven vibrating levels. They all interpenetrate but their general tendency is to align according to the weight of their specific gravity. The thicker they are the closer to Earth they are and the lighter ones

196 IN THE WHEEL OF LIFE, VOLUME II

are outlying, of course. I will explain this through the example of physical nature. Imagine a large transparent container filled with water into which you pour a few different milled substances of different weights. Now you shake it so the elements mix with each other. At first you get the impression that it is one substance coming out. After some time, however, you notice that the heavier contents stay closer to the bottom while the lighter ones drift higher. This is more or less what the entire universe looks like. Everything is spinning according to its weight of vibrating thickness lying close or far from a source, which in this case is God.

I think everybody understands this moderately. Let us go further in our consideration since everything is based on the same principle. Every man in the astral world can move to a chosen place. It doesn't matter if a man is alive dreaming in his astral body or if he is dead and has left his physical body. Everybody can move freely within the astral world. It is only natural for a soul to keep itself on a level that corresponds with a specific gravity or vibrating thickness of its astral body (similar to how you could see the contents of the transparent container).

Transitioning into physicality is a little bit different. An addict in the astral world will move in the direction that offers him the possibility of satisfying his addiction. In such a place those who are spiritual, creators, or in love will not be found. They are not drawn to such places.

People who didn't agree to rearrange the particles of their astral bodies are free to move throughout the astral world. However, they usually keep to their own vibrating zone. All the souls in the astral world create their environments due to the law of attraction. They are drawn to each other, though I should say that they get embedded in the astral world because of the gravity of their own astral bodies.

People with a rearranged astral body cannot move so freely. This is not because anything blocks them from getting onto higher levels or descending into lower ones but because they are fully aware that only the part of the astral world that corresponds or vibrates with the particles of the outer layer of their cocoon. A drug addict could possibly take part in an embroidery course, go to a playground, or see a play but he finds nothing attractive there, nothing of interest.

Colloquially speaking, a good-natured man wrapped in a cocoon will automatically find himself on a higher level of consciousness or vibration than a man wrapped in an identical cocoon who was deliberately bad-natured. They had different values and analogically different vices or emotions that have now passed into the outer layer of the cocoon. A good man, for instance, will look at the astral world through a lens of bitterness while a bad man will hate it or fear it intensely.

The souls staying on, let's say, a middle level of the astral world will know and understand much more about it than the souls staying on the lowest level. Vibrating gravity of the astral bodies keeps such souls in the seventh zone of the astral world, which is located under the physical surface of Earth. The physical matter of Earth doesn't exist in the astral world, of course. A man staying in the seventh zone doesn't sense Earth the way he would sense it if he were physically alive. He percolates it as if it was the air. He is attracted to it, however because his astral matter's specific gravity corresponds to the solid earth. The inhabitants of the seventh zone wander in darkness far from other dead beings who exist on higher levels. Wandering ghosts of the seventh zone can be met everywhere but most often appear in graveyards. People think that they stay there because they feel best within their graves. Living people vibrating on the lowest levels also wander in these layers of consciousness while they leave their bodies in dreams. They dream of graves, night-mares, and graveyards.

The sixth, the fifth, and the fourth zones of the astral world are totally different from the seventh zone and are more similar to the physical world. Most people are attracted to these three zones because they concern the intensity of their attach-ment to material things. Life on the sixth level is quite similar to the usual life on Earth without the needs and obligations of a physical body. We are less interested in earthly matters on the fifth level and even less so on the fourth.

The third, second, and first zone are even less connected to physical reality. They occupy the same space but their inhab-itants are not interested in the physical world at all. They lose their interest in the earthly matters they were attracted to before. Now they are focused only on their internal world. It seems that they don't see the physical world at all and that they are unaware of it as if they are separated by an invisible curtain I call the death curtain. The souls, however, see each other on every level. They can be also seen by anyone who has developed some sense of clairvoyance. A man will see and understand the astral world only as much as is understandable at his level. People who have evolved to the highest level of development can see every zone. The inhabitants of the lower levels can see only one level higher.

You can probably understand why fortune tellers and clairvoyants looking into the same astral world often see it in a completely different way than everyone else. Among other things, the reason is that people in the astral world lack faith. If the beings of another realm visited Earth and one of them went to a church, the other went to a bar, and the third one went to war, each of them would describe the earth differently after-wards. If this is still not clear to you, dear reader, do not worry. All the pieces of this puzzle will fall together in time. Meanwhile, try to accept the possibility of what I'm telling you.

Let us reconsider the way a man who is wrapped in a cocoon found himself on the lowest level the seventh. First he wanders completely alone, feeling lost and frightened. He can, from time to time, meet somebody in a similar situation. Because both of them carry their lowest emotions such as hatred, envy, and fear on the outside they are hostile and either attack or avoid each other. They live in hell they believed in while they were alive. The thing you call hell, dear reader, becomes a reality for those who don't know they died nor how it happened. They were egoistic on Earth and here they reconstruct the same world. It needs to be stated quite clearly that it doesn't have anything to do with hell as it is described by religion.

The seventh level is most often the place where suicidal people reside, even those who didn't let themselves be wrapped in cocoons. It is not a punishment for taking one's own life, of course. In the astral world everyone is equal, there are no courts, no punishment, or crime. The operating system dictates that every man immediately gets precisely what he deserves according to his opinion. The same system is in place on Earth though there is greater delay.

As for suicides: while living on Earth every man senses whether his journey is proceeding in a natural way. When someone takes his own life he opposes or rebels against the natural flow of life. Everything he experienced in the physical life passes into his astral life. He usually has very strong beliefs and no person or thing can persuade him otherwise. Such defiance is sometimes strengthened by love because it comes from love. The defiant man doesn't adapt to his situation and doesn't want to become aware of it. He knows that he is dead and that his defiance will be eternal. Time doesn't exist in the astral realm which is why a man measures it by the quantity and intensity of feelings he experiences and suffers from. Such a man declares he is in hell—he wants to be there and has been there for the duration of his physical life. Suicidal people in the astral world torture themselves because they still want to punish themselves for the things they already punished themselves for in the physical world. Every man has his own hell. It isn't fire and pain for everybody. The real hell is a life wasted by suicide. Don't think that's the only form of physical suffering. There is a bigger threat in so-called death: losing your mind.

As time passes (which can be a long time if a man doesn't get help on time) the outer concentric layer of the cocoon gets worn down and he gradually becomes able to sense higher vibrations from slightly higher levels. There, he meets more and more people in the same situation or who are visiting the astral world in a dream. He also meets angels and numerous spirits of nature. The length of stay on each level depends on the quantity and substance of created zones, meaning the quality and activity of the particles in the astral body (or rather, the quantity and quality of the emotions accumulated during the physical life). In other words, everything depends on the amount of hatred, rage, fear, or any other negative vibration present in a certain layer.

When one of the layers becomes worn, a man becomes indifferent to the familiar vibrations and starts reacting to the vibrations of a more subtle matter. The world and its scenery and inhabitants slowly disperse in front of the man and a new, better world appears in its place. Now, when he meets another man he thinks that his character has grown but he has actually gotten better at reacting to other peoples' subtle vibrations. When we talk about ascending to higher levels it doesn't have to mean that the place itself changes, though this happens. Most often it is only the man's consciousness that changes.

Anyone that lets their astral body be rearranged after death has to gradually pass through every level. It doesn't mean that someone ascending this way is aware of them all. Rather, they see only those levels that make the layers of their cocoon.

An ordinary, honest man puts some thicker matter outside his astral body, which is usually the matter of the sixth zone mixed with small amount of the matter of the seventh zone. This is how, right after the death of his physical body, he enters the astral world with vibrations corresponding to the physical world. Next, he slowly gets rid of the matter of this zone to ascend to a slightly higher level. The time spent passing through some astral level depends on the quantity and quality of each level's matter found in a man's astral body. Everything depends on what the man did during his physical life, including his earthly desires and strong passions. While in the sixth zone a man revisits places and people he spent time around on Earth. He believes that he's still physically alive. It seems as though nothing changed except for that his relatives have suddenly started to ignore him.

I hope many people will understand now why those who have left the physical realm cannot help those who are still there in any way. If we try to attract ghosts to ask them for help we will eventually make them come close enough to be able to possess us. People who used to attract ghosts understand now that they have to stop immediately, forgive both themselves and the ghost, and allow him to have his own life, whatever that may be. It is only then that we can consider how to help the ghost. This is necessary if we don't want to be possessed. He certainly can't help you because he is hardly conscious of himself. Turning to a ghost for help is like asking a drunkard to help you walk in a straight line.

During the ascension process the earthly surroundings

become less attractive to the ghost and his vision becomes blurred. His reality is created by his strongest thoughts at this time. It is only when he gets to the third level that he recognizes that the world he has created is the astral reality, having gotten rid of the cocoon altogether. Now he finds himself behind a so-called death curtain. Dozens of earthly years could have passed between that moment and the death of his physical body. That's why many people are astonished to have problems with their long gone relatives. They're suspicious of me but my readings are absolutely correct. Furthermore, I have happened to meet ghosts that have spent hundreds or even thousands of years in the lowest layers of the astral world and they still held tightly to the earth.

One of the funniest incidents happened to one of my close co-workers. There was an unfamiliar ghost constantly appearing next to him. I looked closer and saw that it was headless. I had never seen a ghost without a head before and it struck me as strange. I looked closer still and saw he kept his head under his arm. I asked him how he had lost his head and he said that it was on guillotine in the eighteenth century. I asked him what kept him on Earth. It emerged that he was looking for his wife and children. I asked that this ghost be helped and shortly thereafter all the souls of his family members came to him. There was plenty of love among them—we could sense it even from the physical side. They departed almost immediately but we could feel their gratefulness for a long time after.

It is possible that you were stupefied by reading about the cocoon. Maybe you asked yourself how God could let such a thing happen. If men were fully aware while living on Earth that they were multidimensional beings and that they own many bodies, they would change their way of living. It wouldn't be in the physical dimension only. They wouldn't let themselves be trapped in a cocoon either. If a man lacks the awareness of the astral body and lets it function independently, he shouldn't be surprised that the same thing happens after the death of the physical body, meaning that our astral body will get rearranged.

The cocoon is an absolutely natural phenomenon. If a man doesn't work on his happiness, his astral body will do it for him though the results will be deplorable. Ignorance is the root of the problem—the cocoon won't happen to the one who understands fully the laws of life and death while living in his physical body.

Some consolation can come from the fact that none of the readers of my book, *Possessed by Ghosts,* stayed on this side and caused any problems to their families. The deceased pass away and the living let them go. They don't despair because they know that death is just a transition from one plane to the other.

THE RESULTS OF REARRANGEMENT

Maybe you realize, dear reader, that these days the Earth is full of lost beings. These are all those souls who, not knowing that they are parts of a larger whole, broke up energetically or let their astral bodies be rearranged, which are ultimately the same thing. During those processes most of them merged with the energetic fields of the living. The living let them take asylum in their bodies without knowing it. I described the details of this phenomenon in my book *Possessed by Ghosts*. Yet living people are not the mere victims of ghosts. Both sides attract each other like magnets, based on the law of attraction. Simply put: each side is attracted to the other's fear of life and since death doesn't exist there is no fear of death, either. There is only fear of what happens next and the mystery of what one's subconscious is capable of creating. The souls of many beings have passed through death and separated from their subtle bodies, and the energetic fields surrounding them. Most often the reason for this is that these people didn't know how to die. Since the astral world looks the same as the physical, people are usually not aware that they are dead. „How can this be possible?" you might ask. Throughout the ages we've been told many stories that, instead of bringing us together, break us apart. We are constantly being told that we are just a physical body that may own a soul. Many people conceive it as a hypothetical phenomenon. Many highly educated people believe in gravity, ether, energy, quarks and many other abstract, temporal, and hypothetical scientific concepts despite never having experienced them with their senses. Why don't these people believe in the existence of the lasting and unbreakable soul which is a much more logical and more important „hypothesis" than all the others?

Your soul is your truth, your direction in life, your knowledge of *Who You Are in Essence*. When you lose the truth of yourself, you lose your direction and purpose. You feel lost and your soul suffers because it loses its connection with your body. Your body loses the map that showed it what to do, where to go, and how to act on Earth. You are unable to use your body in fulfilling your tasks, which makes your soul suffer.

The main cause of this suffering is all the entangled knowledge you got from other people. Such knowledge weakens you and makes you anxious, which makes you an easy target for all those suffering beings known as ghosts. If nothing changes there is a strong possibility that you will become such a possessive suffering ghost yourself when your physical body dies.

The soul starts suffering when men don't love themselves. Instead of fighting for their own truth they put their soul in strange hands. Suffering is a fact. It is not imposed on us however it is a consequence of our own decisions concerning the life we have now.

Maintaining awareness of the physical body only, we

sentence ourselves to die in fear. It can happen only when we believe that all that we are and all we own is a physical body. When we learn about other parts of the soul and the other bodies we use every day it is highly likely that the awareness of those other parts awakens in us. Then, after the death of the physical body we come back to something we're familiar with without the fear of the unknown which could otherwise be intensified by a belief in eternal condemnation for our evil deeds.

My observations prove that the majority of people telling us such stories (dispersing entangled knowledge) honestly believe that they are true. They meet the same fate after death. A more serious consequence of the entangled knowledge is death from illness. Their bodies are intoxicated (with pain killers, for example), and they are veritably poisoned. These drugs are given to them out of ignorance and they are received out of ignorance, too. This mutual ignorance makes it is very difficult to go beyond our limitations and fear of the unknown when the moment of death is near. It is a big problem for our earth and it concerns everyone, even those that study spiritual topics. Merely visiting the church regularly, reading and studying informative books and religious texts, and meditating, won't protect you from the ignorance we are talking about. It is all based on wisdom and living according to it, not on the outer knowledge, no matter how advanced it is.

It's easy to see who confused us so much and why. You could easily find the people responsible for the fact that the true knowledge remains hidden. From my perspective, such searching leads to hatred and we want to liberate ourselves from it. One thing is for sure: the decision to give your life away was yours alone. Such an attitude must be changed and everyone has to decide it for themselves. The fact that you are reading this book is proof of your readiness. You wouldn't understand what I'm saying if it was otherwise.

Anyway, in order to continue living consciously on the other side you need the right knowledge. Nothing will happen by itself, nobody will do it for you, and you are the only one that can live your life.. As you probably know after reading *Possessed by Ghosts*, dear reader, the ghosts, or the astral beings that broke apart or let themselves be wrapped in a cocoon, recall parasites at every level. While they not always take away peoples' physical bodies, they live in their auras and draw their energy. But the living people are not their victims under any circumstances. They attract ghosts themselves (out of many, often personal reasons) and it is when the ghosts possess them. Although many people are not aware of their presence their lives dramatically change after the possession. They feel exhausted, can't sleep at night, have headaches, become depressed, suffer from unknown ailments, and develop strange habits that are intrusive and incomprehensible to others. I described the detailed symptoms in the book mentioned above. To illustrate this phenomenon I am including a letter from a woman who asked me for help. I have received innumerable letters similar to this one.

This is what she wrote:

„Mrs. Pratnicka,

Do you help people inhabiting a dark cruel world where it is extremely cold and very hard to live in? I'll provide some personal details if you could bring me some relief.

If not, then I'm sorry that I dared to write to you and waste your time.

Mary"

Her second letter was different, however:

„To Venerable Mrs. Pratnicka,

I thank you from my heart for your help. Because of your kindness and good will I regained my health. I have always been a sad and nervous person with anger towards the world and other people. I used to oppose everything.

My home resembled my old family home – cold and gloomy, full of yelling and fights. Even visitors felt nervous despite my hospitable efforts. I became ill in 1983 and the doctors agreed that it was a mental disorder. I couldn't sleep at night, had nightmares, and felt tension all over my body though mostly in my head. Every part of my body ached. I sought help from everyone including herbalists and bioenergy therapists. My flat was even refurnished because someone said I was sleeping on the crossing of watercourses – all for nothing. This past July I read an article about you in an esoteric magazine. There was a photograph of you and I could see your warmth and kindness radiating from the picture. I decided to contact you and help came right away. I began to sleep, the pain disappeared, my eyes became normal. I could see this beautiful world and normal people. The people that used to see me as a crazy person now look at me with amazement. People now greet me, smile first, and approach me to talk. Ferns started to grow in my house, whereas before they would dry up if they even grew at all. It all started when my 5-month-old grandson didn't want to come to our house. He would cry loudly, causing my son and his wife to take him outside. As soon as they would close the door behind them the child grew calm. I couldn't visit them either because my grandson's reaction was identical—he would jerk at me nervously and cry. He was so small and his tears were as big as peas. It was then that I understood that there were unclean forces surrounding me. Thanks to Providence, I found you. It is unbelievable that you are able to help people from afar. Such a

Miracle has happened. I am normal again, my children are at peace, and we're able to spend time together. My only regret is that I waited so long to get help. If it came earlier my two sons would probably have more memories of their mother's warmth and goodness. Now they will remember cries, curses, and fights. What was happening to me and my house is impossible to describe on a sheet of paper. It is a great shame that so few people know who you are; if they did there would be less evil in the world. Bidding you farewell and saying thank you is not enough for the help you gave me but I don't have anything else to give.

Thank you with all my heart!
Yours sincerely,
Mary"

You may realize, dear reader, that ghosts are a danger not only to certain people but to the entire earthly population. The frightened souls that became liberated from their physical wrapping block the movement of spherical forces around the Earth. The spherical pathways become blocked and the light that was meant to get to our planet can't reach it. The masses of souls liberated from their physical bodies occupy a large space. They suffer from pain. They don't know where to go nor how to continue to grow because they usually are not aware that they are dead and till they awake they will remain that way until the end. Negative emotions and fear of such ghosts is a common cause for catastrophes all over the planet. I wrote about this in detail in the chapter called „The Fall of Civilization." Our circumstances threaten us with unimaginable consequences, which is why the knowledge presented here is very valuable. If we don't solve the problem we can face the tragedy just like we always have. I'm not writing this to frighten anyone. I'm just trying to enlighten everyone and remind them of the information they carry in their inner being.

LOOKING BEHIND THE DEATH CURTAIN

Luckily, not everyone gets trapped in a cocoon or wrapped in etheric matter. Many people experience a much happier life after the death of their physical body than they did on earth. The first thing the deceased feels is a wonderful, blissful freedom. A human being feels like a wondrous butterfly or a bird flying high towards the sun. He has had no cares or duties except for the tasks he decides to perform.

If I wanted to briefly compare both worlds of an ordinary man I would say that his physical life is spent doing things he really doesn't want to do but feels forced to in order to make a living for himself or his family while the astral world is completely opposite. This, of course, doesn't apply to everybody but we can easily say this is the majority. For example, eating is different in each world. One doesn't need to care for the physically living because we don't need food. It can be difficult for the people who treat eating as a priority, however. They want to eat only for the sake of eating so they easily panic at the thought of starving to death. If only they thought of the things they wanted to eat with trust, the meal would appear immediately in front of them on a beautifully dressed table.

Also, you don't need clothes in the astral world because no one feels hot or cold there. You can dress and even primp and preen only by thoughts. At last, a man gets the chance to spend his time the way he pleases. He doesn't have to clean, wash clothes, cook, wash the dishes, get up early nor go to work every day. But there are no things the ordinary man uses to „kill" his time with either.

As you can see, dear reader, a human in the astral world can be continuously happy, not only because he doesn't have to care about his livelihood. He can easily satisfy all of his desires. He doesn't have to wait for gratification because everything happens in the moment. He thinks of something and gets it in an instant. You don't need a physical body to be happy or feel joy, love, bliss, harmony, and happiness. There are, however, many people who are frightened to leave their physical body and hold on it during death. If we look closer we will see that the object of our deepest desires is a certain state. Happiness, love, or ecstasy, are states that are not comprised of physical matter. All you need in the astral world is knowledge and good will. Do you enjoy the beauty of nature? Now you can spend there as much time as you want. There are no mosquitoes, snakes, or other dangers here. The sun isn't too hot or cold; it is the perfect temperature. Do you like to travel? You can go wherever you want to. You don't need your physical body, money, or mode of transportation to visit the most beautiful places on earth. You can move around the world with the speed of thought, teleporting yourself. You never get tired because your muscles don't have to work to overcome the hardships of travel.

Are you interested in culture, art, literature, or music? You now have access to all the world's masterpieces and you can bask in them as you please. You can do it not only as a consumer (listener or spectator), you can find fulfilment as a creator or virtuoso. And if you cannot do something you can study and learn how to do anything your soul desires or dreams of. All of the world's famous creators are at your disposal. You can learn under their directions even if you are a beginner.

You can listen to every piece of music you dream of whenever you want to. Moreover, you feel the music with your whole self; it moves your senses. You are going to experience it more deeply than you ever could in the physical world. It is the same with pictures. You feel them with your whole self.

To be able to perform all of these „miracles" you have to know that this is possible and be interested in them while living in the physical world. A person that has never been to a concert or theatre in the physical world or who had to put a lot of effort in reading a book will find it hard to find passion for such things within. It is the same with the world of science. Everybody has access to it but only those interested in inventions and science in the physical world use it now. What will come of the fact that the ordinary man has the access to all the inventions in the astral world even these that have never appeared in the physical world if he is not interested in them at all? Any man can visit the greatest scientists. He can discuss them, use their ideas as he pleases, and do his own experiments on a much higher level than he would be able to do on Earth.

This is a paradise for compassionate and altruistic people. They find a wide spectrum of possibilities here. While there are no natural disasters, hunger, cold, or disease, there are plenty of people who are not aware of the fact that they died and need help.

So, dear reader, if a man doesn't give in to rearranging his astral body matter, he will feel only a slight difference compared to his physical life. He can move freely and do whatever he wants to do. The ordinary man most often likes to stay in places he became familiar with, such as the neighborhood of his former home. He will so see not only his house but also his neighbors, family members, friends without colliding with them. The physically living, especially those who are not aware of the higher worlds usually think that they have lost their close ones. A human who has thrown off his physical body doesn't feel like that even for a moment. The physically living who leave their physical body while sleeping are on the same level (in the astral body) as those who left the physical world entirely. When you are awake your etheric body makes it difficult for you (or should we say, protects you from such direct contact). It is a shield against such confrontations. People whose protective net is broken suffer a lot although they usually don't realize the source of their misery. The reason is that the physical body can't tolerate direct contact with higher vibrations. It is as if you touched your body with something very hot or cold or were continuously attached to an electrical current. Your body wouldn't tolerate it. That's why people with a mutilated or destroyed etheric body suffer so much and sometimes fall into madness. The protective cover of the etheric body is extremely useful then. You should guard it so it is always tight by avoiding alcohol, drugs, tobacco, etc.

The physically dead remaining in the astral body are not able to see the physical bodies of those they have left in the physical life. They can see their astral bodies, though, which look exactly the same as their physical bodies. Therefore, they are aware of the presence of their loved ones and that they didn't pass to a distant paradise, hell, or purgatory. They are still in contact with the physical world that was familiar to them.

Shortly after their death, ghosts often come to console us. But we don't want to hear nor feel them. They say „Don't you worry. Death doesn't exist, I am still here, so don't be sad, stop crying." Often enough, even if we sense or hear a ghost, we think that we lost our minds. The ghosts tend to think that the astral world is the creation of their imagination. The living person thinks the same when they get messages from the other world. The ghost is often unable to reach the man so it leaves, not seeing any sense in staying on earth. It says in parting „If I stay here it will kill me and you don't get anything out of it." It knows that procrastination will become a source of misery for it and for the physically living. Sometime after the death of the physical body it will forget that it has died and will try to return to its former life. This is why lack of knowledge about the transformational process known as death leads many souls to automatically reproduce their former lives.

They get up early, cook, clean the house and even build new houses. People who overlooked their death and think they're still physically alive find themselves in the same situation. Their life proceeds among earthly matters and is the exact copy of their former physical existence. It is of no importance for the living since the ghosts do it on the astral plane and keep a distance from the living. Things get complicated, though, when a ghost interacts with home-dwellers and we are not aware of it.

A woman named Bertha called me once. She was smothered by a ghost every night. Since she wasn't possessed, I had to check if it wasn't a ghost residing in her home which was quite difficult. I couldn't locate it for days although I knew it was there. Bertha gave us a long list of her deceased relatives but the ghost wasn't any of them. She eventually admitted that her husband had died with whom she had relationship troubles before he died. He used to work as a taxi driver and his main job was driving women of easy virtue home after they had finished their scandalous duties. „How could he do such things? There were surely other people for him to drive around." she complained. I checked and confirmed that he was the ghost. It was only then that Bertha remembered more details. She noticed that she had been hearing what sounded like the noise of the garage gate shutting every day at the same hour. Then she would hear someone bustle in the kitchen and take a shower. This person would eventually come to her bed, lay on her, and choke her. It emerged that after her husband had died she started to sleep on his side of the bed because it seemed nicer. My assistant took the time to explain to her that her husband was not choking her and didn't want to hurt her. He would just lie down in his own bed and on his side. Bertha's husband died in a car crash and wasn't aware of the fact that he was dead. He habitually lived the way he had become used to. The first thing I did was make him aware of this illusion. In the meantime I suggested to my assistant to persuade Bertha to sleep on her former side of the bed. She found out, surprisingly, that the ghost had stopped choking her. Bertha's task was to forgive her husband for his behavior so her past hatred didn't hold him on the earth any longer. After that, Bertha and I worked together to wake her husband up. He passed on to the other side sometime after that. Many people in similar situation have the biggest problem with forgiving. They would rather persist with wrongheadedness even though it causes them to suffer.

A man that is physically dead (and aware of it) sees the astral bodies of his living relatives and knows he didn't lose them. Most often, however, he cannot contact them or influence them even if he used to do it while he was alive. He doesn't know either your or his own higher and nobler thoughts either. It is because they don't belong to the astral body but to the mental body. A human staying in the physical body can have a higher vibration than the ghost's vibration. Let's say that a man gives himself to noble high concepts. He resides in his mental body then. The ghost, on the other hand, resides in his astral body so he maintains a different level of vibration. I think everybody now understands that they don't need to be afraid of any ghost even when they see one. First of all, a ghost remaining in its astral body can't influence physicality. This is completely different range of vibration. A ghost can only influence our astral body, meaning it can manipulate our emotions. We can, however, control them if we know our emotions and control our thoughts. Remember, emotions always follow thoughts. The deceased has difficulty connecting with the living because the communication takes place in the mental body a ghost doesn't have access to. When you leave your physical body while sleeping and you find yourself in the astral body, you can meet your dead loved one on the emotional level the way you did it while he was alive but I will write more about that in a moment. If you don't want this meeting you should raise your vibrations. How? Forgive yourself and him no matter what he did to you. You can also try to feel gratefulness or genuine love if you are able to. They are definitely above the vibrating range where a ghost resides. Your roads will never cross then. If there was a higher imperative such as the fulfillment of unfinished business, the ghost has certain methods for contacting the living but I will say more about this later.

Since I mentioned pacts and contracts I would like to share a story with you. For four years and a half I tried to help a man named Jack. A ghost would surround him, leave, and come back and I couldn't figure out who it was. It seemed the case was hopeless even though my experience has shown that such things don't exist. Jack was working hard on himself but the ghost wouldn't go away. I intuitively felt that it concerned some trading business, that the possession had something to do with Jack's job. As time passed the ghost remembered more details that I relayed to Jack—it emerged that many years ago Jack went to the other end of Poland to meet a contractor but she never showed up. „It happens," Jack said and eventually forgot about the incident. The contractor didn't forget, though, because she counted on high profits. Unfortunately, while driving to the meeting place she got in a fatal accident and didn't realize that she was dead so when her memory returned she still wanted to finalize her contract. I advised Jack to sign the contract symboli- cally and the ghost left him immediately after that. It didn't pass to the other side of the death curtain but it has never haunted him again.

All the physically dead can watch their living loved ones if they wish. But not every dead soul chooses to make a contact, knowing that some people would be frightened. The souls that are self-conscious can show up and communicate with the living at will. They only do it immediately following their death, however. They can do it through some special spiritual faculties. There are many ways. Some use the force of their sight and show up in their former physical shape. Others use their energy and move objects by telekinesis. They leave signs that the living can easily read, telling them that their soul visited them. This is a kind of a loving confirmation saying, „Look, my physical body is dead but I am still alive. I am here because I love you and I will never forget you." However, it happens that people reading these signs go to a psychiatrist and start taking psycho- tropic drugs or start looking for ways to cast the ghost out. The ghost just wants to pass on the message that he is still alive and then go away. Since the living react nervously, most ghosts become disheartened. They give up after a few trials and leave.

Only the souls that are aware of their death can leave but it doesn't concern those who hold on for dear life. It is very important information because a contact can have various consequences. One type of ghost will give you love and consolation while the other can possess you forever with tragic results.

The soul that is physically dead can show itself and look identical to the way it did while living, even down to its clothes. Mostly, however, it makes spiritual contact. Sometimes it leaves a message that seems coded but the recipient understands its meaning although the contact is only spiritual. It is as though he understood it inwardly.

I know this from my own experience. Every time one of my relatives died they contacted me. It usually happened during or just after his or her death; once it even happened after the funeral. It is usually a one-time connection. We both discovered what we were supposed to share with each other to make the deceased go away. I knew I shouldn't despair, although I grieved deeply, of course. Despair makes the journey of the beloved soul even more difficult. The passing one must settle accounts with his life and make decisions concerning the next one. Giving him more burdens seemed cruel to me. Many people, however, think of themselves and their grief before everything else so they stop the ghost, sometimes forever. When we stop despairing we usually want the ghost to go away but he is no longer strong enough to do it. This is when both sides suffer.

The astral body of the deceased can take various forms depending on his or her present self-image. The ghost can also take on his former look from the time before he came to the earth. If you make a contact, even if the ghost looks different and you don't recognize him, you will be certain this is the person you think it is.

It is common for the astral body that got used to a certain physical shape to keep its shape and looks. Most of us believe we are younger than we really are. Since the astral body is very flexible and becomes however we want it to be, it can change shape, heal, and look much younger than it does at the moment of death. People open to such contacts can meet a prettier, younger, and healthier version of their beloved deceased. Nobody should be afraid nor doubt that it's the person they think it is.

I would like to discuss these contacts in dreams now. When you fall asleep, your astral body leaves your physical body and goes to the astral world, where all the ghosts reside. We are all equal there because we are all ghosts. If you are on the same level of vibration you can meet easily. However, if your vibrating levels differ much, there are other ways to make contact. Everything is possible for someone who wants something to happen, especially in the astral world. You can easily move in astral bodies and when you find each other, you can spend time together, or more precisely, share emotional sensations. The astral world is built on them so every emotion is possible there. I repeat: these are the possibilities available to these ghosts only that undergo the phase of renewal and are fully aware of the astral world. Additionally, not all living people have their astral bodies fully developed enough to be aware of it. The same issue concerns the dead ones even if they don't let themselves be wrapped in a cocoon. It doesn't mean that you can't communicate. It just makes it impossible to remember this fact.

THE PERMEATION OF BOTH WORLDS

The astral world permeates the physical, but because there are different states of matter in these worlds, their inhabitants are not aware of each other. Only in abnormal conditions can the inhabitants of one world be aware of the beings from another present. This is what happened in the case cited below.

A famous man came to me (let's call him Robert) who during the communistic period in Poland built a large villa with a swimming pool for himself. It was a rare investment in those times. Robert was rich and influential so he could afford it. He was so busy with his work that he didn't notice the constant turnover of the building crews. After the family had moved to the finished house, some weird things started to show up. Robert claimed that his wife, three kids, and many of his workers would sometimes run outside in fear and didn't want to come back. When his work stopped him from coming back home, his wife and the children were waiting for him outside, sometimes even late at night.

They told him about a woman lurking there with a huge club – she eventually attacked them. At first he thought they were imagining things. When he had to leave home to go on a business trip his family slept in their neighbor's house. They ran there at night, more than three miles through the February snow. At that time his frightened workers left their job.

„Tell me please, Mrs. Wanda," he said. „I walk around the house undisturbed and but when my family and workers are left alone weird things start to happen." These are not their whims, they are frightened to death. Nobody could fake such fear. It is only now that I understand why my workers escaped the building place although I paid them double."

I checked and found a ghost, though it didn't reside in the house, only on the edges of the residence. Robert declared this was an empty, vacant lot and he was sure that nobody had died there. I told him that even if the physical building wasn't there the energy would still exist on the astral plane. We had to consider the possibility of a battle, murder, or suicide taking place there. Robert called me when he learned from the local priest that there was a famous border conflict there in the eighteenth century. The trial ended abruptly because one of the participants, whom he even knew the name of, died in a courtroom. The other side of the conflict moved out with the whole family but nobody knew why. I checked the name. It emerged that after almost two hundred years the ghost of that woman was still fighting to move the border – the place that was currently the driveway. The woman built herself a house in the astral world. When she saw her new neighbors, her old obstinacy awoke and she took up the fight as she had with those people in court. She was stubborn and pugnacious and we couldn't persuade her to give up. I came to the conclusion that it was useless to waste time persuading her to leave and that we should make an agreement with her immediately. I asked Robert what is placed on the piece of the property her ghost was fighting for. He said that this was the backend of the garden. I suggested that he mark out the driveway to the woman's house for her. „This is crazy." „You want me to make a pact with the ghost?" „I will take care of the ghost. You just mark out the driveway where I show you, unless you want to continue to fight with her?" I said. Robert agreed. He marked out the way and from that moment a deathly hush fell. The ghost hasn't appeared since. When she got what she wanted there was no reason for her to stay on the earth so she went on.

The next example is of a slightly different matter. A woman named Cheryl called me asking for an intervention. She said she didn't have quite the strength to clean her house any more. Every time she vacuumed it, within fifteen minutes dust clouds began to waft. „Mrs. Pratnicka, I have been a tidy person since my early childhood and I get angry watching this dirt. I haven't had guests for years and when someone visits me accidentally they immediately ask if a bomb has fallen or a tornado has passed through my house." There were some more ghosts but I managed to identify only the ghost of her uncle. I wondered what could be the reason for this weird phenomenon. Unfortunately, I couldn't get any information from the ghost. In such situations we ask the living what their relationship with the ghost was, what unfinished business might be keeping them here, suggest forgiving him and ourselves and ask for forgiveness in return, and we tell the ghost it is dead. Nothing helped though. I tried to learn what the uncle's profession was. It emerged that until the moment of his death he worked as a pyrotechnic expert in a quarry somewhere abroad. Also, in this case there appeared to be an anomaly and the astral world got mixed with the physical. The uncle wasn't aware of the fact that he had been killed during one of the explosions. Coincidentally, he moved to their house and returned to work. He got a big company going and employed several workers. I started a long process of waking him up. He needed to be told that he is dead already, how he died, and commanded to leave Cheryl's house. Because he was killed in the quarry, he was still in shock and didn't accept what I was telling him. His employees, however, apparently understood since they left him one by one. When he was alone he got to wondering if Cheryl and I were telling him the truth. He woke up one moment and left almost immediately. „You know, there is a positive aspect to this," Cheryl told me in the end. „I have once and for all let myself free of excessive cleaning and started to enjoy life. Life isn't all about cleaning after all."

CHARACTER

As you have probably noticed, dear reader, human character doesn't change at all when the physical body dies. It has the same thoughts, feelings, and desires it had before. A man is the same man as he was in every respect with one difference – he doesn't have the physical body anymore. That is why among the dead there is the same variety of intelligence as among the living.

Nevertheless, it often happens that people who died don't realize that they are free from the necessity of earning a living, eating, or sleeping. They don't recognize that after the death of a *physical body* it is not a new and unusual beginning, that this is the continuation of the same method of existence but in basically different surroundings. This is the most important fact we should be aware of. Unfortunately, only a few are able to see it. Usually it takes a lot of time for a man to slowly, gradually notice the conditions of a new life. He starts to notice things about himself, such as not being as tired anymore or not feeling pain.

His happiness or misery depends on the way he experiences the loss of the physical body. If he desires it he will probably suffer. The suffering will be deeper if he has addictions or desires. These will reveal themselves in the astral body as a vibration or force field. While we are still in the physical body, the biggest part of this force field is busy moving heavy physical particles. When we don't have it anymore, the whole force of this vibration moves only the astral body only and then every desire expresses itself in the astral life much stronger than in the physical. In other words, we feel it with multiplied intensity.

If a man doesn't learn to control his desires and addictions while he is physically living, he will suffer deeply after his death because he won't have a chance to satisfy them for a long time. If you want to see what you will have to go through, try to stop your addiction immediately and forever. You will get a poor substitute for a desire that will strike you. I say a poor substitute because you have still have your physical body and the intensity of the desire doesn't reach you with the intensity you will feel when you have only an astral body. Now imagine the future when you completely lack the possibility of satisfying your addiction. Shouldn't you start working on it now?

It doesn't matter if it's alcohol, tobacco, drugs, sex, work, or anything else you cannot live without satisfying. Yet you are in a worse situation when your addiction is stronger than reason, common sense, decency, or family bonds, then think what will happen to you later. While entering the astral world you will experience your desires one hundred times stronger and you won't be able to satisfy it. This condition will boil over into true hell. Many people stay there. We cannot say, however, that this condition is a punishment for wrong deeds. They just harvest the effects of their actions, thoughts, and emotions that grew to be strong addictions from normal habits. So we deal with the consequences of our behavior only. You probably agree with me on the matter, dear reader.

And though one day of great suffering seems to last forever, this great desire not fed by a new energy will weaken very slowly until it disappears completely. How long is it going to last? Time doesn't exist in the astral world. Everything is measured by the intensity of one's feelings. so the feeling of an unsatisfied craving will last very long. It may seem to the soul that it lasts for ages. Meanwhile we begin to understand that the false concepts of hell and of eternal condemnation emerged from the image of a man tortured by his own unfulfilled desires.

It may seem that the suffering described arises in extreme cases of addictions only. Nothing could be more wrong. Unfulfilled desires coming from different bonds to the physical world become a real torture for many. This category includes total engagement in business, spending too much time on social activities, habitual TV watching and shopping, games, sports, computer games, internet, everything one does to „kill time." For such a man the astral world would be a place where he doesn't know what to do with himself, full of unspeakable emptiness and boredom. There is no time here nor activities that make it to pass quicker which the physical man chases and desires greatly. There is no gossiping, judgement, or small talk like there is in the physical world.

WHAT DOES THE ASTRAL WORLD LOOK LIKE

The astral world, however, seems to be heaven, paradise, or Eden for many people. Some people can create everything they want there. „Here" the astral world is so enormous that everyone can have his own universe made of more than houses, gardens, parks, theatres, museums, school, cities, or villages. The inhabitants of the astral world don't need all of this to live, of course. Many of them imagine or paint their surroundings in order to feel safe. Everything depends on thoughts and feelings. Everyone can change their choices at any given moment, of course, and choose whatever they want. Some do it unconsciously though they eventually begin to understand that matter is an illusion and that thought is the only real thing. From this moment on they begin to create consciously. I repeat: such acting is reserved only for those who are self-conscious and who accepted their death understandingly.

In the astral world everyone imagines his reality differently, so there is a lot of diversity there. When a group of people wants to be together they „paint" or create their reality. They have to create it together otherwise any individual creation will separate them from each other making everyone stay in their own self-created world.

Everybody actualizes their surroundings and creates landscapes at will. A man chooses things he believes to be beautiful which contain everything he needs to live anew. There are no rules to live by there. That is why it is possible only in the astral world to discover who we really are and what we want because everything materializes immediately after the thought appears.

If we could see it with our physical eye, we would see beautiful lakes, wonderful mountains, and rich gardens surpassing the beauty of everything that exists in the physical world. We would also see wonderful things that too many of us living in the physical world would describe as fantastic and unbelievable. For inhabitants of the astral world, though, reality is as real and tangible as our houses, churches, and schools built of brick and stone. A vast majority of people live happily for many, many years in a fantastic, whimsical setting, created continuously by their own thoughts.

Unfortunately, most people created their version of the astral world according to the concepts they acquired while living physically. They believed this was going to be their fate. These are thought forms of a different nature—hell, fire, devils, Satan, beasts, various annoyances, purgatory, tortures, etc. If you want to look closer at these various concepts realized in the astral world by its inhabitants, I suggest, dear reader, that you watch the movie *What Dreams May Come*. It is a very realistic picture containing many details, warts and all. You will realize then that there are much less people that are self-conscious and creating their destinies than there are people that allow themselves to be programmed during their physical life for cruel conditions after death. Because the astral world is only an extension of our physical lives, anybody who feels guilty or unworthy won't find themselves in a happy place after physical death because both conditions are opposed to each other and incompatible.

Although souls can move throughout the entire region" of the astral world, they can sometimes get stuck in their thought forms, unable to break free. They are attached to it by their own fear. This is what happened in the example below.

Lucy, an educated, married woman, a mother of three little kids, came to me because she suddenly started to feel terror and panic without a clear reason. She had already visited all the therapists she knew but they couldn't help her. She felt tremendous fear and didn't know why. I suspected that it might come from some traumatic experiences in her previous incarnations. I discovered, however, that a ghost was attached to her. It emerged that it was her beloved grandpa, who was a warm, kind, and helpful person while living. He remained the same after death. His body hadn't been rearranged so I couldn't understand where his fear came from. He was in a state of powerful fear resembling shock. I had almost no contact with him because I couldn't reach him. I was doing my job as an exorcist though and Lucy was supposed to do tasks assigned to her. First of all, I told her, like I tell everyone in such a situation to forgive herself and her grandpa and to ask his forgiveness. I explained the fear was not hers but her grandfather's. She had to learn how to distinguish her own fear from fear that comes from the outside and how to avoid getting them confused. It took her quite a long time. I started to ask her about her relation with grandpa—if she was afraid of him when he was alive or if he had tried to hurt her. She said they loved each other deeply and

that she grieved after his death and still missed him a lot. I asked
why she would be afraid of him now if she wasn't while he was
alive, since his soul had remained the same. Besides, her
longing didn't let him go; she kept him by her side as if he was
on a chain. It was only then that she understood how she was
the cause of her problems and started to distance herself a bit.
That made her fear to diminish. Until then Lucy and her grandfather had been so tightly bonded by their longing and fear that
I was unable to help either of them. When Lucy let go a bit I
was able to take care of her grandpa. At last I communicated
with him and he told me the reason of his terror: he was in hell
and there was no way out. „Why is there no way out? Hell
doesn't exist" I said. But grandpa persuaded me that since he
was in hell he knew what he was talking about. I checked again
and confirmed that he wasn't wrapped in a cocoon. It was the
first time that I tried to free a man from his own „hell". I
thought it would take weeks but took only few seconds. „Don't
you understand this is all illusion?" I asked him. „Your imagination is playing games with you. Look around, you are surrounded by light." The devils and hell disappeared in the blink
of an eye. Lucy's grandfather finally saw a beautiful light. It
was there all the time, only covered by his illusion. He expected to be punished for some reason and this expectation
created it. „How is it possible that I'm in heaven?" he asked
with astonishment. Since he wasn't interested in anything
besides his happiness, he left immediately. Even good people
can go to „hell" if they cannot forgive themselves. I hope you
realize, dear reader, how important it is to forgive yourself and
others. Lucy called me after some time. She said she felt
wonderful that her fear had dispersed. She asked if this condition was permanent. It was. When her grandpa found himself
in a better world, he didn't have any reason to hold tight to his

granddaughter because he wasn't afraid anymore.

As you can see, dear reader, what we experience in another world depends on our ongoing experiences and perspectives. It is up to us whether or not we see things the way they really are or if we give in to other people's suggestions who may not know much, if they know anything at all. It is necessary then to cast away other people's visions and reassess or filter things they say or describe in both this world and other worlds. Be aware of the fact that even your knowledge can mistake you. Doubt everything until you find the truth. Never listen to the ghosts' opinions because they will surely mistake you. Everything is relative. Few people that are seeing the same thing can describe that thing very differently, because everything depends on the level of your consciousness. All our visions depend on consciousness as well. Even if they seem frightening to us they are not so in reality. Every one of us decides on what we perceive.

In the physical and astral worlds many people bask in various atrocities and create corresponding thought forms. Their authors are often pleased with them and experience some satisfaction upon creating them. This is like watching a horror movie. Some people may feel disgusted because they invoke fear and they will try to avoid them. Others may bask in the horror, it all depends on their imagination. That's why there are so many versions of various beasts, devils, and hells in the astral world. People imagine life after death in various ways. It is of no importance if they did it out of guilt, fear of punishment for their sins, the feeling of unworthiness of anything better or they actually enjoy being frightened. The fact that they like it doesn't mean that you have to give in to such visions. Creating these atrocities was their own decision.

First of all, such thought forms come from the followers

of various religions. They mostly think of themselves as hardened and unworthy sinners prepared to be punished, condemned for their sins, and sentenced to fire and brimstone. More devout people imagine their life in paradise and create the thought forms of various deities depending on the religion they follow. Others go to the imaginary purgatory where they suffer from many tortures.

Nonbelievers in the physical life, who were convinced that there was only emptiness and nothingness after death, have it just as hard. They often feel lost and are unable to believe that they are still alive, not to mention other options that would become available if they allowed the thought to enter their minds. When they leave the astral world and go to the mental world for a while, it will unexpectedly turn out that they were completely wrong in their beliefs but I will write about that later. In both the astral and physical worlds people gather according to various categories such as religion, nationality, and interests. The members of those groups can visit each other, nobody forbids them that, but they most often spend their time with groups of friends. That's why in the astral world nobody lacks company. Everybody shares common goals or interests. People feel attracted to each other and gather as they used to do in the physical world and tend to create small limited groups that not only avoid but are afraid of „strangers". This is becoming a source of prejudice and common hostility while our task in this and the other world is learn how to become closer not only to the people whose vibrations are the same as ours but to those whose vibrations are different.

THE INHABITANTS OF THE ASTRAL WORLD

The astral plane is inhabited by beings of various types. The first group is made of the dead who have left the earthly world. They reside in the density corresponding with their maturity level. The more perfect, noble, and pure the being is, the subtler the astral density it resides in. One third of the astral world is inhabited by the living who leave their bodies in sleep and move within their astral bodies for a limited time.

There are many other beings in the astral world that are not human, some of which exist on lower levels than us and some on much higher levels. There are called *elemental*—beings with only one or a few characteristics. They live off vibrations that people send to the astral plane.

Another kind of beings is called *larvas* and they are created by intense emotional thinking. These are not real beings but forms that live on the lowest astral plane because of human passions. Their life instinct attracts them to the zones of humans with similar or identical emotions. They try to invoke dormant emotions in people. If they succeed they feed off them and strengthen themselves through the emanations created by man. A physical man burdened with many negative emotions brings with himself to the lowest astral plane many *larvas* that he will fight with throughout his life.

Another kind of beings is spirits of nature. They have nations and different types like we do in the human kindgom. They can be classified by four great categories: spirits of the earth, water, fire, and air. There are a lot of them and they can be found anywhere, not just in the astral world. This huge kingdom exists also in the physical world. Many types own etheric bodies and reside very close to the physical range of sight. You can see them in many lonely places, especially where people once strongly believed in them.

The beings of fire are called salamanders; of the air, sylphs; water, sirens or water nymphs; and earth, gnomes or goblins. These beings form the connection between the astral plane and earthly elements.

There are also many beings such as fauns, dryads, water elves, etc. You can think it is unbelievable, dear reader, but they are as real on the astral plane as plants on the earth. Many clairvoyants can not only see them but also communicate with them.

The spirits of nature don't have the definite shapes but they often resemble small humans. Since they are not individualized yet, we can imagine them as little humans or etheric and astral animals. Many of them are intellectually on a par with the ordinary man.

The representatives of the Angel's kingdom, known as Devas, also live in the astral world. These beings are more highly evolved than humans and only the lowest parts of their world connect with the astral world. Their members are on a par with humans who, we are certain, have good character. The role of this group of angels is to help and guide the souls entering and leaving the material world.

Angels are always ready to help the inhabitants of the physical earth also but this is not always possible. Firstly, in order for the angels to be able to help in any world they must be called. They cannot help by themselves because people have free will and they cannot break it. Secondly, if a man gives in to a negative thinking, the angels can't help him until he changes his vibrations. Finally, people sometimes ask the angels for help on someone's behalf but this person may not want to be helped.

Additionally, most people cannot get the help they need because they are not able to balance their vibrations enough for the Light and the Truth to abide within them, which is the Angels' reality. A man may even consciously wish to act right, but he hasn't developed his thinking process enough to move his soul. His aura is blocked, as are the majority of people's. His spherical forces are near stagnant and not directed towards any goal. It is disadvantageous for this man, as for all the others who get in touch with his aura.

Angels want to help suffering people at all costs, of course. However, because the difference between the low vibrations of a suffering man and the high vibration of an angel is too big, there often appears to be friction. The angels even sometimes reach the outer edges of the suffering man's aura and try to get inside to cleanse it. They are blocked, however, by the friction, intensified by the presence of the ghosts attached to him. Such friction sometimes ignites a spark and a man's aura begins to move more quickly. The process is sped up by the brain of the man possessed by ghosts, which raises the level of confusion and entanglement. It is a vicious cycle.

And here we have the law of the universe confirmed. If you are healthy and have high vibration, the angels can reach you. They will help you if you ask them. As the Bible says: „For to everyone who has more will be given". If you feel bad, however, the angels or any other help is made impossible. While suffering you have a negative vibration that separates you from everything that is good and the angels cannot get through it. The phenomenon is described by the succeeding part of the quote from the Bible: „Whoever does not have, even what they have will be taken from them".

The situation is even more dramatic. The ghosts of the people that don't realize they are dead emanate a negative force, drawn to the suffering one by the similar vibration, and can impersonate and take the place of angel sin people's auras. Ghosts in such situations have a lot of strength and possibilities and can even control people fully, which I wrote about in *Possessed by Ghosts*.

And *this is exactly* what happens in most cases. Because people are so open to receive help in these moments that they willingly let the ghosts in (vainly, of course), hoping that they will receive assistance. This is only possible when the soul loses its balance and, in extreme cases, gives in to a confused thinking, meaning it forgets *Who It Is In Essence* and why it came to this world. Such a soul then suffers and its spherical forces become very sticky. Due to the law of attraction, it attracts equally suffering souls and this is how the possession takes place. A man can have one, a few, or even hundreds of suffering souls residing in his aura. Some people know they have problems but they don't realize how great they are. The mind is a powerful force. People use it to forget everything, wanting to minimize their suffering (which is a completely wrong strategy in this case) but I will come back to this subject. Have you ever thought, dear reader, how many people ask if they have any souls hooked to their auras? I assure you that not many do yet and it's a problem. People suffer and they don't know where their suffering comes from so they don't know what needs to be changed. There is much confusion within them.

GHOST'S HELP

Are ghosts able to help us? *Yes*, if they limit themselves to showing us a way. *No*, if they do something for us. They not only don't help us then but disturb us because every soul needs to live its life on its own, otherwise it is going to waste its incarnation and a ghost will receive bad karma. Let those who nevertheless claim that I am wrong become acquainted with the examples below. I quote them here because many readers of *Possessed by Ghosts* wrongly believed they are in a better situation than most others. They came to the conclusion that regardless of possession their ghosts are of different nature and don't disturb them but help them.

Once, a wealthy businesswoman who was at the peak of her career became suddenly ill. She dedicated all her time to her business, totally forgetting about her family. When she was approaching death she found herself completely alone, physically and mentally. Her family was nearby but as absent minded with her as she had been with them. This family gap was filled by a poor girl, Veronica, who was hungry for attention. Her job was to help around the house. These two developed an unwritten but strong bond.

The more curt or indifferent the family was to the dead woman, the stronger the bond between them became. It didn't help that the woman threatened to help only Veronica and get revenge on the family from the tomb. What had been in place for years couldn't have been healed despite these threats. During a sudden attack Veronica drove the ill woman to the hospital. When she regained consciousness for a moment, she blamed her, furious that she wasn't going to die in her own home but at a hospital. She died in that condition. The girl lost her employer and a roof over her head. She spent all days sitting at the grave grieving, not knowing what to do with herself. She didn't have a place to go and once making a good income through that family she suddenly became homeless. Her life changed from then on. The ghost began to help her as she promised. Things appeared to happen automatically. Something would tell the girl what to do and she followed. She began to earn money in an inventive way. To make a good amount of money all she had to do was to work a few hours a week thanks to some good ideas. She graduated college that way. She started a career and was on the making to the top very quickly, as did the ghost while she was alive.

The family of the ghost lost everything and Veronica gained everything in some miraculous way, making an exceptional career for herself. The door stood open for her but closed for the family. They failed at everything they did. It was clear to the outside observer that this was the ghost's revenge. It lasted for many years until the point the family was on the verge of poverty. This was when the help of the „caring" ghost suddenly stopped for the girl. Until then she was a puppet in its hands.

Having no part in her success she couldn't find herself in what she was doing. For all those years she was getting it for free but when the ghost left her, she almost instantly lost everything she gained in this „miraculous" way. A year and a half passed and still she cannot regain her wealth. Thanks to the ghost she was „somebody great" Now she refers to herself as a great „nobody".

Here's another example of a man who voluntarily gave his soul to the proverbial devil. A mother called me asking to help her son Michael, who showed the symptoms of a very strong possession. Almost every day he changed beyond recognition and became a completely different man. It disturbed not only his mother but also his work. Less and less people wanted to use his services although he was an excellent professional (when I began helping I didn't know what his profession was). As his mother suspected, there were many different ghosts near him. To my surprise, all the ghosts left immediately once I started cleansing, clearly happy with their freedom. Such collective departure happens very seldom, especially with so many ghosts involved.

I probably never would have heard of the matter ever again if it wasn't for the fact that all of Michael's abilities left along with the ghosts. It turned out that he previously spoke as many as eight languages so perfectly, he could translate any of them simultaneously. He supported the biggest conferences and hardly anyone could match him. When the ghosts left, he lost that ability. He spoke other languages very clumsily, not even able to build simple sentences. „Give me my ghosts back", he shouted. He had no profession and didn't know what to do. None of the ghosts wanted to return, though. Michael had his own way of contacting the ghosts from different countries and trapping them, that was similar to being taken into possession and was done only by him. He presently lost the ghosts and the ability to bind them to him.

I could give many examples of such „ghosts' help." Each one of them ended in a similar way. The ghost left and the abilities left with them. It is sometimes the cause of tragic consequences. Many parents, for the sake of this dependency, don't want to agree for cleansing of their children. First of all, they don't want to lose contact with their Mom, Dad, Grandpa, or other person possessing them. Secondly, they know that their child wouldn't be as eloquent or intellectually efficient as they are. They wouldn't be able to show off their child. But this is going to be so only for some time. When the ghost wants to leave it will find a chance to break free of its prison. Unfortunately a child that was possessed for a long time often cannot operate independently and subconsciously searches for an „alternate" to the previous ghost that is usually less clever and well-mannered. They then call and cry: „Help, Pete was so intelligent until now and now he curses and cannot count to five." If you are in a similar situation deal with it today because tomorrow may be too late. Besides, we can forget about how greatly a child can suffer, not to mention the ghost connected with the possession itself. Consider the physical diseases the ghost could have had that could appear in the child's body. Realize that a possessed child doesn't behave as spontaneously as other children. It is internally old and doesn't feel like doing anything.

THE ASTRAL DEATH

When all the lower emotions based on the egoistic thoughts, dissipate in the emotional body, the astral life of a man comes to an end and the soul passes on to the mental world. We can assume then that we constantly pass from one life to another. First, it is from the physical to the astral life. If we learn our lessons in the astral world, we go to another dimension and another life in the mental world. In order for the soul to go further, however, it has to understand everything in the astral world. It doesn't mean, of course, that it moves in any space. Everything is based on a constant raising of vibrations, from the thickest astral matter of the soul to the most subtle. During this climb the soul crosses many planes and reaches the level of the mental world.

While passing from one world to the other, the human astral body doesn't break in one moment although the process could have started already. The soul leaves a so-called astral corpse behind, exactly the same as before when she had left the outer physical coating.

There is an important difference between those two processes we need to note considering further consequences. When someone leaves their physical body, it is important that they are separated from it completely. If not, there can be painful consequences, such as being wrapped in the etheric body or a cocoon.

During the astral death the processes occur a bit differently because we deal with much subtler matter of the astral body. An ordinary man identifies himself by his lowest desires and wraps himself in energy similar to the astral matter so tightly that a soul receding from the astral body can't be completely liberated. When it finally succeeds and breaks free of the astral body, passing on to the mental body, it loses a part of itself in the bondage of the astral body. This phenomenon resembles trying to pit an unripe fruit. There is some flesh on the pit because it is difficult to peel away.

The chunk of vitality detached from the soul and left in the astral corpse can still move as freely as it did when it was whole. Such a chunk is often believed to be a whole man by the people who are not aware of this phenomenon. It is difficult to recognize because this part of consciousness thinks of itself as of the soul and speaks as if it was. This is a phenomenon similar to a hologram, where every particle contains the whole picture.

This part of the soul's consciousness often participates in séances. It is as if the rest of flesh on the pit believed it was actually the whole fruit because it tastes and smells like a whole fruit. Although this chunk is just a tiny part of the soul, it preserves all of its memories. But just like you cannot say that the part left on the pit is the whole fruit, you cannot claim that the tiny part of the soul left in the astral body is the whole man. It is only a shadow or an image of the former human. The soul, meaning the real human, resides already on the mental level.

This part of consciousness of the astral body eventually leaves and doesn't return to the soul but disappears irrevocably. We call these remnants „the astral corpse" and when the remnant of life has left it we call it a „shell."

THE SÉANCES

I wrote about séances extensively in my book *Possessed by Ghosts*. I am coming back to the subject because it is only now that we can understand what exactly happens during the séances. As you know already, dear reader, many people get wrapped in the etheric body after their physical death. It is them who are most often the cause of possessions. When they get called somehow and appear in such a séance, it is only to possess one of the participants. This is why so many people come home after the séance with a summoned ghost. It also happens (though less often by far) that the summoned ghosts stay with the medium. It is not easy and sometimes even impossible to recall or channel such a ghost because it is not aware of what is happening to it. All it wants is to conquer a body that it can function in. People, being the living proofs of this dependency, come to us almost every day. Within this group of the deceased we won't find ghosts moving tables during the séances.

The representative of the second group of the deceased wrapped in a cocoon cannot move nor visit a séance even if it is summoned by a medium. And if we could, our Mom, Dad, or husband would present such a negative attitude because of the cocoon that we wouldn't be able to talk to them. We would state that this was the ghost of someone else and not of our loved one.

The representatives of the most numerous third group are totally unaware of the fact that they are dead and think they still exist as they did during their physical lives. If we somehow pulled them to the séance they wouldn't answer our „stupid questions" because we think they are dead and they think the opposite.

There is a final fourth group made of the more conscious representatives who immediately go behind the death curtain. They left the physical world and nobody's call can bring them back. It is not because they don't care about us but because it would be of no advantage to us and would be damage to them. If they came back they wouldn't have the strength to return and they would become the cause of someone else's possession, maybe even yours. I doubt that you, dear reader, want to harm both of you. I hope that after reading this book you will let your loved ones go because you will understand that you never lose them.

I decided to write about séances because I've seen a large interest in contacting people's dear loved ones. At various esoteric fairs crowds of people visit mediums. It can take the form of a performance sometimes and it's hard to fit all the people in one space. Despite charging a lot for tickets, such séances disappointed most attendees. Most people that left the séance prematurely, left accompanied by ghosts. They were too open to ghosts, regardless of whether they went there to contact a loved one or just out of pure curiosity. Luckily, such séances are not as trendy in Poland as they are in western countries. This „trend" is most popular in Great Britain. That's why so many young people leaving Poland to work in Britain become the victims of possessions. I'm often asked to help the people that have taken part in such a performance.

As I mentioned before, ghosts can always contact the living. They will only do it if they have to tell you something that you absolutely need to know. They never do it during séances. They are always able to find a way to let you know directly what you should know. They can show themselves to you (if you are open to that), talk to you via feelings, show you symbols connected with a certain case, or use the mental or spiritual way. You would know then, without a doubt, who sent you a message and what it concerns. Such contacts can only happen shortly after the death of a physical body and the longer the time after a death the less a ghost is interested in earthly matters. It is a natural course of events for the soul and doesn't have anything to do with its indifference. If you need to contact the one who had left physicality because you love them and miss them, you can meet in dreams or during the day using the love in your heart. You will feel then that you have never lost contact and that you are together constantly. You won't hold them with your grief and you will avoid the high chance of becoming possessed in the future.

In regard to séances, it needs to be repeated that our deceased loves ones can't come to such a séance (besides the ghosts that want to take an advantage of the situation to possess us). That is why séances are often attended by the beings mentioned above, that are left after the separation of a real man from the astral body to satisfy their or our curiosity and sometimes just for fun.

The misapprehension of the dependency mentioned before is the reason for our utter astonishment on meeting such a partial being at the séance and wondering how it is possible that a parent, friend, or child changed so negatively after death. The only nature of such an astral corpse are low emotions such as anger and fear and that is why they can manifest only in this emotional range. There is neither love nor kindness in them because these passed with the real human to the mental world.

Then there are the astral shells. A shell itself cannot operate during the séance, but the spirits of nature that can move in such a shell for some time and animate it do it for fun. Such a creature can purport to be the original owner. It is possible because some characteristic traits of the owner or his memories can remain in the shell. Now when they are called anew by the spirit of nature, they exist just to have fun at the expense of the séance participants. I wrote of such games in detail in my book *Possessed by Ghosts*.

The sense of the séances needs to be understood correctly. At one time a spiritualist or medium was much needed since they played parts of discoverers/inventors. They proved to other people that there is something more than a physical world. They should be praised for their efforts because it is thanks to them that our understanding of reality has become more enlightened. Not many contemporary people, however, pay attention to the fact that all of them paid an enormous price for their studies (such as Maria Sklodowska-Curie, twofold Nobel prizewinner, who died because of perennial radiation exposure to radioactive roots). People studying the ghost's world suffered not only during their lives but long after the death of their physical bodies, even through many incarnations. They didn't realize that they become the victims of possessions by studying the ghost's world. Many of them lost not only their vital forces but personalities too. And how many of them died in agony because of madness or various physical diseases caused by the ghosts? It is not only the possession (meaning wasting of a certain incarnation) but stopping in the growth process, which is definitively a larger consequence of such studies. The effects are more serious, however. Many of them will not be able to come out of the disorientation, stagnation, or attraction to ghosts for as many as seven incarnations. This is the cost of the fascination with spiritualism. It is one thing to sacrifice your present and future life for a higher ideal, which was turning people's attention to the existence of the non-physical world. It is another to mindlessly expose yourself to things that have been proven a long time ago. There is no need to reinvent the wheel because it already exists.

Many people show determination in wasting their lives contacting ghosts. They don't realize that their attraction to ghosts comes from the mistakes of earlier incarnations. Like addicts, they cannot break free of this vicious circle. They need to show sturdy perseverance in breaking these attractions, which is the only way they can liberate themselves. The attraction to ghosts is the same as any other addiction and it needs to be treated the same. Either you oppose it with all your might or you give in and hit rock bottom.

Many people could protest at this point. They say, Mrs. Pratnicka says not to contact ghosts but she does it herself." Some people think that I want to keep the exorcisms for myself. They would like to be able to do what I do. They assume the exorcisms are something unusual and the people performing them are exceptional. But I am neither a spiritualist nor a medium. I don't do anything out of curiosity and the ghosts as personalities don't interest me at all. All that exists to me is the higher part of man, his soul. That's why I try to help the soul first and the body second. It is one thing to know everything about ghosts and stand on hard, safe ground. It is another thing to see, hear and feel ghosts (be aware of them). You will admit the difference between the scientist who knows everything about electric current and a person realizing what the electric current is by experiencing an electric shock. To haul anybody out of the astral swamp (possession) you need to stand on solid, safe ground. By standing in the swamp yourself you cannot help another person inside of it.

If I was remotely interested in ghosts I would submerge myself in their abyss like a swamp. If you see or feel ghosts you have already passed the safe border. The highest priority is then getting out of this astral swamp now and refraining from being interested in its content. Freeing oneself of ghosts can be exclusively done by a person that is absolutely free of them, standing on solid ground. The knowledge concerning exorcisms, or rather wisdom came to me without any effort on my part. I could say I was born with it. Maybe I came to this world just to make people aware of it. If I thought I risked becoming possessed while performing exorcisms, I would never do them. I think that for many exorcists it is very dangerous to perform this job. They confirm it by coming to me for help.

People easily get involved in the various games ghosts play and they are later surprised that this phenomenon consumed them, that ghosts possessed them and they cannot control themselves. They often say, „Mrs. Pratnicka, please help. A man closes the stable door after the horse has bolted." The experience shows, however, that this wisdom doesn't fall on those who are interested in ghosts in most cases, even if they suffered. They get easily fooled and give control of their lives to the ghosts. It's reminiscent of a man who lies himself down on railroad tracks with the irrational belief that the coming train will not run him over. I hope that when you have read this book, you won't be interested in ghosts no matter what they promise to you and that your life will become more meaningful.

MY ADVENTURE WITH EXORCISMS

I have always been interested in helping people but I became so engaged in doing it at some point that I forgot about
myself completely. I groaned under the weight of other people's
problems and, like many readers of this book, I didn't want to
change anything in my life. I thought that I had to help them
because this was important and nobody else would do it. It was a
mistake, of course, but I understood much later. I always try to
keep my balance. Of course, I sometimes lose my center of
gravity and my moods swing one way or another. It usually
doesn't last long and I regain my balance. I strive for it to be the
basis of my work. While studying the problems of the most
needy I discovered that people experiencing the blues were
always possessed by ghosts. I didn't wonder then if they were
the cause or the effect. I thought it was reminiscent of asking
what was first, the chicken or the egg. I came to the conclusion
that since the possession led to such catastrophic consequences,

260 IN THE WHEEL OF LIFE, VOLUME II

I had to try my hardest to help people. This was all that mattered. Additionally, I was aware of the fact that most of them didn't realize how complicated the problem was and that ghosts can sometimes influence people in such a tragic way. I saw that many people would fall into the proverbial pit so deeply that they could not get out of it without help from the outside. I am talking of a physical, tangible form of help here since they have always gotten offers of non-physical help from Angels, Masters, and other beneficial beings. Most of them couldn't see a hand reaching out to them, let alone use the help. Seeing this, I became a missing link between what was physical and what was non-physical. Nobody wanted to undertake this task in those days. I became a teacher of life on both this side for the living and the other side for ghosts. My therapy concerned the souls of the living as well as the dead.

My observations confirmed that when both sides are ready for a change it can happen almost instantly. I often had cases where only one side (either a ghost or a living man) didn't want to let them part. My job was to teach people and ghosts how to liberate themselves from the need to be a victim. With understanding there came freedom. And what if the other side didn't want freedom? The ghost would find another person or a person would find another ghost and fall into captivity once again. Some will ask, „How can one not want freedom?"

Possession is like any other addiction. Some people become so accustomed to their malaise that they don't see the advantages of well-being. They simultaneously fearing changes and facing the consequences of their creativity or the power of what they could become. In order to pass from one condition to another first a decision is needed, and then the will to persevere in this resolution or a new condition. It is only when the new condition solidifies that it becomes as natural as the previous one.

This was wonderful and exciting work. Miracles, in the full sense of the word, happened every day. A miracle resulted from each one of my cases. Sometimes the deliverance was permanent, sometimes temporary. One way or another, everybody was helped.

Wherever I found myself, even if it was the gas station I had to accept that someone would come over and tell me what I did for him. I always help remotely so I don't see my clients though they know my face from television, magazines, and the internet.

Some people didn't want to remove ghosts but rather wanted to indulge in the drunkenness that possession entails. This is a kind of addiction and what matters to the addict is not a light daze but a total loss of consciousness. Every addict knows that and if he wants to get rid of an addiction, he has to find and eliminate the cause that impels him to it. The wish to feel better is motivated by the realization that he wouldn't like to feel bad anymore.

There are also people who constantly ask for help for themselves and others. I helped them and it was a relief. On one hand, they enjoy the relief but on the other, something pulls them back to the old condition. What kind of force is that? Every habit is like a pothole on the road that drivers fall into at the moment of the slightest inattention. To keep on the even road they must stay very focused. The deeper the pothole, the harder it is to get out of it and the easier it is to fall into it again.

When I help a certain person for the second, fifth, or tenth time or even the fiftieth time, it means there is something wrong with that person and not the ghost possessing them. These people know and feel that I help them every time (they wouldn't ask me any more if it was otherwise), but they fall into the old pothole after some time. Over the years a group of people has emerged that want to use my energy constantly but they don't want to do anything to change themselves. They can't or don't want to understand that ghosts come to their need, that the ghost is not the cause of the problem. Remembering how I helped ceaselessly earlier, I groaned under this weight. I thought that I had no right to say no. I asked, God, do I have a right to refuse? I am tired of offering help that is unproductive. My help doesn't do anything for them because they don't want to change anything." And I heard the answer: „It is not your job to rescue everyone. See people with love and compassion and don't worry about the effects so much. Higher wisdom worries about the effects and knows the time destined for all things. Their free will coexists with their destiny. Reach out your hand with love, do all you can, and don't care about the results so much." This simple concept sounded very true and was a balm of understanding that I needed so much. It was only then that I could refuse to help people that wouldn't help themselves. I also understood that it is not the exorcism that is ineffectual in such cases but it is the person refusing to allow themselves to feel good because they are addicted to malaise. I lead the ghost away and they immediately bring it back.

To make this scheme clear to some suffering people, I continued searching for real causes for so long that I would finally reach the heart of the matter. Every time they were speechless. Some of them said, „Mrs. Pratnicka, how can I let myself feel good when there is so much poverty around and so much misery all over the world? Isn't it better when everybody is unhappy than for one man to be happy and the other unhappy?" I replied, „ Isn't it better to give the unhappy one an example of how happiness can exist?"

Others declared, „Mrs. Pratnicka, I have heard since I was a child that suffering makes you noble. When you help me and I am well, I feel I start to miss something, which I suppose is the suffering. Then I begin to feel miserable because I am so worthless and not noble." Other people said, „ Why do I have to forgive in order for the ghost to leave? Oh, no, I will never forgive him! I'd rather suffer than let it go..."

It is difficult to persuade such a person that he or she forgives for his own sake not for the others. Forgiveness isn't about saying to the other, „It's all right, go on" but about understanding that we both participate in the same lesson and that we equally need to learn it. I repeat: forgiveness doesn't serve the other side (man or ghost), it serves us so we can understand the lesson, finish it, and go on. Lack of forgiveness equals attaching to this „something" (man, ghost, or situation) and this is going to oppress us in this and another world. And if we come to this world again, we will come back with the same challenge, though it is most often much more difficult in its nature (for we had already proved that suffering we had to bear wasn't enough). We will come back so many times that we finally understand a certain lesson and we will be able to forgive. I repeat once more: we forgive so we don't suffer anymore and stop others from hurting us.

There is another kind of person that honestly, from the bottom of their heart, says, „Mrs. Pratnicka, all of what you say is true but it requires change that I am not ready for." I think this speaks for itself. Dear reader, people suffer because they want to and even if my assistants and I tried our hardest to help them they wouldn't take this chance or would use it just for a while and then fall into their old habits. Such people call after some time and ask for help again. They don't understand, however, that possession in their case is the result of their own wrong beliefs.

If someone doesn't attract a ghost by the subconscious emotions and thoughts they haven't worked through, it is easy to break the chains connecting two souls. A man liberated this way becomes „normal" in an instant.

This work generally liberated me but working with people resistant to change restricted me. But I will start from the beginning… I started to work with exorcisms by „accident." I wanted to help a woman in need (unbeknown to her) and I didn't even know that my help was considered an exorcism and that what I took off her were ghosts. Maybe it was better this way because otherwise I could get a fright or think that this was church domain. I acted in good faith but totally in the dark. There was not much literature on the subject and even less about the priest's exorcisms. In some countries there were one or two exorcists at the most and in most of them there was none. The need, however, was huge and numbered in the thousands. I thought that this woman was a single case and it didn't occur to me that more people may need such help. However, God wanted otherwise. Someone noticed this woman's metamorphosis and started to ask questions aloud and discuss the subject. This was the reason why another man soon came to me, this time by himself, asking me to try helping his mother. He claimed that doctors had given up and deemed her a lost cause. I helped her successfully so then another person came for help, and then another, and another, and so it became my new profession.

People that found their way to me had witnessed (sometimes unwittingly) someone's metamorphosis or healing or someone else told them about a person who got such help. After such a recommendation I didn't have to explain anything or persuade anybody. They knew perfectly well what they wanted from me and I could give it to them. It didn't matter to me what their ailments were or how long they suffered, whether it was a mental disease or a physical one or how many people have already tried to help them. When I ascertained ghosts, it was enough for me to start helping. Since I always help remotely I never realized how efficient my help was or if it was even efficient at all. I knew for certain that positive changes followed every cleansing (usually once a day) but I didn't know what the physical effect on people was or how long it lasted. I wanted to know, of course, how the cleansing of ghosts contributed to the lives of single people and whole families. I received information about the positive changes from some people. Most often, however, my clients wanted to forget very quickly that they had ever even had a problem with a ghost. Sometimes I even resented them for thinking of themselves only. If they felt obliged to notify me about the changes, the documentation would be gathered from the physicians, psychiatrists, and scientists. Meanwhile, my help is usually sought secretly as if there was something to be embarrassed about. People don't quite think of others that are in the same situation. I thought so because I was very enthusiastic then, seeing that it was so easy to help so many people. Today I know that I expected too much from them. They would have to wish for common good and they haven't matured enough to be able to change their way of thinking so radically. They remain thinking of themselves only.

I needed the feedback very much and it didn't have anything to do with curiosity, of course. I am always aware if a certain man still has ghosts around him. The point was that I started to closely examine the causes of possessions. I was mainly interested in how and why the possession takes place and why a disease develops along with it, what the connection between cleansing and curing is and why some people undergoing this process get well while the others don't. I was especially

266 IN THE WHEEL OF LIFE, VOLUME II

interested in the reason for which entire families are susceptible to possessions. What are the emotional and physical burdens for such large groups of people becoming possessed? That is why I asked for accounts of their progress, test results if they existed, etc. I got very limited information, though. I knew it had nothing to do with the efficiency of cleansing since I got this information first-hand and, I could see for myself if people still had ghosts. The reason for their minimal cooperation is very simple. People ask and beg for help when they are faced with problems. They promise the moon and unlimited cooperation. They pledge many things. However, when they get a bit better, they forget everything instantly. It is very hard for them to go to „unnecessary" trouble and inform me about the progress. Not everybody is like this, of course, but the majority is. I don't care for gratitude, of course. But I wrongly assumed that people are aware of the fact that it is everyone's business to build common good and that everybody should learn things they haven't taken into account until now.

God, however, found a solution for that, too. When people called me, many conversations started with accounts of the physical success the caller or their loved ones had. They were feeding me stories: „You know, I am talking about my friend's husband who suffered of leukemia. He was on the verge of dying, the doctors didn't give him any chances for survival and now he is absolutely healthy", „This Mrs. Smith, you know, the lady that was schizophrenic, is totally normal now", „The child that chased his parents with a knife is absolutely quiet", „The girl that didn't say anything talks so glibly as if she wanted to make up for the lost time", „The breast tumor has disappeared altogether." And so on. This is how I knew not only about a ghost's departure but about the effect on someone's physical well-being also. More than once I was very astonished that what I did caused such a big change.

As time passed there came more calls for help and every day my assistants were besieged by questions that repeated themselves no matter the position, educational level, religion, or way of life of the person asking. The rich and the poor, educated and not educated, great and small reacted the same way. It was difficult to understand why such a wide variety of people were suddenly unable to deal with simple events or everyday duties that had been easy for them so far, why the drugs don't work, and the diseases came back. What phenomenon is causing them to struggle day and night?

One question instantly led to the other. This knowledge is so broad that even the longest conversation couldn't answer every question and callers got frustrated when this happened. I spent most part of the day instructing my assistants how to answer the same questions. This knowledge has been hidden until then, disavowed by human consciousness and almost every person that called thought that what happened to him (personally or to his loved one) was a sparse, unitary case. I saw that this problem concerned a huge part of the population and that the majority wanted to sweep it under the rug so it would never see the light of day.

Meanwhile, my time was limited because in addition to conversations I also performed cleansing. How could I find the time for my private life, children, family and ongoing job? I had many other duties. However, people demanded some detailed explanations. Several people called me multiple times a day for at least an hour each time. Such was my life.

I then had the idea to write a booklet I could give the clients to read, which was the basis for *Possessed by Ghosts*. I wanted readers to find out the answers for themselves while I could provide consolation in moments or despair, trouble, or tragedy. That book, however, gave me new responsibilities instead of taking them away. Lots of people read it (it was a bestseller) and recommended it to people they knew. Even more people began to call me. Instead of answering existing questions, the book led people to new questions, giving me more work to do.

Until then people had come to me because they had been recommended and knew the effects of my work. They were very disciplined and willing to change. It awoke forces within them that guaranteed success. Now came people who, although they read my book, were of a different kind. I thought about employing more assistants. However, people didn't want to talk to some random assistants. They pooh-poohed them, treated them unkindly, and were even vulgar sometimes. But when I definitively decided to work with exorcisms exclusively, my assistants took care of the questions. I didn't leave anybody helpless that way. For those seeking knowledge I offered and still offer lectures during which I answer questions. I organized lectures in various towns and paid high prices for this. Many people declared the need to participate and then didn't show up. The reason was simple. Since ghosts had already left them they didn't need the knowledge anymore. The true experts on this subject were few and far between even though this knowledge is fundamental. So I have stopped organizing the lectures by myself once and for all. I gladly accept the invitations of independent organizers and people interested in this knowledge, however. It turns out that there is bigger interest in such lectures abroad. Maybe the principle „the grass is always greener on the other side" applies here.

My current experience is based on tens of thousands cases of people I helped and hundreds of thousands ghosts that attached themselves to them. Were physicians or scientists interested in the subject then? Well, those circles would lose a lot on understanding and implementing this knowledge. They are profit-oriented and do not care for the common good. I understood that people who are not possessed themselves or are possessed but not ready to face it don't want this knowledge at all because of the fear of losing possible profits. I think the following examples explain what I mean.

A long time ago, a young woman named Myriam came to me with her autistic son, Barry. This was my first contact with autism face-to-face and the toughest case I've seen yet. I was deeply moved by this meeting. The child was constantly howling like a hurt animal and wobbling and flinching intermittently. „Does he always behave like that or is he stimulated by a new situation?" I asked. „Now he's even calmer than usual because he is afraid of you. While he's at home he really gets it going. You wouldn't like to see it. The worst thing is when he doesn't sleep at all. It is an hour or an hour and a half at night at most. Although our whole family helps us, we are dead on our feet because we stay up trying to deal with him. I don't work myself but my husband is exhausted", the young mom answered. It emerged that Barry had his grandparents within. „How did they die?" I asked. Ghosts don't usually behave that badly after death. It turned out that they had an accident and didn't regain consciousness though they were in a great shock. I won't describe the process of cleansing and therapy here because it is not important now. After I helped this child, he immediately contacted his surroundings and started to talk even though he never had before. Myriam was so happy she wanted to share her joy. She wrote letters to many people but nobody reacted. She appeared before Poland's congress for autistic children where there were doctors, parents, etc. Instead of getting their interest in the chance for therapy of these children,

Myriam was mocked and attacked with vulgar epithets. And the parents? They would shout in panic that she was insinuating that their children were possessed. They said that she should know they are not possessed but ill and they also claimed that she was mentally ill for saying such things.

Two weeks later Myriam got a letter from the foundation for autistic children ordering her to give back all the money she had ever received. This was a large amount of money covering the cost of medical consultations, therapy, travel costs, etc. „Mrs. Pratnicka, I am glad that Barry is well but what shall I do now? Where do I get the money from? I have spent it all on Barry, his doctors, and therapists" she cried to the phone. The ghost came back to Barry after some time (which is normal with autism and why a long term cleansing is needed) and the foundation doctors, seeing the improvement was temporal, waived the order to give the money back. Myriam learned a lesson from this incident and doesn't officially display her son's progress anymore. She wrote under a pseudonym to various institutions but hasn't awoken any interest. The source of Barry's healing was known to the family and a therapist who once demanded an explanation. The doctor taking care of Barry every day wasn't interested in his improvement at all. She asked various questions but Myriam felt that they didn't concern his illness. Barry went to school and the difference between him and the other children gradually decreased. He occasionally needed my help since various ghosts come to such a child. As I wrote before, when the etheric net is disabled, ghosts have an easier time accessing someone. After some time, Myriam was invited with Barry and his therapist to the capital. Barry's doctor and therapist, both of whom had been working with Barry for years, were honored for their merits on behalf of autism. The doctor gave a lecture on autism and told how she contributed to Barry's healing. Myriam and the therapist called me afterwards, feeling guilty. „Mrs. Pratnicka, what should we do in this situation? If we tell the truth, they will demand their money back once again. This doctor did nothing for Barry. She prescribed him medication that I didn't give him," Myriam said. „Be happy that Barry has regained his life, Myriam," I told her. „Let us not look for contribution. I couldn't take credit for this success either since I am only the „intermediary", a channel through which the healing came. Everything else is in the hands of God." Today Barry is just like everyone else. He has graduated college, started a family, and holds a steady job. I should mention that I deal with many people who were offered help in autism when they were grown-ups already. Ghosts left but they are not able to lead a normal life. Their rate of growth is at least several years behind healthy people. Therapeutic work is extremely important here and it has to be the same as what is offered to babies. These people's bodies are mature but their minds operate on the same level as an infant's. They need to be taught the basics. Unfortunately, there is usually nobody to take care of it since the families get easily discouraged. Only a few actually succeed.

Shortly after I dealt with Barry's case I got another call from a Canadian mother with a similar story. „Mrs. Pratnicka," she said sadly, „the doctor taking care of my Kate wrote an academic article based on her in which she proved that she had invented the method of curing autism. When I made her realize that the help came from the exorcist from Poland she got paranoid, started to shout through the phone, and threatened to deport my family and I if I announce it. She claimed she had some adequate contacts. The news about Kate getting well spread throughout Canada. I get calls from reporters all the time asking about the details. What should I do? I don't know what this doctor is capable of but on the other hand, if I lie I will harm

272 IN THE WHEEL OF LIFE, VOLUME II

you and other children that could benefit from this knowledge."
I suggested that she listen to her heart. She also had the option
of not speaking at all

These examples concern autism but believe me, dear
reader, such things happen in every part of our world. Let's take
the example of a reporter on a very popular Polish TV show
bashing me and an editor of a popular Polish newspaper which
thoughtlessly perpetrated several crimes. They assembled
falsities about me only to step out and win a prize at a festival.
The person handing them a prize declared they got it for an
entire list of things they faked in a film. It is worth mentioning
the premeditation—the reporter committed his crime knowingly
by all means. The fact that he, from the very beginning, wanted
to incriminate me without regard for the obviousness of facts in
my favor and claimed until the last moment that he is reporting
information about me is the smallest of his crimes. I talked to
him repeatedly, describing the exorcism in details for hours. To
my surprise, he understood many things correctly though he
used it against me and people in need by saying „claw your
way." He wouldn't reach his goal if he made a report about an
unknown person. He made his point—the special edition of his
program attracted over four millions of spectators, twice as
many as usual. It didn't upset me, though. It only strengthened
me.

I wish to thank the hundreds of people who, after the
emission of this disgraceful program, called me, left messages
on my answering machine, wrote emails and letters trying to
console me, and defended my honor before the court. Thank you
for being with me in those harsh moments.

Maybe you wonder, dear reader, what the cause of such
attacks is. I think this letter from a Polish priest living in
Britain will help you understand. He doesn't perform exor-

cisms himself but he knows what they mean to people:

„Mrs. Pratnicka,

I am glad that you touched on the subject of exorcisms and not by virtue of me participating but because it is an extremely burning issue. It has more antagonists than followers because most people think it is nonsense in the midst of progress in the twenty-first century, to believe in ghosts. Believing in their existence is important but not as much as acknowledging the fact that ghosts (bodiless beings) influence human life so much. There is a big group of people, each alone in their suffering,, that others either will not or cannot help. Although, when we look at the facts we suddenly see with horror that this is the truth. It is not a phenomenon, however, that a normal man or even a priest would like to believe in. It invokes fear, irritates with irrationality, and seems completely crazy for many. It is easier to mock this phenomenon and call it a superstition or misconception. It is but burying one's head in the sand hoping (usually in vain) that it will never concern us or our loved ones.

God bless you,

Rev. John from London"

I have gotten many such letters. Physicians, psychiatrists, psychologists, judges, lawyers, teachers, and uneducated people write to me. They wonder how to spread this knowledge, how to put it into practice, if at all possible. They declare that the knowledge I present is true and extremely important. The fear of the reactions from their colleagues, scientists, and various practitioners causes them to be silent. There are a lot of sapient people but most of them have to consider their reputation. It is the fear of criticism that often stops them from doing anything.

THE EXORCISMS

The book *Possessed by Ghosts* was intended to show people how profoundly life is affected by ghosts that haven't passed through the death curtain and how to deal with them. A good deal of readers, however, perceived it differently than I had intended. Many people think that possession is a phenomenon beyond their control and they liken exorcisms to dental treatment in that all they have to do is to submit to it and the doctor will do everything for them. Others are under the impression that an exorcism is a kind of magic pill in that they communicate their problem to an exorcist and they don't have to worry about it anymore because it their job to „chase" the ghost away. Sometimes they don't even want to know who the ghost is and why it stayed with them. You can have such an attitude towards possession only if a contact with a ghost happened „accidental-ly." Such a case can occur if you lose consciousness and the ghost uses the 'open door' to enter you unwittingly. Nothing unites us then. Both sides are dissatisfied with the ensuing situation and want to disengage. There is no mutual attraction. The exorcism is then permanent (for it's always effective).

All the other cases, although they experienced an effective exorcism, are impermanent, meaning they work for a shorter or longer time. It results from magnetic attraction on human, ghost, or most commonly, both.

The ghost that is led away then comes back, regardless of frequency of exorcizing, and the group of people that thought Mrs. Pratnicka would do everything for them feels disappointed. This kind of lack of independence or lack of responsibility for one's own choices is prevalent in our world. Many people expect that someone will do this or that for them, which is intrinsically an illusion. When these people are made aware that they need to work on themselves and break the bonds uniting them with ghosts they sometimes ask, „Why am I supposed to work on myself? Mrs. Pratnicka hasn't written about it in her book." If you are in such a situation, know that I did everything that was needed. It doesn't mean that you must do the rest on your own but that you have to cooperate.

I simply cannot eat your meals or sleep for you. Analogically, I cannot live your life for you or learn the lessons for which you came into the world to learn, one of which is possession or breaking bonds with a ghost possessing you. I can help you cut the chains that were connecting you with the ghost and I can lead you through this process but you must work through the rest yourself and break free of your cycle of negative habits. It is not that I wouldn't like to do it but because I must not do it. This lesson belongs to you and the ghost that possessed you, not me. If I didn't commit to it and broke the Universal Laws, I would concoct you even more distressing experiences than the ones you have had so far.

There are people who treat our recommendations as a form of punishment. Instead of following our suggestions that can help liberate them from ghosts and improve their health or comfort, they say, „I cannot do it. I don't have strength. Can you do it for me or suggest something else?" Luckily, many people fulfill our recommendations. Ghosts go away and they quickly return to normal health and mental and physical balance.

Of course, everyone has their own will and doesn't have to follow directions and still suffer. It is important, though, dear reader, to recognize the difference between suffering from an unknown source and suffering that is realized. While you are reading this book new knowledge reaches you. You recognize that suffering doesn't end with death and you will see from the following pages of this book that things you don't work through in this life you will carry to the next one. Is this what you want? Isn't it worth it to hunker down now, oppose ghosts and your strayed personality and get away from the „pit" where you are perhaps stuck now, once for all? You will suffer more in future than you do now, because your suffering will overlap. The suffering of this life will add up to suffering of the coming life, meaning it will get bigger. The fact that it is so hard for you now is because you have no way of knowing how many former incarnations you went through in which you didn't fix your situation. However, know that only at this very moment, in your present life, can you do something about it. Only now, in the physical reality, can you transform your life and fate. You must do it on your own. Even God Almighty cannot do it for you. You once chose your existence as an independent, self-creating being and it is unreasonable now to escape from being aware that only you are responsible for the conditions you find your-self in.

I, for my part, reach out my hand and offer you help, but

you must reach your hand too in order to catch it. Everyone has to eventually walk their own way. Don't complain that you have to forgive everything you and everyone else has done. This is the only way leading to freedom. You will understand it better when you read about further events following life after death and you recognize the cause of your next birth. Of course, everything I say is directed at people that are self-conscious, not those who cannot look inside themselves and find evidence of ghosts and go outside themselves to find the source of their bad moods.

Among the readers of *Possessed by Ghosts* are people who sought my book not out of need but out of curiosity. Their life flows harmoniously. Some of them got the wrong impression that it is the ghosts that are responsible for everything and that we, the living, are their helpless victims. This is nonsense, of course. This was not the intention of writing this book. I understand how this could be a first impression of the book but in the deeper layers of our being NOTHING happens without a reason. We will never face any phenomenon in the physical life that we didn't pay attention to earlier by inviting it to our life. Also, nothing will happen if we forbid the thing that comes to us to enter.

The fear of ghosts is invalid since we find ourselves in physicality, out of the reach of their influence. Dear reader, if you have never met any ghosts before then don't panic. Live as you have thus far and they will never come to you. We often receive calls asking how to stay secure in the future and how to prevent ghosts from possessing your body. Everything happens for a reason in this and in all the other worlds and you experience what you created only. Don't be scared of your future. Pay attention to the good things you do presently and no ghost will possess you.

Higher Intelligence (or God) created a perfect Universe, where everything has its place and where nothing happens randomly. All the ghosts used to be physical humans, the same as we are now. It was only their ignorance and erroneous thinking that makes them suffer now and wander about.

If more people knew about ghosts and the diseases connected with them they certainly wouldn't have to suffer so much. None of the people that had read my book and died stayed on this side of the death curtain; they all went on. It was the knowledge itself that did its part and saved many families from suffering. When a man understands the knowledge of ghosts in-depth, he automatically knows that he never dies. He once and for all gets rid of the constant paralyzing fear of death we are usually unaware of. Hidden deeply within us, it consumes and disables us and takes away all the energy necessary to live and experience life.

Anyone that is subconsciously afraid of death is automatically afraid of living, too. They live furtively and partially so that they don't accidentally die. We have the tendency then to do foolish, absurd things. We think that we need to snatch everything we can from death and to live life to the fullest (but in a safe, limited way).

Did you know, dear reader, that the fear of death isn't an innate human emotion that primitive people were born with? The priests of old times planted the idea in the minds of people in order to control them. It was them that introduced the idea of sacrificing human lives to the gods and decided who would live and who would die. Such ceremonies were performed irregularly but quite often; any reason for celebration was good. People never knew who would be next or what the criterion for the selection would be. That is why people lived in constant fear that grew constantly until it spread throughout humanity like a plague. It is still present and influences our every move although most people are not aware of it since they erase it from their domain of thinking and feeling. Every so often I deal with people who track down memories of how they were sacrificed to gods and died by cruel torture. It happened to everyone—children, elderly people, virgins, rich fathers of large families, etc. They were killed in a variety of cruel and unusual ways. The system worked because you didn't even have to die yourself. It was enough that the others died and you feared that this could happen to you or your loved ones. This fear operates in most people as a hidden, constant fear of life that no amount of money or effort can neutralize. It is the main cause of misery in this world and beyond it. If it wasn't for this fear most of the dead would have passed to the other side of the death curtain. The phenomenon of possession wouldn't exist. Most of the dead loved their dear ones deeply and didn't want them to be harmed. If people knew that life didn't end at the moment of physical death they wouldn't hold on so tightly and with such determination. This enormous fear would disappear completely and each one of us would automatically step into the consciousness of living a great number of times before. This would settle down the frightened minds and hearts. It would change the quality and the type of life on earth, too. People would see beyond the doubt that there is only one world in which the same divine laws govern all its manifestations, both visible and invisible to the naked eye. Being conscious that life looks the same in this and other worlds, they would experience neither fear nor the feeling of surprise or strangeness while passing from one part of the same world to the other. They wouldn't feel uncertain concerning their fate behind the curtain. We would all realize that the new, wonderful possibilities open for us in the higher life. That's why a man, understanding death, would welcome it without fear and rebellion, even when it was taking his most loved one from him. Instead of focusing on the loss, he would concentrate on the advantages that his loved one benefits from.

Furthermore, a man with a consciousness free of fear wouldn't let himself be exposed to the bombardment of bad news in the physical life. He would realize that every negative message directly exacerbates his life because it attracts everything he focuses his attention on. Knowing that there is no death, he would select everything that is to appear in his life and then he would become the master of it. No longer would he be the one who was given life for some indeterminate time and from whom life can be taken away at any moment. He would certainly not watch rapes, thefts, and disasters because he wouldn't want them to be a part of his experience.

You cannot influence other people's experience, dear reader, but you can determine everything that concerns you personally. Without fear you can become an excellent example to follow. As you can see, every man is his own employer and creator of his own glory or darkness, the judge of his own life, and distributor of prizes and punishments.

Until he understands this, he is like a puppet that doesn't know whose hand remains inside of it. Don't believe me? Turn on your TV or reach for a newspaper and you will immediately learn how many people were raped, deceived, and robbed. Watch the news, a movie, or even cartoons for children closely. You will see violence, blood, and lack of respect for life everywhere. What you focus on is what you invite into your life. Are you sure that you want to experience all those things? You probably don't. However, you let yourself be fed these visions. The authors of these programs would say that people don't want to watch anything else, that this is the only product that sells. I tell you, however, that maintaining the fear of death brings profits. Don't you, fearing death, want to know at all costs what can happen to your life and the life of your loved ones according to worldwide prognosis? We make ourselves participate in this bad fate when we follow these visions, however. Don't we as humanity find ourselves on a slippery slope leading us to disaster? The world became crazy and we became crazy with it. People should wake up. Will it be you? You will read about what makes disaster possible in the chapter „The Fall of the Lost Civilization."

It may be, dear reader that you don't agree with me and watch all those atrocities thinking the hard times came and they are the reason for the present hardships of living. After all, wherever you look you see apparent evil and callousness and it seems that only bad people live in this world. Those who believe it is so gain reasons to complain more and more. What ghosts will they become after leaving the physical world? Wouldn't they, by any chance, hold on to dear physical life, fearing the evil, misery, and punishment awaiting them?

We fear death (and life) so much within us, that we willingly project this enormous fear onto the outside world. That is why we like horror movies and scenes of people dying so much. We're pleased watching it happen to film characters and not us. In order to hide our paralyzing fear from the outside world, we express it through anger. That's why we've always allowed the media to portray angry people as models of behavior. We put our minds at ease, thinking that everything is okay since everybody is angry. The rage assumes the shape of the most righteous anger, that of the heroes that were somehow hurt in the end. We learn that anger is justified, that one can even kill because of it. Such pictures do us enormous harm and this is sufficient reason to eschew them. They translate to our daily life. Don't believe me? Young children have been participating in robbery and bullying other children at school. They don't respect life, and it is us, the grownups, that teach them that. The anger coming from the fear of death brings violence, wars, and suffering, which in turn intensifies the fear we project onto others. It is a vicious cycle. Isn't it time to break free once and for all? When you stop focusing on these images the people that create them won't have anyone to consume their work.

You may want to ask how God can let this happen. I think He didn't lose control over anything. Even the fact that ghosts don't pass to the other side serves some higher goal. On one hand, they intensify the subconscious tendencies of people they possess so they can recognize that they have this or that negative emotion. This becomes a basis for healing and evolving their soul. Moreover, ghosts provide evidence that there is life after death and help them understand the process. My practice proves that families that understand that there is no death due to their own or a loved one's possession don't get possessed anymore. It concerns even the families in which the dead, generation after generation, stayed on this side and became the cause of possessions. Reading of my book *Possessed by Ghosts* only makes those who died in the meantime go to the other side of the death curtain without fear. As you can see, dear reader, this knowledge helps the living as well as the dead. It provides incontrovertible proof of how much it is needed.

A great number of people tell us the same story of how they entered a bookshop and left with the book *Possessed by Ghosts* in their hands without realizing it. These are often people who wouldn't reach for it consciously because their beliefs wouldn't let them. Others claim that reading books is a rarity for them, that the last time they visited a bookshop was when they were in school. And others claim that they found the book in various places—at the bus stop, in the lounge, on a train. From my perspective, it is some operating force that wants these people to gain this knowledge.

A great number of readers give the book as a present to someone who needs it or they pay us for it and ask to send it to a given address. Such packages are sometimes returned to us. There are various reactions from people who received it but didn't know what it was. Some are moderately quiet while others are outraged and shout, „How could such a book be sent to me?" When we calmly explain why it was sent, we hear various reactions: „So that means someone still cares for me?" and „I can see that I am not totally alone on this world." Every time I realize that people who turn to me think they are the only ones who are in the throes of this problem and that nobody under-stands them.

I am most pleased with these cases of possessions, in which the main merit of breaking free of the ghosts is not my work but the decision and the persistence of people calling for help. I showed them the way but they walked it by themselves. They previously thought there was no way out for them and now they are recovered. They gave themselves a gift, the biggest one possible.

There are also people who, for whatever reason, didn't want to put in any effort. This happens most commonly when people closest to the person possessed are the ones asking for help on behalf of the suffering. It may be a surprise to you, dear reader, but the exorcism is often effective and permanent even if the possessed doesn't know about it. It does not happen in every case, unfortunately. Some clients don't want or can't take the advantage of this wonderful gift of fate and so they return to the same place they left. This may be because they actually desire suffering. Furthermore, by failing to see the cause of their improvement, they were not able to maintain a condition of permanent freedom from ghosts. If they had become accustomed to their previous misery, it is much harder to capture them after they've tasted freedom. You can't win. I think that Providence arranged it purposely so that resistant people find the motivation for changes, too. It may not happen instantly because of their strong resistance, but in time (when they don't want to suffer any more) they will try independently to help themselves. Who knows, maybe there will be someone in their neighborhood who has already dealt with the problem?

Unfortunately, many people want changes only when their suffering becomes unbearable. Don't judge such a person, though. Many people have chosen to learn with the help of suffering. Many possessions by ghosts serve to amplify suffering and it concerns both sides. When the pain is not strong a man decides to bear it. Everyone has their own scale of resistance to pain, of course. There are also people that find pleasure in pain. However, there is a certain limit for everyone, with no exceptions. When it is crossed, people find the courage to change. Pain at the top of their endurance scale is their teacher then, their lifeblood.

I hope that since we discussed the astral world it will be much easier for you to understand the intricate and mysterious subject of possessions and exorcisms. You probably do understand by now why it is sometimes so hard to free a man from a ghost or a ghost from a man. It sometimes resembles untangling of a rope tied in a knot. This procedure, as you know, is not up to me but depends on the attitude of a man and a ghost. It is even more up to a man because a ghost is always led away. The ghost, however, has his own free will and a right to stay. It can be fear of the unknown, the longing for the physical world and loved ones, guilt, and many other reasons. Nobody should break such will. God gave it to every soul (I will write more about this later) not without reason. A man has free will and a right, even a duty, to prevent the ghost I take away during exorcism from returning. If an exorcism doesn't work, one should search for the reason of the ghost's return within himself.

I will try to explain it using the example of vibration since, as you know already, everything is vibration. When a ghost is at your side, you vibrate on the same level, or more precisely, speak in the same rhythm or cadence. That's why you've become attracted to each other. To break such a connection, it is necessary to find a way to vibrate on a higher level. It is then that the ghost finds itself on a different level than you. The process of forgiving (ourselves, ghosts, everything, and everybody) serves to permanently break free of the emotion and vibration. Forgiveness also has this wonderful effect of causing you to rise up to a higher vibration. It usually has an immediate effect if you practice forgiveness for quite some time. Sometimes, considering the psychotherapy I give to the ghost, it raises its vibration, which breaks the relationship between man and ghost permanently. However, I always impel the man to work on himself because he is the only one that can influence it. The ghost's decision is its business. The man has everything that is needed to permanently break free from any ghost.

It happens very rarely that a man and a ghost work on themselves simultaneously. Although they both ascend, they are still together. A man can feel resentful because he doesn't break free from a ghost even though he put work into it. You should note, however, that in this situation the mutual relationship and influence are placed on a completely different level than they were before. In place of former hatred, compassion appears, and in place of fear and alienation, certainty and understanding. It is only a matter of time now. It needs to be said clearly, however, that lack of freedom in this specific situation results from the desire to stay with the ghost for as long as possible, especially if it is a close family member or friend. It is necessary to search the subconscious then to find a reason for captivating the ghost (this is the most correct term) and not letting it go. Then, even if you are at the same vibrating level, you won't be chained to each other, you will be independent of each other. It is like in a well-functioning family. You are together yet free.

Sometimes we get calls in which people claim that absolutely nothing has helped them. When we check such person we usually see that he has accumulated a completely different ghost than he had before. We ask then: „How did you feel in the beginning of the cleansing?" They say they felt good then, even great. „And a month after the cleansing?" we ask again. „I still felt good then," they answer. We dig deeper and ask when they started to feel bad. Usually they say that something trivial, such as an argument with a spouse, has triggered them to feel bad. It is somehow normal since the man that the ghosts have returned to is convinced that he has always felt the same way he does at this very moment. This is the ghost's belief and he deduces that he'll feel this way forever. It is easy to forget or underestimate the fact that he felt good for a long time before he started to feel bad.

There are also people who control themselves so poorly that they let the ghosts act or talk through them. We can recognize it immediately, of course, and declare to the possessed person who called us, that we are not going to talk to a ghost. We continue to help but we limit contact with them. There is no other way. Such people often resort to threats of blackmails of a different kind. We have even been threatened with arson, death, and other atrocities. We know that when the ghost leaves, the man will apologize, wondering how he could let himself be the channel for all those terrible things. It doesn't always have to reach such extreme point that we're required to stop a conversation or a correspondence. It doesn't mean that in such case my help is being stopped also.

Who are those disobedient, strongly rebellious ghosts that influence people so powerfully? These are most often the dead that remain deeply unconscious and under the control of earthly desires. They don't want to wake up and acknowledge the death of their physical body since they desire physicality above everything else. They need an explanation that will direct their thoughts toward higher goals and away from abstract matters. That is why we often ask their living loved ones to talk to them (only those that remain on this side of the death curtain, of course) and tell them that they are already dead, the circumstances and details of how they died and where their bodies rest in the cemetery. It serves the purpose of awakening them to the awareness that they're not physically alive anymore.

It happens sometimes that when they finally come to their senses (wake up), instead of acknowledging the present conditions as normal, they suddenly give in to their old beliefs. They begin to be full of fear of the future awaiting them, mostly of the punishment they expect. Such was the case of Lucy's grandfather, who thought he was in hell after he awoke. This always happens if we believed in theological education and took its allegories literally during our physical life. It materializes later as a fact, according to the rule – you receive what you believe in.

When we experience the exorcism and we are not aware of complicated dependencies and what I mentioned above, we usually become very frustrated. We cannot understand why it gets worse instead of improving, especially since we're doing everything that we were told to do. We forgive, tell the ghost that it is dead, and nothing happens. We begin to think that the exorcism might not be working.

We should be aware of the fact that us humans have worked on our beliefs for many, many incarnations. It is impossible sometimes to pull such deep roots out in a short time. Changing such deep erroneous beliefs can sometimes take months or even years. This is also true about changing a ghost's beliefs. This is not an easy matter, all the more since a ghost is often in shock. Nothing gets to the ghost because it is so convinced that what it sees is the absolute truth. Perhaps you are a step away from being free from a ghost. The point is that instead of being angry with it and yourself, you need to be more patient. Even a ghost, despite being the cause of your suffering, needs your consolation and support, not your fulmination. Such an attitude can only have a wise man, the one who knows the natural laws, and not a person that presents themselves as a victim.

People and ghosts can be helped exclusively with the help of intelligence and a good heart. On one hand, ghosts desire knowledge about their situation but at the same time they tend to panic when they learn the truth. Such a condition can persevere for any length of time. It all depends on how much the man is rooted in his thought forms and how much he believes them. Some ghosts are so deeply caught in the net of their own images that it is difficult to break or eliminate them. Although they are born of erroneous concepts, they are consolidated by one's own faith. These ghosts can only be liberated by a being that knows their environment and realizes the truth at the same time. Such a person can help them distinguish the true reality of the astral world from false concepts that they adopted or created during their physical life. This task belongs to spiritual guides and angels, those who undertook it and are not indifferent to other people's misery, in other planes. People like me do the same job in the physical realm.

There is a group of ghosts that deliberately manipulate humans in order to be with them and draw their energy for as long as possible. The example below will explain what I mean better. People often come to us claiming that living people are influencing them and taking their energy away. Such a case happens very seldom. In most cases, it is ghosts operating.

A woman named Martha turned to us, saying that she had participated in a seminar for people interested in the esoteric arts. She claimed that the leader of this seminary, a man named Kevin, had hooked himself to her. When we investigated we found the presence of some very strong ghosts residing alone. She didn't want to believe it since she felt very strongly the influence of that man. She subjected herself to the cleansing, though. The ghosts left and all the manipulation stopped. The conclusion was that it was not that man influencing Martha, but the ghosts that were present at the seminary. Nothing was happening for few months till something began to happen again. She called us and I „accidentally" took her call. She asked for help again since this time it was a woman known as Pratnicka that possessed her. She spoke for a long time without interruption I finally asked if she knew who she was calling. She said of course she knew she was calling Wanda Pratnicka the exorcist, who had helped her once and went on to continue the story of how this Pratnicka kept her from living peacefully. I wondered if it was a convergence of names or a ghost that had possessed her so powerfully that kept her from noticing that it was my name, too.

I asked her then if this Pratnicka was currently near her and if her name was Wanda. She confirmed. I asked how it was possible for Wanda Pratnicka, the exorcist, to manipulate her if she is talking to her by phone at the same time. The ghost then

couldn't stand it anymore and started yelling to Martha, „Don't
listen to her, I am Pratnicka, she lies to you, I tell you the truth,
hang up the phone..." and so on. I understood what was happening and started to talk to her calmly. It took a while to make her
understand. Unexpectedly, Martha said with astonishment that
the Pratnicka in her head wasn't the one she was talking to. I
wasn't sure, however, if the ghost had stopped possessing her. I
began talking to Martha but I directed my words at the ghost.
During this conversation, the ghost understood what was happening just like Martha had earlier and left, never to return.

I knew, of course, that ghosts impersonate people and
manipulate the living in this specious way. Martha's case,
however, made me realize how powerful a ghost can be and that
the man cannot distinguish the truth from mystification. A
clever ghost can pretend to be someone else and manipulate for
long enough to reach its goal. There are many people who have
such a problem. The power of the ghost is not what it says it is
and can influence people similar to the way hypnosis can.
Living people can also have such an influence and you should
be aware of it because they can have awful intentions. The point
is not to get paranoid at every occasion but to constantly keep a
healthy distance from people, matters, and our own former
decisions and considerations. Separating ourselves from everything is as equally undesirable as too much credulity or naivety.

My assistant had a similar case once. The ghost of a
man who called her was so convincing that she even went to
check what I was doing at the moment. It was only when she
saw that I was engaged in a conversation with a group of
people that she understood that I couldn't influence this man
at the same time, as he was claiming I was. Once you become
acquainted with that game, everything else is easy. My assistant gave this man therapy and the ghost capitulated immedi-

ately. It remained for some time but knew that he was uncovered.

THE MENTAL WORLD

As a man is dying in the physical world and waking in the astral world, so too is he dying at the end of his astral life and waking up in the mental world. Finding himself in the mental body, he feels much joy, happiness, and ecstasy as he enters unspeakable bliss. This is caused by the single fact of residing in the higher subtle world. The higher the world, the greater the bliss, ecstasy, love, happiness, and joy.

As you probably remember, dear reader, the astral world presents the possibility of living in a state of much greater happiness than is possible in a physical body. It is possible only for those who have accepted death and ceased to hold on to dear life. It is similar with the next level of heavenly life—the mental world and body. It is incomparably happier than the astral but only when a man accepts his second death, an astral death this time. He can let himself experience this happiness or bliss then.

Otherwise, he is pulled out of the astral life with unpleasant consequences for the soul. The experience of an increasingly greater state of happiness repeats always at the moment of ascension into the next world. Upon entering the first one, a man believes he has found himself in Heaven. When he reaches an even higher world he ascertains with astonishment that his former feeling of happiness was only an ersatz. Every time the bliss within him increases, wisdom deepens and greater love awakens. It happens independently because this feeling is the answer to God's Love he has found on this new level. It is the same Love as it was on the earthly plane, but it is felt more intensely since the soul puts away particular bodies in turns that separate the soul from Love. How does it look in practice?

A man in the physical world is constantly worrying, carrying, bustling, preventing. He most often pivots on the same things. He thinks that this way of acting makes him the most wise and provident. When he passes to the astral world he suddenly ascertains that he did many unnecessary, pointless things in his former life. The astral world seems much more broad, beautiful, and wise than the physical world. While he is entering the mental world the experience from the astral world repeats itself. This new mental life is so much more broad and intense than his astral life, that it is impossible to describe or compare them to each other.. It is very difficult to talk of these states of consciousness. Language creates a linear message that is two dimensional but the phenomenon itself is multidimensional. We have no words to describe the phenomena that appear there, because there is nothing on earth that would convey their meanings. Only poetic language, the language of symbols and comparisons, can be helpful here. Only this language can convey the poor substitute for what happens in the higher world. I have had difficulties many times before in this book trying to describe certain things. Until we find ourselves in the higher state of spirituality and understanding, deciphering the cosmic laws is an easy, light, and pleasant task. It becomes downright unfeasible once you begin translating it into human language. Why is it so difficult? Well, you could compare it to trying to push a big inflated balloon through a key hole. You can say that the balloon's mass is not big, but pushing it through a keyhole turns out to be impossible.

Looking at this matter vaguely, you can say that the mental world is the world of thoughts and their networks that create an energetic system. A man is a part of this system. His mental body consists of energetic coverings (similar to many clouds of different sizes in the sky, differently illuminated by the sun, such as during a sunset) that make up our thoughts. There are many layers of creative thoughts resting on them that connect with higher knowledge of truth and light. On Earth, every time single thoughts become thicker in the thought form, they are surrounded by some medium covering creating a kind of a wall. Presently, in the mental world, a man is surrounded by the walls created exclusively by thoughts—wall after wall—that head into infinity. An ordinary man surrounds himself with plenty of thought forms during his life. He creates many walls then, but I will write about it more in a moment.

As it happens in life, a man gives much attention to some thoughts or thought forms and less or even none to others. Thought forms that don't get much attention or energy pass quickly or disperse as clouds in the sky. It is different with the thought forms that are important to a man for some reason, that constitute the core of his interests, worries, and various tactics serving to prevent his fears from coming true. These thoughts don't disperse like the first ones I mentioned since they are constantly powered by the energy of attention and the emotions connected, becoming increasingly powerful.

The thought forms connected to an egoistic attitude towards life (either one's own or in general) are usually connected to strong emotions. They belong to the astral world and dissipate completely while staying there. A man enters the mental world with the thought forms that are totally unselfish, altruistic, filled with unconditional love, high, subtle, noble, and created during the earthly life. Thanks to such high thoughts only a man can presently recognize the mental world. If he hadn't had such thoughts during his physical life, he couldn't truly live in the mental world because he doesn't have a properly built body that would make it possible for him. I remind you that the mental body is built exclusively on thoughts. The egoistic ones belong to the astral world and only those that are unselfish and filled with care and love serving higher goals in the physical life belong to the mental world. Presently, only such thoughts gather around a man residing there, surrounding him with a covering of some kind—meditative, which helps him answer to vibrations or stimuli flowing from the mental world. Every high thought or group of thoughts becomes a window or channel through which a man can feel or contact the mental world. Lack of such thoughts causes lack of the window and therefore contact. Such a man, although he resides in the mental world, remains behind the walls surrounding him without windows making contact possible.

Staying in the mental world is diametrically different than staying in the astral world. A man used a body there and he has become accustomed to it. In the mental world he lives within a body most people have never used before, that is hence poorly developed if it is developed at all. That's why, instead of letting a man see the world he just resides in, it separates him. As if he found himself at the most fabulous concert inside a soundproof box.

There is an infinite fullness of Divine Thought in the mental world full of unlimited richness given for the sake of every soul. Everyone, without exception, can use this endless ocean of richness without limits. The only one that can use it, however, is the one who is open to that richness and ready to receive it. Such a man believes in the power of thoughts and strives for it during his physical life. The soul residing in the mental world can use only as much of its richness as it is able to draw. Most people have no idea, however, that the place they just reside in is this treasury. Not realizing this, they don't appreciate its contents. Since everyone takes as much as he is able to take during his physical life, every man has different abilities there.

In mental and higher worlds, every man finds himself among the greatest treasures, not only those he is able to imagine but the ones totally exceeding human imagination. I remind you that this unusual beauty and glory can be seen only through the „windows" that we create during our physical lives. Lack of „windows" means residing among the greatest treasures without realizing their existence and the possibility of using them. If, during his physical life, a man turned his attention mostly to material or sensual objects, he couldn't have opened many „windows" through which the highest glory and God's grace can fall. However, cross your bridges as you come to them. Everyone, even the worst among us, has had at least one selfless reflex in his life and this feeling will presently be his „window".

An average man is not capable of any broader activity in the mental world. Although he vaguely feels that outside of him there is some wonderful arch, he doesn't realize it and cannot participate in it even though he is surrounded by helpful forces on all sides, such as powerful angels residing in this world. They are very sensitive to every human pursuit and if they get called, they answer immediately. The only one that can utilize this richness is the one that is aware of it and who used it during his physical life.

There are many directions that can be followed by a high thought, filled with love, perfection, and harmony. It will always be a noble and high thought and can be either personal or impersonal. Every impersonal thought is attributed to art, music, or philosophy. Everybody that is interested in these domains can have his fill of them in the mental world. For such a man nothing changes, he can still continue and cultivate his passions. He was able to do it in the physical world and astral world and now he can do it in the mental world.

Higher personal thoughts, however, are connected to love and devotion to another person, personified divinity, or deity. If someone loved deeply during his physical life, this love is in his mind and within him forever. When we love somebody much, we somehow create and keep in our mind a very powerful, loving mental image of that being. It stays with us for eternity and when we die, we take it with us to heaven. We don't need to do anything with it, it all happens independently. The quicker the thoughts of love and gratitude vibrate and move, the higher the value of it. For everything is energy, and love contains all energy. That's why everything is love. When we understand love it's also possible for us to understand the nature of God. How does it work in practice? Let's assume, dear reader, that you love somebody very much. When you think of them, your heart is warmed. This is love energy. As you know, energy is constantly moving and when you thought of your loved one, you made it move. It spreads and reaches the soul of the dear person. Remember that the dear being is the soul, not the physical body, which, as we know, emerged from thoughts (or images) of the soul. The thought forms created this way act in the higher part of the mental world and influence the real human here. When energy reaches the soul of a loved one (no matter if this person is physically alive or not), together with this feeling of love your image is being born. Your loved one felt their heart become warm and thought of you with love and gratitude. Then she added her love to yours and the energy was returned to you. In this way the energy of love becomes stronger and strengthens the people emotionally involved.

When we think of someone that is gone already with love, they will always feel it, amplify it, and send it back. Everyone feels loved in such a circle, and that brings the souls even closer. Love's confession is always directed at the real human, no matter what state his physical and subtle bodies presently reside in. He will always answer, even if the soul has already been incarnated as a new man.

We sometimes wonder how we will recognize our loved ones in heaven or in the next incarnation. Don't worry, dear reader, you'll just know it. It is not a matter of looks (which can sometimes be deceiving), but of vibration. The souls in heaven immediately sense the energy of mutual love. It is always the same after all, it is the energy of someone dear and close to you. Recognition of the soul can happen through internal knowledge, sensing of this special energy, light, or vibration of a loved one. You love them, and so you *feel them* with all your heart and soul. You recognize them in your intuitive wisdom in an instant, without a doubt.

Living in Heaven is much easier than it is on Earth. Your loved ones can help you recognize who you loved in a past life by temporarily inhabiting the body from their last incarnation. You see them the way you recall them from their earthly journey, though they are usually younger and perfectly healthy. You will certainly meet your loved ones there. You will not be alone. They will know about you and they will even know your name. They will take you by the hand, bringing healing and consolation to your heart.

It is similar on Earth. Sometimes you meet a stranger and on a deeper level, thanks to internal knowledge coming from the heart, notice that this is a loved one. The eyes of the soul see first, and sometimes you can't express the certainty of spiritual recognition with words. There is neither doubt nor chaos in it. Each incarnated body can differ greatly from its previous one but the soul remains the same. It is the soul being recognized beyond the slightest doubt. Spiritual recognition can sometimes begin in the mind before the heart has the chance to recognize it. This may cause a person to believe that they are crazy because the soul longs for a newly introduced stranger while the mind says that this is ridiculous. After a short time, however, the souls will definitely recognize each other.

In the mental world, a man having a great number of friends can communicate with all of them simultaneously and send and receive love. On the higher level there is no number of images that could exhaust the infinity of the soul. In the heavenly life, the real human has all the friends he wishes around him, even those who are still alive in physicality (it doesn't matter if they are awake or asleep). He sees them in the most perfect possible form because it is him who creates their thought form (or „window"), through which they manifest in front of him.

In the limited physical world we are used to thinking that our loved one is only what we know as a physical body. Initially, it is difficult to imagine that it can be different. We will eventually come to understand, though, that we are closer to our loved ones in heaven than on Earth. The same applies to adoration. In heaven, we find ourselves two worlds closer to the person we adored than we were while physically alive. That's why experiences are of much more direct or real nature because they are tangible.

THE MENTAL WORLD DIVISION

In the mental world, as in the astral world, there are seven spheres, also known as levels. The mental body contains the matter of the seventh, sixth, fifth, and fourth sphere and within them the heavenly life progresses. The third, second, and first spheres are the causal body. A man doesn't pass through every sphere, as he did in the astral world, because in the mental world there is nothing that is comparable to the rearrangement of the astral body. Rather, a man is immediately pulled to the level that corresponds best with the level of his growth and it is there that he passes through the entire life of the mental body.

In the mental world, people create an infinite amount of various states in which they desire to live. Generally speaking, you could say that souls reside in the seventh sphere, which is mostly characterized by the feeling of unselfish family love. It must be unselfish because otherwise it wouldn't exist. If an aspect was egoistic, it would have dissipated in the astral world long ago. The sixth sphere contains souls whose dominating characteristic was religious devotion while the fifth sphere contains souls that expressed devotion through active work. Basically, the seventh, sixth, and fifth spheres contain souls that were devoted to someone such as a family member, friend, or deity from the religion they followed. Souls that devoted themselves to all of humanity (in the broad meaning of the word) reside in the fourth sphere. They gratuitously searched for spiritual awareness, engaged in philosophy and knowledge of a high level, or had literary and artistic faculties. They created exclusively for the sake of others and devoted themselves to humanity because of love and the intrinsic need to serve.

Despite how joyous, blissful, and happy living in the mental world can be, it must eventually come to an end. There comes the time when causal body separates from the mental world and a man enters the causal world.

LIVING IN THE CAUSAL WORLD

A man doesn't need „windows" anymore because he is finally living in his true Home. All the former walls of the mental world have collapsed. We returned Home, where we had once set out from. We could stay in it forever if we were fully aware of where we truly were and if we were capable of living there. There are a lot of people like this, who during their stay in the mental world lived behind the walls with zero or very few windows.

What does it look like here? This phenomenon hasn't been correctly described in esoteric terms yet. You can call it Heaven, but also Existence, an Absolute, Nonexistence, Nirvana, Quantal Field, or Chaos. It would be more correct to call this a state of awareness because at this level all the events of the universe are so subtle and passive to the average man that he would call them fictional and unreal. Why? Because they are

like a trace on a water, a smell in the air, just simply impermanent. They can be perceived as partial states of awareness only.
They are all important, as well as not important at all. For an
advanced soul, the state of awareness of a plant or a worm
crawling on it equals the state of awareness of a highly developed cosmic being, known on earth as a master with capital M.

In the causal world there is no evaluation whatsoever.
Things and states simply are. Nothing more. There is no good or
evil here. There is only a certain variant of reality which is not
real at the same time. There is no judgment here: good, bad,
pretty, ugly, worse, better, desired, undesired, etc. What we call
the opposites, such as love and hatred, occur side by side simply
as possibilities. If we used a language on this level, it would
contain only nouns. The terms of polarities such as perfection
and imperfection exist only on Earth. On a heavenly, cosmic
scale, there are no such opposites, there is only more or less
good there. I will write more on this subject in the chapter
concerning universal laws. According to this contradistinction,
every soul is ultimately good and finds itself on the road to
understanding.

In terms of an absolute awareness, evil is not punished
and good is not prized. There are only lessons (I will write about
this further later). It seems unfair, but there, in „the cosmos",
there is no specified prescription for justice. We independently
choose the worlds we want to reside in if we are fully aware of
them while worlds choose us if we are ignorant. This process
runs according to a certain key of frequencies in which the
information about us is coded. If we are synchronized with the
frequencies that carry love with them we react to these vibrations and they react to us. This phenomenon is similar to mag-
netism. If we don't have love within us and we vibrate on
another, lower level, there can be the whole sea of love around

us but we will not feel it. We all vibrate on different levels which means that there is no attraction within us. For an example in the physical world, think of two children. A mother loves them both dearly and equal. However, one of them may feel loved and the other one may not. One of them may have opened themselves to love and the other may be unable to receive it and feel it, no matter what the mother does.

It is the same with most people. Love is all around them, they are born from it and live because of it, but they are unable to receive it. They close themselves to it and don't feel it. Most people haven't developed love with the capital L within themselves. That's why, while residing in the causal world, they cannot come into their own in this reality. During their stay on Earth they didn't understand that everything was love. If they loved, they would understand life, because understanding comes from love only. Out of understanding comes patience and then the time stops: everything becomes present, eternally now.

Most people coming back Home don't recognize the laws of the universe and often don't even realize that they are Home. It is not out of lack of love (because love is everyone), but out of being closed to love during their physical lives. Remember the first volume of this book. The soul left its Home and put on certain bodies. After coming to earth it forgot *Who it is in Essence* and started to live as if it was just a physical body. It didn't understand the love it was born from anymore and didn't know how to grow further. Now, coming back Home, it is stuck in forgetfulness and is unable to use the magnitude of riches found there. It resides in a wonderful vault filled with valuables and still feels as if it was a forlorn beggar.

And so many people can't do anything more than rest passively, or rather, vegetate in isolation born of ignorance. While in the physical body they didn't use their causal body and didn't even know that they had it. This, however, is constantly changing because every stay on earth and return Home diminishes this ignorance. Every man loves himself more throughout each incarnation and ends up loving others more, too. Then the *real life* in the causal body becomes broader and fuller to him.

Some people begin to notice that out of the cosmic stock, which is absolute awareness, it is possible to create literally everything: all worlds according to one's own preferences and caprices, even new laws of nature. This act of creating doesn't depend on desire only, but on abilities, too. God, the Absolute, allows everything not by gracious allowance but by undisputed law. It is human destiny to take as much as he wants of the cosmic stock and desires to whatever extent his abilities and imagination allows him to.

Those who can use this level use it to the fullest. Education in the spiritual state of being happens much more quickly and accelerates more rapidly than it does in the physical body. However, here on earth and there in *heaven* it is us who choose what we want or what we are going to learn. When you have gained love, forgiveness, and self-respect, you begin to learn love, forgiveness and respect for all other souls. If you had already worked on every aspect of what the Earth can offer you and you feel love, respect, forgiveness and compassion for yourself in every situation, you can *break free* of the Earth's limits and the necessity of incarnating further. It is only then that you are ready to stay and grow in the spiritual state of being only. You will reach that point when, while growing you become able to not only receive but to give before anything else. You will understand that giving and receiving are the same. Energy should be allowed to flow from us and to us. Love with capital L, meaning unconditional love, becomes a constant, natural condition of a man and not a sensation appearing from time to time.

As you can see, dear reader, love and compassion are not some orders coming from God or some master power. Someone with advanced awareness perceives them as conditions advantageous and viable for every being. Translating it to an earthly, human language: the soul's evolution has created something like a moral economy. Using love with the capital L, we create the world as safe, joyous, and pleasant and this supports creative growth. By seeking cruelty and violence we create a destructive reality for everyone, including ourselves as creators. On the higher levels of growth (here on Earth or in heaven) nobody uses this. It is not because he cannot use it but because it is not viable. When you are in a union with God, you are in a union with God's law independently and you don't want to do certain „nonviable" („bad") things. Being in harmony with Him, you don't want to bring disharmony since one excludes the other.

You may be wondering, dear reader, why these higher laws don't operate on material Earth. Why does evil win over good so often? Why is goodness so nonviable here on Earth? Well, the law operates here correspondingly as it does in heaven. We have free will that we're able to use. Those who obey the law do it only because they understand it and profit from it, and not because they are frightened and think they have to. No good comes of it then and disharmony is being formed. Everybody on Earth should not only know but realize fully that acts of violence and of injustice towards other people will never be forgotten. Sometime, somehow, they need to be paid for (if not in this, then in the next incarnation). Imagine how much less anger and the desire for revenge there would be.

Everybody should also know that only through the knowledge born of love can we get closer to God. What would be the meaning of material values or authority to the people if

they were an end itself and not the means to gain such an attitude? Greed or the desire for authority is of no value as they are.
Instead of bringing us closer to the desired goal, they take it
further away from us.

If disharmony or „evil" influences you in any domain,
dear reader, know that you need it for some reason. It is a lesson
that you brought on yourself. Even if you don't experience
„evil" now, but you see it around, know that what you pay
attention to will manifest sometime in your life. If you see only
goodness around you, you will experience more and more of it,
but if you see only „evil", you will experience disharmony and
nothing else. You will avoid negative influence in your life
when you understand the law that holds that evil (poverty,
misery, disease) is as necessary to humanity as goodness is.
There are many people of different preferences and „appetites"
for various kinds of vibrations. There are also many people that
can't exist outside of an atmosphere of fright, violence, disease,
or grief. Both sides – the violently acting and their victims—
need each other and complement each other. They cannot exist
without one another. When you understand the naturalness of
these desires, it won't bother you anymore. You won't complain
or ask how God can allow it. You will understand that these
people still reside on a relatively low level of consciousness and
don't know what is really important in life. They don't understand, apply, or use the requirements of the universal laws.. It is
easy to imagine what would happen if everyone's moods and
pursuits (which are often in opposition to each other) suddenly
began to become fulfilled, especially if this process was as
immediate as it is in Heaven. The physical world would be
rocked to its foundations because most of people haven't grown
enough yet and still have to limit themselves for the good of
themselves and others. Their free will is very limited and the

results of their choices are delayed. It cannot be otherwise, though. If it wasn't for those limitations, the worlds would become unstable or may cease to exist. However, there is no limit to the ability to understand others. They become limited only in the range and time of manifestation, meaning that the creation is sometimes very delayed. It can even be transferred to the next incarnation. We all change the world and have influence on our lives, which affects the present, earthly measure of time. These affects are quick, but seldom immediate. Think of what would happen if everything manifested in an instant? How many people in a rush of fury or hatred would eliminate half of humanity in a second? But once they calm down, everything goes back to normal. At most, they feel guilty that they got carried away with these emotions. Then one desire replaces another, causing many people to live in apathy from day to day, pretending they're doing the right thing.

I experience the workings of these laws in relation to ghosts almost every day. On the other side, my thoughts become reality instantly. For example, a family that a ghost is asking for appears immediately. Everything happens at the same velocity as thoughts. The ghost couldn't find its family for hundreds of years because it didn't believe it was possible. I didn't have such doubts, however, and so it happened in an instant.

Long ago I started to notice that it is similar in our physical world. Many people don't experience this because we are limited by our own beliefs. If we believe that one has to work hard and wait long for some things, the sudden appearance of the desired thing or a condition would most probably cause a shock. We wouldn't receive the thing after all, wouldn't see it, or would subconsciously believe it was a dream. Our thoughts create our truth, whether we realize it or not. It is the thought that is real and the matter is its derivative, ergo the illusion. It seems like a paradox, but it is not. Everything happens in the mind. However, for most people the impossible is what they have never seen before.

When the job on earth is finished and there is no need to come back unless you want to,, you continue with your growth. There will come a moment when you understand that you don't need a form anymore because you are complete and full of light, wisdom, and love. You will feel energy flowing throughout your body that is also vitalizing everything else. You will be absolutely sure that it is wholeness containing light, love, and knowledge and that you are a part of it. When this becomes your life and diffuses into your consciousness, you will enter the state in which you won't need a vehicle or body to exist, only the education your soul has gathered until that time.

You will start to perceive your „Self" differently. Among the occultists, mainly yogis, there prevails the opinion that the „Self" can disappear completely. I really don't know what these people mean. Describing this phenomenon as disappearance is either illogical or inadequate in this situation. The „Self" doesn't disappear—our profundity, the perceiving reality, still exists. Ego with capital E is still aware of its existence and perception. It is the personal traits that cease to exist, the things that distinguish us from other people. The ego then becomes impersonal and void of sex. This condition, however, doesn't mean nonexistence. It doesn't weaken the feeling for yourself and your own value in any means. The value of the ego simply cannot be compared to other egos anymore. The value in itself, in reality, doesn't exist. It is only when we compare one trait with the other that the evaluation starts and this is the phenomenon that disappears in higher conditions. Everything becomes equally beautiful, perfect, harmonious, filled with love, etc. for everybody. We currently live in a world where there is always something that is more or less beautiful, perfect, etc.

It is only then that we notice and understand that in the whole or multiplied universe only one soul exists, like a huge pyramid, and that all people simultaneously share all experiences. In the condition of absolute awareness its levels are not perceived. This doesn't mean, however, that they don't exist. They do, but beyond the condition of the general awareness. They serve to indicate the levels of the growing individual awareness still present in the independent consciousness. The more developed the human consciousness is, the higher it stands on the pyramid. The basis of the pyramid is the lowest, broadest, and most populated.

I realize that not everybody will adopt this knowledge at this moment. But to those that are advanced enough to understand, I say this: when you look into someone else's eyes and you see your own soul there looking at you, you will know that you have reached the next level of awareness. In any other case, the things I write here will seem nonsense to you. In this state of awareness we understand that reincarnation doesn't exist because all incarnations and experiences occur simultaneously. Apply this knowledge in a way that is full of love is wisdom that you cannot gain any other way.

I should end this book at this point. The soul has marked out the full circle and returned to the place it once set out from. If this was everybody's case I would have called my book „The Wheel of Life". Unfortunately, not many souls are ready for it. What about the rest?

RETURNING TO EARTH

For an average man, time spent in the causal world is only a tiny part of his life. It results from the fact that his soul
hasn't reached an adequate stage of growth yet and has forgotten
Who It Is in Essence. It hasn't woken up enough to be able to
live in the condition of an absolute love, in both the causal body
and the higher worlds. Although not every soul is aware of life
in this higher state of consciousness, every soul, however, has
the honor to have such life. It returns Home only to see what it is
like and to feel or taste what real Love is. Although it doesn't
realize it until later because it doesn't consciously remember it,
somewhere in the deeper layers of its being it keeps the memory
of this stays and subconsciously longs for this state. You can say
that it is internally attracted to it. When it enters It, since it is not
fully aware of this state, it loses its sense of fullness of life
simultaneously. It is then that a vague wish to try the physical
life again is born within a man. The kernel or an incentive that is

316 IN THE WHEEL OF LIFE, VOLUME II

pushing the soul in this direction is its unfulfilled desires from the previous physical life. These desires grow with every minute and prompt the soul to descend into physical matter. At first glance, it seems that the main reason for being reborn is a general desire to live. The true reason, however, is the unfulfilled or suppressed desires from the past life. They attract us back towards the earth so we can realize them at last. If you have desires or if you wish for something but you don't realize it, you make a big mistake that will affect you in the future. That's why various religions claim that desire is the root of all evil. However, please note, dear reader, that a life without desires, in the full understanding of the nature of earthly desires, means something totally different from suppressing desires.

Buddhists believe that when you don't desire anything anymore you are spiritually progressing. There is a seed of truth here. When you satisfy all of your desires or wishes and pay all your earthly debts, you are free and can go on. Remember, though, that when you satisfy your wishes you bring them into the past and break free from them. As long as you have desires you must satisfy them. If you suppress them, you can create problems for the future and will have to return to earth for them later. Isn't it better to find the courage within yourself and watch carefully what the fulfilling of your desires brings to you? Are your wishes important enough to decide on your return?

Desires vary between people, of course, but the most common desire is that of accomplishing a goal by relating to other people that are either already on Earth or coming in the future. It is us who choose when we enter and leave our physical state. If we wanted to incarnate instantly, we could do it right after the death of the physical body (I will write about this more in the chapter „Castaways"). If we decide to journey through higher worlds, we need and adequately long for time to stay in each one of these worlds. Therefore, when a man has rested and recharged the batteries of his soul, he begins to miss esoteric stimuli and the wish to live on earth awakens within him, rooted in the unfulfilled desires from the previous incarnation.

The souls that hesitate or are not sure about the new incarnation can momentarily lose the chance to return and fulfill the things they believe they need to accomplish or experience life in a physical state. There is a far greater number of souls than physical bodies and when a soul misses its chance, it can sometimes wait a long time for the next opportunity, but I will write about it in a moment.

If a man wants to accomplish or receive something and he doesn't do so during his life, he dies with the feeling of unfulfillment. The condition of ascension (as I wrote about above) is attainable only for these souls that are truly, totally free from earthly desires. In this sense, the religions are right. Everyone else will be drawn back to Earth by their unfulfilled desires. That's why I wrote that one should put all their matters to an end before death, so they don't leave their unfulfilled desires on Earth.

There is no other possible way to stay in the higher worlds, even if we wanted to. The inner being of a man, also known as his soul, begins to think about the unfulfilled desires that automatically begin to create a new body. That's why it is so important to know what you desire and, more importantly, what the subconscious desires. You can also say, „Consider what you desire because you will definitely get it" in this or a future life. However, is every desire worth returning for? I have met many people who could not understand the cause of their earthly stay completely and couldn't find the purpose of life. When they saw what desire attracted them here, first they cried with laughter and then regret because they were so foolish, as you'll see in the case below.

You probably understand already that heaven doesn't exist as a place. It is a condition of resting, in which you don't have to *chase* freedom anymore. Every time you accomplish something (even here on Earth), you are in heaven for a while, because it is a condition of rest and happiness that exists on the subjective plane only. And although the generally accepted concept of heaven is erroneous, your soul can always touch heaven whenever it wants to but only when it's internal light allows for it.

If reincarnation doesn't exist from the spiritual point of view, then in the three dimensional physical world, it is as real as the ground, mountains, and oceans in the physical world. It is energy, the same as other energies, and its reality depends on the energy of an observer. If you can live without earthly desires, reincarnation doesn't exist for you, and if you can't, it is reality to you. That's why, dear reader, you need to answer the question whether it is or it isn't yourself.

In other words, reincarnation is real as long as a man perceives the physical body and solid objects as real. The main subject of his lesson on earth is still *attachment* then. There are many things on Earth that a man desires but he mostly desires a place where he will be able to manifest himself while experiencing earthly lessons. If a man sees energy instead of a physical body and solid objects, he also understands that everything progresses in an eternal present. He doesn't desire his physical body anymore, nor the place would he manifest in.

Reincarnation wouldn't be necessary in such a case because we could accomplish everything in one life. It is possible to understand instantly and contact God instead of constantly circumnavigating Him by being born and dying. From this perspective, reincarnation can be called a failure, an ever-repeating mistake of a human who is unable to reach the central point, God. This mistake chains him to the turnstile of ever-repeating incarnations. Look at this book cover. God is in the center, in light, and people circle around instead of going straight to Him. That's why Jesus said, „Know the truth and it will make you free." Humanity is stuck in this constant turnstile for millions of years already, totally unaware of the fact. That is where the title of my book comes from.

Dear reader, you can have the best teachers, gurus, or masters, but sooner or later you have to walk along the path leading within alone. You are never alone, however, as you are not deprived of help. How long will this journey take? It depends on you. Time doesn't exist in this respect. If you must count the time passing, count in lessons you've learned, not in minutes, hours, or years. If you gain the right understanding, you can heal yourself in five minutes or fifty years. It remains one and the same lesson for the soul. It is like with a poem: you can reflect on it for a few hours or a few minutes. It is the effect that is important to the teacher, not the time you spent on learning.

Regarding reincarnation as the turnstile of life, I say the following: many people think that you live only once so it is necessary to have a blast and make a pile of life as big as you can. Some want to live their young years in blissful laziness and idleness. For many, the peak of their accomplishments is fun, drinking, sex, meaningless discussions, and killing time. On the other hand, others drive themselves to accomplish things. When they get exhausted from chasing nothing and realize they would like to live differently, they are already too old or sick, simply an empty shell with no energy left. They don't strive for anything anymore and don't know how to change their lives. So they die and when they are there, on the other side, they want to be reborn since they recognize their mistake. They believed that they only lived once so when they come back to Earth they begin to live just like they had before. And so it goes 'round until the moment something happens that awakens them they get out of the rut they were stuck in.

If you believe in one incarnation only, it is impossible to understand existence on Earth. Many will protest, claiming they don't believe in reincarnation. I am not trying to persuade anyone or detach them from their religion. On the contrary, I just want to show the deeper meaning of life that a man has probably never suspected. I wish for religious people to understand it and live according to it. I am writing about reincarnation because its understanding can restore lost faith in many cases and provide enlightenment. We are suddenly able to understand many questions that could not be explained otherwise. We begin to understand all those apparent wrongdoings and injustices of fate regardless of if they've happened to us or other people. First of all, we recognize the existence of the Great Law – Life Principle that regulates everything in the midst of apparent chaos.

During all my years of practice I've noticed that people who don't believe in reincarnation are much more frightened that something bad will happen to them or their loved ones, which, of course, comes from the fear of death or nonexistence. And when they don't have a choice and have to die, they hold on to life with great determination for as long as it is possible. This in turn leads to possessions and misery but it happens only to those who live according to the patterns followed earlier by the dead. People who understand reincarnation live more peacefully and joyfully and when a death comes they go away in trust. They know that after the death of the physical body they don't disappear but return

Home. They can always come back here, whenever they wish.

THE IDEA OF REINCARNATION

According to the dictionary, reincarnation is the belief that in every man there is a particle of energy independent of his physicality that can be reborn in another body after death. It is pervasive in Eastern religions. Reincarnation and the phases between incarnations are also the foundations of Kabbalah literature. Christians believed in it long ago as well. It was Origen (circa 185-254 A.D.), one of the most influential Church Fathers, that taught it. Reincarnation theory was confirmed many times in the Bible but condemned and deleted from the doctrine of the Catholic Church during the second church council in Constantinople in 533 A.D. The Church rejected the reincarnation doctrine decidedly and still does. Christians are presently taught that eternity starts from the moment of birth which is a contradiction. That way, a man doesn't depend on self-knowledge in order to master himself. Then there came the times of inquisition when they killed off those who knew any-

324 IN THE WHEEL OF LIFE, VOLUME II

thing about the subject. Today, even those who loudly protest against reincarnation know little to nothing about it.

What we should believe in and what we shouldn't was once again decided by the Church for us. Think of how few church representatives are presently at the stage of growth that makes it possible to live in light. Then the idea of reincarnation truly disperses. That's why reincarnation is an undeniable fact for most people. Important historical and clinical evidence confirms it. Many doctors, psychiatrists, priests, and people like me face such evidence almost every day. However, many of us deny it out of fear or being called crazy. It often happens on the basis of „It is better not to talk about what I know. It is better for me to save my reputation, job, position, fortune, respect, etc." This is the main reason so little is being said about it.

Nevertheless, if you give in to delusion and believe that you are living for the first time, please know, dear reader that you incarnate to experience creation and understand it as a whole. I suppose you don't think that you chose your life and experiences and this is what life is about? This would be like looking out a window and saying, „I know everything about the world surrounding me". You can, with a little effort, start to expand your limits and realize that there are many things that we need to learn as humanity. Every life has its sense and its glow.

Know that I am not trying to persuade you to perceive things the way I do. Whether you will believe in reincarnation or not is totally up to you. I think, however, that if you didn't believe it on the intuitional level, you wouldn't be reading this book or my earlier studies.

It is no wonder that so many people reject the thought of reincarnation. Both religion and science seem to have conspired to make life after death or immortality a taboo subject. It didn't happen out of nowhere, of course. The Church authorities once discovered that an increasingly large number of people reject church so they came up with the idea in order to join forces with the world of science. From that time on, they began directing their followers' attention to the fact that it is science now that will give solutions to all problems bothering humanity.

On account of this, people have wrongly believed for a few hundred years that when technology reaches a certain stage of development it will solve the problems of humanity. Science was supposed to become the escape route from diseases, poverty, suffering, and pain. We know now that science and technology themselves cannot solve these problems. They can be used to achieve both good and evil goals. Technology can be truly helpful only if we use it consciously, wisely, and most importantly, moderately. That's why humanity must find harmony and balance within. It is not possible to give harmony and balance to someone else, even using the most advanced technology. Not everyone is aware of the fact that the foundation of this balance or harmony is love, and that we can only find it within ourselves.

Giving so much power to science caused even more disorders in the educational system, which contributed even further to the complication of human minds. Such disordered education is the reason why materialism is the only explanation for the world taken into consideration. That's why materialism seems so unusually attractive to many people and they don't consider other possibilities. You cannot blame science or scientists here, of course. Every individual has agreed for those superficial visions to conquer our thinking and gain an increasing number of followers. They contain nothing apart from what can be seen, tasted, touched, heard, smelled, measured, weighed, bought, sold. This is the human heritage that we are so proud of. We don't realize that it leads us into a dead end, which we realize only after the death of the physical body when it is too late for any reaction. There is such proverb that says, „A Pole is wise after the harm is done". It should be changed to, „A man is wise after the harm is done," since this phenomenon applies to everyone.

However, many people try to escape the darkness that humanity has been stuck in for ages. The limitations of the material world still hinder most people, especially educated ones. They are based on the evaluation of the five senses only. It is so with individual people as with entire institutions. At first glance, it seems that only people impervious to reason reside there. How can we depend on people that never doubt their beliefs or religious systems? Our minds blinded with beliefs and antiquated ideas, keep us from absorbing new observations and knowledge that we gain ourselves or learn from other people. This is why people pay so little attention to their fundamental roots before birth and in the future which, as you know already, dear reader, reach far beyond the death of the physical body. Although we have so many scientists, we skim the surface of the phenomenon of the matter of life itself. Often we rely exclusively on what we know already and this stops us from realizing the nature of things that we perceive with our five senses. For example, scientists search for life on other planets and while it certainly exists, they cannot see it. That's why they remain unaware of the wonderful spaces expanding into the furthest horizons. I get so many letters concerning the subject. Individual people see nonmaterial worlds or note anomalies they see but they are afraid to talk about it openly. They write, „Mrs. Pratnicka, you are truly brave. I agree with you, but I am too weak to change anything in regards to human understanding."

The readers of my books comprise a relatively small group of people. Deep inside, they believe in life after death and accept their own immortality. Skeptics still burst into disparaging laughter at the thought of life after death and arrogantly deny the world they are unable to see. They shrug, preferring not to engage in what, in their opinion, is a distant and uncertain echo of another world. Besides, all their doubts will crumble sooner or later. At the latest, it is after the death of the physical body that they will learn how things really are. The older generation says, „How can we know that what you write is true? Nobody has come back from there yet." The people that have come back, however, are those who have survived a clinical death or a long and hard narcosis. Regardless, you cannot prove anything to a person who doesn't want to believe. Others, not noticing these spaces, subconsciously deprive themselves of their cosmic identity and consequently deny their spiritual essence. By rejecting this heritage, they deny their sense of their own existence at the same time. I know this from my daily practice, since I often deal with cases similar to the examples below.

I met a professor of physics once. Let's call him Ken. He was an unrepentant materialist that didn't believe in life after death at all, let alone reincarnation. He spent many hours discussing the subject with me or in a larger group with his colleagues. He often eagerly brought scientists and priests to meet me. Ken was the traveler type. He constantly moved around the world, visiting various academies. All of it was happening in the communistic time and the subject was totally unknown. After a few years of these meetings we grew apart from each other in a weird way, overnight. He stopped coming to me without any clear reason. After a long time I learned that he fell down the stairs to his apartment and died before the ambulance arrived, even though he was less than forty years old. He didn't visit me after death, either. In the meantime, many people from scientific circles as well as family members that I had never met before started to call me for help. They constantly described the same phenomenon. It turned out that professor, the tireless frequenter of every discussion, still participated in them even though he was physically dead. He died suddenly and he didn't understand that his physical body didn't exist anymore. On account of this he acted exactly the same as before. He often aroused fear and confusion at home, at the university, or in various clubs while actively participating in the discussions mentioned above.

When he had finally awakened to the consciousness of transformation called death, he nevertheless didn't want to go away. His present goal was to make everybody he used to have discussions with realize that he had been wrong and present himself as clear proof. Most of them didn't hear him out of fear or lack of faith in life after death. I was unwittingly forced to mediate in many of his conversations until he accomplished his goals, meaning he brought this home to his friends, colleagues, family, and neighbors. In most cases, I messengered to his large family, many of whom were also academics, and they mediated further. I had to „deal" with the more resistant people myself. And again, they started coming to me in groups in order to understand what he wanted to tell them. Ken was determined to make his point and wouldn't leave until everyone close to him understood that life after death existed.

I am trying to show you from various perspectives, dear reader, that life and death are the same. The soul is eternal, and its yearning for knowledge and enlightenment exists both in the material and spiritual worlds. Reincarnation, meaning the process of letting the soul circulate between those two domains, makes this search easier and possible for the soul to continue its education as it strives for perfection.

A man that is aware of further existence after the death of the physical body, lives quite differently than he did before.

When he deeply understands that he never really dies, his every thought, word, and desire takes on a completely different meaning than it had before. He changes the perspective of his perception because he knows that whatever he did can't be obliterated by time or space. He begins to understand cause and effect better. Until now everything was transitory and tangential to him. He lived believing that he couldn't influence what was happening to him. Now, looking from a different perspective, everything gains much deeper meaning. The conditions and dependencies that he sees are not only transitory phenomena, but meaningful events rooted in a certain cause. He doesn't expect the end of his earthly journey with fear anymore. He treats death as a return Home that presents the possibility for revival. Awareness is the reason that every moment of life becomes unusually important to him.

THE SCHOOL CALLED LIFE

I suggest we look at life from a broader perspective. As I mentioned before, beams of energy once pumped out from the Source of Everything That Exists, also known as God. Their interaction caused an inception of matter on various levels of experience. Every human soul, including yours, set out to new spaces. Each one decided to gain new experiences through constant learning and expressing. This process we call involution. Every journey (even the longest one) will end sometime, however. The same applies to the journey of a soul. It eventually comes back Home to God, Source, Light, whatever you want to call it. This is what the evolutionary process is about and the development of the universe as well since everything that lives is a wave. I will write more about it in the chapter „The Laws of the Universe."

The task of the soul is to descend into the thickest matter that the physical body and Earth are made of and ascend back into higher spiritual worlds. Every time the soul comes back Home it takes rich crops with it consisting of accomplished and resolved experiences. In other words, a soul is neither constantly dying nor being born, but leading a continued, eternal life.

What we call death is only parting with the lowest physical plane. The soul as a real human doesn't submit to change on higher planes in the same way that a living man doesn't change when he takes off his clothes every day. If we want to understand life and its purpose, we have to look at it from the spiritual, not physical, perspective. Looking from the frog's perspective, we don't see much. However, looking at the same phenomenon from a higher point of view, we see the physical life completely differently. An entire life is recognized the same as a single day in the earthly school. It begins with physical birth and ends with physical death. We also notice that we have many such days behind us and many still before us.

From this perspective we see that real human life lasts forever. Life in the physical body is just a tiny section. And afterwards it has stays on the astral, mental, and causal planes. It is like a proverbial blink of the eye in the endlessly long existence of the soul. Look at it like this: the stay in the physical body is like morning, the astral body is like noon, the mental like afternoon, and the casual is like evening, all in one day and leading up to one incarnation. Without exception, everyone has a very long story of such incarnation behind them. An average man has a lot of lives still to live because he has a lot to learn.

With each incarnation a soul puts on a new physical body as well as subtle bodies and learns lessons in the physical world. What lessons? Everything depends on the person and what they want to learn. Such a choice is given only to souls that are self-conscious and willing to learn, of course. Everyone else is somewhat forced to learn their lessons but I'll write more on this subject in the chapter „Castaways".

The ultimate human goal is freedom gained through love, kindness, and self-respect. If we look closer at those traits, we will see that they are the same. When we gain love, respect, knowledge, kindness, and understanding of ourselves, we begin to learn these traits in relation to the rest of humanity. How long will our lessons last? Try to answer this question yourself, dear reader. When you look around, you will easily recognize how many of us truly have self-respect and how many have learned to value themselves as exceptional, perfect souls or individuals. You may be astonished to discover that almost nobody has such an attitude and that most of us mistake dignity and love of our true Self for egoism.

That's why, dear reader, the soul must learn the truth from all sides in order to understand Life fully. It applies to all of us. This is why in some incarnations we change religion, race, or nationality. We live through our incarnations with unusual poverty and richness throughout health, sickness, fame, disgrace, high, and low. During subsequent incarnations we change our sex, too. Sometimes we have children and sometimes we have none, although we would love to have them. We are executioners and victims, criminals and almost saints. We experience this only to gather the knowledge from all sides like we do in school. Does it make sense to judge others if we were in exactly the same situation once?

It also happens that the soul fails to learn anything after having lived the physical life. Many souls learn their planned program only partially, to use the language of an earthly school, with a lick and a promise. No matter the quantity of experiences, however, the soul eventually takes off its bodily clothes and returns Home to rest and gain some strength. During the „morning" of every new life, in the time following birth, the soul

334 IN THE WHEEL OF LIFE, VOLUME II

realizes exactly where it left off in the previous life. When it comes back to Earth it feels like it faces something entirely new and unknown.

This dependency is very well illustrated by the film „Groundhog Day" from 1993. The premise of this movie is that a man lives the same day over and over again, prompting him to reconsider how he lives his life. It is worth watching, even if to understand the repetitious patterns a man goes through. For example, he learns how to avoid falling „into the same puddle" he fell into yesterday and on many earthly days before. He learns that it takes a while to remember lessons and walk through life „dry-footed." That's why a soul learns some lessons within one day and other lessons over many more days until it adopts them well enough to pass the exam on a higher level.

What does the soul have to learn presently? First of all, that a man that is physically dying doesn't take „things" with him but his deeds only. These are the fruits coming from the wisdom of his heart. Often a man entering his earthly life forgets this and stands, after his physical death, on the verge of his further existence empty handed. There, in the real Home, he swears that when he goes to school „tomorrow", he will behave differently. After many trials, he finally succeeds in remembering, it becomes a new habit, and changes the flow of his life. This is what the film „Groundhog Day" shows.

Most people don't remember their experience the first time. That's why they have to go through death and birth many times (with all the trials and troubles that come with the process), until the memory is so embedded within them that they become what they learn. The main lesson is understanding that the foundation of human family is spirituality, not materialism. When this lesson is learned, death will cease to exist for the human race. I'll say more about this in the chapter titled „Life in the Lost Civilization".

How do we remember our experiences? First of all, we need to realize that we are a soul that puts a body on like a body that puts clothes on. If this is difficult for you to accept then please refer to the first volume of this book. The soul descending to earth can be compared to a discoverer entering unknown terrain. It reminds me a diver who has to don a heavy outfit to deal with the conditions of the ocean floor. The mission that a soul comes to earth with is always the same—the gathering of experience and expansion of knowledge on the grounds of these experiences that eventually transforms into wisdom. When it gains it, it is obligated to help others reach the condition it accomplished itself. When the journey of a certain incarnation comes to an end, the soul puts away its physical body and continues to learn on higher planes. This part is the real You that lives forever.

A man that accepts this fully ceases to identify himself with the body so strongly. He will know that he is a soul that owns the physical body. He will remember from now on that being *everything*, he is inextricably connected to the Whole, God, with his Source. He will also understand, with the help of intuition that everything, not just him, is constantly learning, getting to know itself, and growing because of it.

A man who understood this, knows, and never forgets that every time he leaves Home on the other side knows that he comes to earth only to experience and learn from it. He needs this in his constant striving for spiritual perfection, for Perfection. He also knows that before he comes to Earth, nobody imposes anything on him. It is he that decides who and what he will be, even writing down his own pattern or plan to guide him through the lessons he wants to learn through his experiences in the short journey outside Home. He realizes that there are many ways to reach his goal. He can play many roles to accomplish his desired, ultimate purpose of the earthly stay: *freedom from wants and needs present on Earth.* It is just like how Jesus was intended „Be in the world, but not of the world." He repeats his lessons as long as he needs to in order to gain full freedom.

More than one reader will probably ask if we should really return to earth to learn anything. Why can't we stay there and learn in the spiritual state of being? Of course, we can and we do since there are different levels of learning. As I already mentioned, however, we don't want to stay there at all because we are attracted to physicality by our unfulfilled wants. Moreover, we realize that interactions between people residing in the spiritual form rely on something other than the physical form. We can learn some things only as physical beings. It is only then that we make interpersonal contacts, through which we feel pain and can hurt others, which is impossible in the spiritual form because pain doesn't exist. You may realize that most people are able to learn through suffering only, and they cannot understand anything otherwise. It is very exhausting to live like that, of course, and is impossible to live that way permanently. So the soul comes back Home, rests and revives. This is the rejuvenation, mobilization period. And as you already know, dear reader, it is easy to gain the energy and motivation to act on the other side. There is only happiness and the sense of satisfaction at the Source. After the resting stage we come back to learn again.

However, not everyone you meet during your earthly journey goes through this scheme. There many people here, too, that came only to teach others and bring them help since they have forgotten *Who They Are in Essence.* An old begging woman can be such a person, whose task is to teach love and compassion. Many come to Earth only to live in the impurity of the physical world and not to moil in it. Some succeed in that, while others don't. Then they have to learn their lesson from the beginning. You should know that the fall from higher awareness is much quicker and it is possible to reach the bottom in an instant. The more advanced the soul, the more unbearable pain it is able to feel. This pain can blind the soul, causing it to lose its sense of direction and go astray. Sometimes the body cannot stand the pain any longer and throws the soul away. The man dies then. Anyway, the course of earthly lessons isn't imposed on us, we choose it ourselves. If you don't like what you chose earlier, forgive yourself, make a new one, and your life will subsequently change.

The most difficult thing is for a person to understand that their present experiences in earthly school are their lessons. And since they are just learning something, it is only natural that they make many mistakes. The deeds can sometimes be foolish, bad, or even blameworthy, though only under human evaluation. The soul can grow and submit to remodeling even during the lowest or most disgraceful incarnation. It can learn from it and use the abilities and knowledge acquired to help other souls in the next life. It can be oppressed in one life and helpful in the next. The feeling of guilt coming from a disgraceful incarnation is not important It is important to learn from the past, not to think of it constantly and feel guilty. It is the education that is important, not the evaluation. That's why we need to learn how to get rid of prejudice and hatred. Those who remain prejudiced and hateful because they either don't understand or can't forgive,, simply change sides, returning in new incarnations with the bodies of mutual enemies. This is supposed to teach them how to understand a certain lesson. Every action is only a way of expressing ourselves. Our actions are never fully us so we shouldn't identify with them.

And so, a man shouldn't demand much from himself,

338 IN THE WHEEL OF LIFE, VOLUME II

judge himself, or condemn himself when he is not able to do something well enough or when he acts wrongfully. He shouldn't judge others either since they are in exactly the same situation as he was once in or will find himself in later. When a man as a soul understands this, he won't get frustrated and that will hasten the learning. He won't judge himself or others anymore. When a man finally understands that something is wrong, he just stops expressing it and his perspective changes at once. His actions follow this.

While in the school of life, even if we realize that we are a soul and not a body, it is still difficult for us to remember this fact. If we remembered this even occasionally, it would disperse much delusions and illusion. It would be much easier to live peacefully among other people. We would realize more often that whatever an individual person's journey looks like, we're all going to the same place – Home, the Source, God.

As a pupil in the earthly school, the progress of the soul isn't always linear. The soul can excel in a certain domain by being caring, protective, compassionate, but fail in others by being angry, envious, and impatient. If a soul is an eager student in the earthly school, it learns everything very quickly. It learns things it should be learning but also additional curriculums. It tries to understand its rights as a student while learning the school's regimen at the same time, which is determined by universal laws. After studying them, it knows how to adapt to them in the most efficient manner. It starts to flow with Life on one wave, unresisting, upstream, like it used to. It also understands that these laws concern the whole Life (on all of its levels) and not just physical existence.

The school life will be relatively short on the physical plane for such a student. When it ends they will pass with the whole supply of his knowledge and wisdom to higher worlds.

As I mentioned before, the education goes on there and the life in the three lower worlds (physical, astral, and mental) are the only preparation for real life. It reminds me of passing from elementary school to middle school, then high school and higher.

Some souls, unfortunately, fail in living in the physical body. They try their best but no good comes of it. Some find it difficult to learn since their lessons are still too demanding, though they may learn them the first time. The second group's problem is the burden of karma. What they sowed before over-weighs them now. They undertook this task through their own decision, of course. This group embraces souls that are too ambitious, that came initially to help others but overplayed their hand. The weight of the task undertaken outgrew their human or physical capabilities. Behind the death curtain, it is very easy to accomplish everything one dreams of. It seems to some of the souls that they are capable of anything in the physical realm, which is actually a much harder task. It is learning in a sense, too, since they were told to look before they leap while on the other side but ignored because of hastiness or arrogance.

There are other students that cannot understand their rights or the school's regimen at all. That's why they constantly disobey the rules. Some, even if they have learned the school's rights already, cannot overpass their own resistance or rebellion to act accordingly. Such students stay in the earthly school the longest, delaying entering the higher worlds because of their actions.

Earthly life is a school that no student can drop out of. Everybody must go through his education, whether he wants to or not. Some extremely resistant students are forced through the education, though it is very unpleasant for them. You'll be able to read more about it in the chapter „Castaways." However, the time it takes to learn and the ability to excel on higher tests totally depends on an individual decision.

If a soul is a wise and resolute student, it understands that the stage it presently finds itself in, meaning the school in physical life is the only way to prepare to live in higher worlds and is therefore the only opportunity to achieve a true goal. It tries with all its might to understand the laws governing the universe and adapts its life to them. The soul regains its light then and shines while entering its kingdom, true Home.

OUR LESSONS

Every lesson we learn in life is learned so that we can we can become more like God by experiencing it. In this way, we come closer to Him and we can, eventually, stay in our true Home forever. It is possible only when we have learned every lesson, meaning that we have broken free of human desires (through understanding, not superseding). As you already know, our desires are a force that pulls us back to Earth. I hope that this knowledge brings you an explanation for many questions that you were perhaps struggling to solve, not knowing why they appeared in your life. This knowledge can remove many diffi-culties that you face every day, too. I hope that you will stop perceiving the world as filled with „injustice" and grievances since you will know that they are apparent. When you integrate this completely, the world of the common order will show in the apparent chaos of the modern world in front of your eyes. You will still see the beings that are unequal because each one of them bears a completely different wealth of experience due to their own talents, abilities, and energy present from various incarnations. On the other hand, dear reader, you will know that we are equal as souls and that we are all students in the same school. We share one goal—to reach the level of enlightenment, enabling us to pass the exam to the next level. Then we will see plain and clear that despite all the differences, each man's path is basically the same. In the physical condition, we all have to learn the same truths and integrate with them until they become our second nature. Each of these lessons consists of the same factors for all the people. There is, however, a variety of them that many people get confused about while trying to distinguish them. Let's take mercy, hope, faith, and love as examples. There are so many ways to learn how to express them. With every stay on Earth we learn only bits of these virtues since, considering their complexity, we are not able to accomplish mastery in one lifetime.

As you already know, before each soul enters the world it writes down something similar to a scenario for its future incarnation, designing in detail everything that will help it to learn the lesson desired. One soul can plan to learn only one aspect, even this one can turn out to be too difficult to realize. Other souls don't have much of a problem with that and its difficulty appears to be in another domain. This is like with many things here on Earth. A man can play or sing beautifully, but he doesn't have fine motor control. He is a good student of science but has problems with expressing himself, and so on.

The physical body is the concentrated energy, your soul's reflection. This is a kind of a vehicle, an apartment or temple, in which the soul realizes the role appointed in advance. You can also think of your body as of a gate through which you enter the coexistence with the earth. It allows you to unite with the planet since it is made of exactly the same elements that occur on the earth.

Coming to Earth, a soul connects to a core (of the earth to learn power through the thinking mind and love through indebtedness. You are indebted and you pay or others are obliged to you. The earth is neither the place of the highest power nor the highest spirituality. It is just an adequate place to gain knowledge through love and compassion or through suffering. Although a body is a reflection of a soul, it doesn't mean that an ugly, broken, or stoop-shouldered body presents an ugly, broken, or stoop-shouldered soul. It only means that the body reflects or performs a job that the soul undertook to complete during its limited time on earth.

I previously wrote that in order to get to know a man's soul you should look deeply into his eyes. It doesn't mean, of course, that blind people don't have souls. It means only that they perceive the world with eyes that aren't physical. Analogically, we can see that a wise, beautiful, and rich man, perceived according to earthly criterions, may not have a grand or wonderful soul or a compassionate heart.

It's often difficult to figure out which lesson we should work through. We can use a woman that has had many miscarriages yet still wants to give birth as an example. It turns out that the man she wants to be the father of her child is sterile. She could have a baby with any other man, though. Any choice she makes will be wrong because she will either be without a baby or be without her beloved man's love. The lesson this woman is working on is finding happiness within and not making it dependent on having a certain man or a child.

Feelings and matters of the heart are very important elements of living on Earth. In many universes, feelings don't exist. That's why so many beings come to Earth to learn through feeling. That's why these sensations come from your body, among other things.

As you know, we learn pain through the physical body. One of the first lessons in life is learning how to feel. Fire, air, water, and other elements of earth that comprise both your body and the Earth's systems are some of your teachers. It is them who create temperament, meaning they indicate the traits you must still learn or unlearn. The body is the limit. Everything that exists on Earth has its limits. The heart is the limit within the broader system of the body. The limits are lessons too. We ultimately learn to cross the limits of physical existence. However, in order to learn our lessons we need to be completely honest with ourselves and our selves in every situation we find ourselves in, no matter how much it hurts to face our own inadequacies. In this way, each lesson in the body will strengthen the direction and meaning of the soul.

When a soul takes a certain direction, the necessary activity comes to it in the form of thoughts. If you are supposed to walk in a certain direction but you don't, you act against yourself and begin to suffer. You learn about life on earth from Earth itself, so you need to follow her rules. In order to face up to these, you need to be self-disciplined. If you don't sow or harvest, you don't build and balance your mind constantly and you fall on both the plane of the mind and matter.

Each new lesson passed while on your individual path on Earth opens new channels of knowledge enabling you to reach into deeper and deeper regions of yourself and space. Your energy as an individual connects to the collective energy with an all-encompassing Light. In order for you to learn, you are connected to the forces of the universe—truth (knowledge), light, and kindness. This universal movement of the spherical forces is connected to the energy of every individual soul.

Imagine a lucent web in which we are all connected to each other.

A soul isn't a separate, lonely being, and learning on Earth wouldn't be possible if we were to accomplish it alone. That's why we get the help of people closest to us (both friends and enemies) and participate in their learning, too. The physical body makes you feel isolated but this is an illusion that needs to be recognized as quickly as possible.

Before we come to Earth, every one of us knows where we will go and why. We agree to certain tasks and terms. We live with our family or we leave them and walk the road our way. One way or another, we play our part according to the script written in advance. Life is a stage of a theatre that we play our parts in. We learn this way.

Everyone has probably gone through some particularly tough period in their lives, asking himself or God why it has to be this way, Think harder about what you're going through and ask yourself if you would learn anything if your life was easy. Difficult challenges offer the most possibilities to learn and progress. As you know, the teacher of knowledge on Earth is pain (although it is not the only option). Most lessons of knowledge and truth are taught that way. Together with pain an individual grows.

Each soul is different and experiences pain differently. You will never know the pain of another person since everyone needs a different kind of teacher. We can identify with another's pain only through our own pain. The more advanced the soul, the deeper the pain it feels because it understands much more. The greater the awareness of the understanding heart, the deeper the compassion, and sometimes pain, too.

OUR TESTS

As you know, dear reader, living on earth is a school in which we all learn. During class, tests are sometimes taken. They take the form of new challenges, problems, unpleasant people, and situations. No man or object appears without a reason. In order to secure an adequate amount of spiritual growth for yourself, you choose your parents, family, time and place of birth, and even your genetic heritage. You create what you presently experience yourself. Many relationships have their source in the choices made before the present life, of course, but this doesn't change the fact that this is of your making.

How do you attract things and people into your life? This it easy. Your thoughts make it. They are a magnet attracting everything that is part of your experience. The source of thoughts in turn is your beliefs. If you attract something you don't want then I advise you to look at your beliefs. It is only when you completely consent to the thought that you chose everything yourself, attracted it, or created it, you are ready to take full responsibility for your life. If you feel like a small, miserable victim or a pawn in the hands of fate or other people, you are stuck deep in this swamp. You attract every person and phenomenon on your path through your own effort in order to receive your next lessons from them. When you deeply consent to this responsibility, you will begin to gain more power over your life and you will be able to make changes. So if an unpleasant accident happens to you and all the appearances suggest it is someone else that is guilty, you need to consent to the realization that it was you who attracted it. Ask yourself why you did it, how, and if your anger wasn't accidentally a magnet that attracted this incident to you. Maybe it was your fear. Which one of your beliefs was the reason for this? Or maybe you refused to listen to your body for so long that it finally refused to be compliant and you got ill? If you didn't listen to it, why was it so?

When you come to the understanding that it is you that chooses despair instead of joy and fulfilment, you will begin to wonder what are the causes of this condition are. The karma law says you get only as much as you give. If you give goodness to *yourself and* others, you receive goodness. If you give disharmony, you receive disharmony. The world is just in that matter, more than words can express here. You always get what you give, although justice of this kind can only be realized in further incarnations or after you graduate from the school of life.

Before coming to the world in your present incarnation, your soul was ready to confront the unsolved problems of the previous incarnations (school days). Every traumatic incident, no matter what it is, is like a new task to complete. In order to liberate the body from the bonds that are binding it, it is necessary to finish and understand these events in a broader context.

That's why it is so important to forgive ourselves and others. Without forgiveness we constantly carry a thorn within us that causes us pain. Isn't it time to pull it out so our body can heal at last?

Each man has a dominating vice. It can be greed, desire, envy, etc. Whatever it is in your case, it is necessary to pay the debt to the people you did harm to. Besides, you need to take control over this vice in the life you live now. If you fail, you will carry this and all the other vices to the next incarnation. The burden will grow. Each incarnation without paying the debts will be harder. If you pay them, your life will be easier. In this aspect, it is also you that decides what life you have. Also, when you enter higher worlds in the next phases of life, you will answer for the life you live. It is you that decides everything.

If you did something „wrong" to yourself or others, you will choose a lesson that will enable you to repair it. You can become a victim of the same „evil" or meet the consequences of entering the energy of „evil" in other ways. You may learn how to stop hurting yourself, take care of yourself, or stand up for yourself. In other words, you learn how to become a master of your life after being a victim.

If we do good, goodness will certainly return to us. In human understanding, the one who does good receives more and more good, while the one who does „wrong" receives more and more disharmony. It doesn't matter if he does wrong to himself or others. What we devote ourselves to, or pay attention to, returns to us multiplied. Indeed there is nothing like „evil" or goodness but a smaller or larger good only. You will discover that later when we discuss universal laws. Right now, I will just say what you have probably heard before: „Every cloud has a silver lining."

A soul must sometimes come back to Earth just to receive from others the good that it once gave. It is common for a „good, helpful" man to ail at the end of his life in order to avoid coming back to receive goodness. Everybody thinks it is unfair. It has nothing to do with evil fate, though, but with a lesson such a man must learn. Harmony reigns in the universe and it must also exist in a man since he is a part of the universe. A „good, helpful" man that gives only all his life and never demands anything from anyone and who even shies away from receiving when something is being offered to him breaches the harmony mentioned. It is of no importance why he does it. Maybe it is the sense of duty or own ignorance. Maybe he hasn't learned the law yet, saying that every energy must get balanced in order for harmony to reign. Maybe the cause is arrogance since it is often easier to give than to receive. Or maybe it is out of constraint since he feels the need to be a victim. Maybe he sacrifices himself in order to be able to feel sorry for himself. The soul that gives from the heart, out of the joy of giving for the sake of itself and others, without thinking of the reward, open to receiving what they have given, will never get ill.

The soul that gives without receiving can balance itself in later incarnations by receiving and giving nothing. It often doesn't want such a development though. A man like that, attached to bed during his illness, is forced to receive from others what he gave them all his life. It could cause him to suffer greatly. It is not enough that he is ill; he has to learn to receive from others, too. Suffering comes from impertinence, lack of submission, lack of understanding the law, guilt, the need to be a victim, self-pity, and resistance to forgiveness. It would be enough, however, to accept this situation and the disease wouldn't appear at all. It was so with my mother. She was convinced that she had to help everyone who had less resources or opportunities than she did. She gave only all her life and when she got ill, people crowded to take care of her, to pay their subconscious debt. Before she got ill, she didn't know where poverty came from. She thought that by giving she would help people liberate from it. When she was dying, she understood that everything is necessary on Earth and that people learn with the help of painful experiences. Poverty wouldn't exist if it wasn't needed it on Earth.

Whatever happens, happens in accordance with the spiritual laws. That's why no disease, disability, fire, burglary nor success, welfare or other „positive" thing happens by accident. Nobody has the power to do to us anything that would be discordant with our deep will or the allowance of the Higher Self. It's true for the smallest and largest occurrences.

Most often, the excess of some negative thing or apathy is the sign signaling that it is time to change something in our lives. For people unwilling to change, resistant to this signal, it is repeated many times. The abundance of something is a basic test. What is the lesson from this? I think you would agree that it is more reasonable to choose the education program yourself than to complain, lament, and wait for the second lesson. Let's take fire for example—it always suggests anger and the feeling of being stuck in an inflammatory situation. Explosions, burns, and fire are signals of the anger manifesting to those who don't want to look at it more closely or realize it. The universe will find a way to force you to understand but it is better to try to deal with it yourself.

THE PURPOSE OF A MAN'S LIFE

We are taught on Earth that money, power, prestige, material wealth, and tangible and earthly comforts are the basic purpose of life. This is nonsense, of course. The physical life is only a small part of our real Life, in the end. Relying on something you cannot take with you reminds me of building sand castles. Does it mean that one should disown beautiful things and live in poverty? No. God gives us good, beautiful and wonderful things to they can serve us and we can enjoy them. They are to bring us joy and fulfilment. It means at the same time that we are their temporary users only. So we don't have the right to become attached to them since they are not our property. Everything that we love are unable to live without belongs to God and we will have to be able to leave them behind when we go on to the next stage of life.

In the spiritual world, behind the so called „death curtain", we get everything and more back from God. The same things we had before are better if only we wish. It was written in the Bible, „Truly I say to you, it is hard for a rich man to enter the kingdom heaven. Again I say to you, it is easier for a camel to go through the eye of a needle, than for a rich man to enter the kingdom of God" It is harder for a rich man because it doesn't let him take the riches possessed from the physical to the spiritual world. If a man wants it, there are the same things there that were in the physical world but they are built of subtle spiritual matter vibrating on a higher level. That way, most people are not able to see them. Maybe you belong to them, too. Don't worry about it at all. If after having left the physical world you accept your death, all those things will become as tangible to you as material objects are now. By getting attached to the physical things we become their captives. We can become captive to people, too, as well as knowledge, power, respect, success, happiness, etc.

On the other hand, total rejection of physicality is just as disadvantageous as attachment. Rejection comes from the fact that a man subconsciously remembers that he once had to once leave what he was attached to. And since he suffered a lot for this reason, he doesn't want to possess anything in his present life in order to avoid a painful feeling of loss. It is not a conscious process for many people. It often happens that they envy things that rich men have although they work hard, they accomplish far less. When they realize that they once disowned material goods and let themselves not possess but to use them, they can suddenly use everything God offers without limits.

One of the cardinal mistakes is inordinate caring for the results of our own activity. We get so absorbed with the results that we forget to enjoy what we created. This awakens anxiety and depression. The anxiety may concern many things: How will we manage? What will happen if the result accomplished won't fulfil the expectations? What if we fail? What will others think? The effect is that instead of enjoying what we have in the present moment we judge ourselves harshly.

Sometimes it is the other way round: we do nothing since we believe that if we fail we will be rejected, hate ourselves, and become lame ducks or losers. We don't realize that we are that way already. And how does it work in your life, dear reader? Maybe, instead of worrying about the results of your activity, do just what feels right, help others with joy, and imagine a better life.

We are taught in the modern world that we need other people's sympathy and respect as well as need objects, clothes, and gadgets in order to be happy. But people come and go. We cannot influence the length of their stay since everyone has his own lesson to work through. At the same time, we should realize the undeniable fact that all of us, without exception, have eternal, spiritual partners and families. We are immortal beings that, because of energy, will never be parted or separated from those whom we truly love and who love us. There is always someone who loves us and protects us; we are never alone. We are always protected by God and the army of spiritual beings adoring us as members of our spiritual family. So always re-member that truly no one and nothing can hurt us because we are immortal beings and not just physical bodies.

Our individual spiritual family is constantly guarding us. Spiritual guides constantly direct us. Everyone that looks deeper into his heart will discover that he is never alone. The feeling of safety comes not from people or material goods outside of us but from internal peace and knowledge of a true essence of The Highest Being that we are. And since we all come from the same essence, there is no reason to worry. This truth is the secret of feeling safety and joy. If we love each other with all our hearts, we don't worry any more, and the more we give, the more returns to us. If we could understand at last that we all are spiritual beings, not only would our value system change, we would finally accomplish peace and happiness.

Since we often forget this, we turn our attention outside instead of inside. We endlessly search, chase, and create external idols (of things, people, money, sex, etc.), and make it our purpose in life to attain them. It frustrates us because we try so hard to get these things and then we are afraid to lose them, and life shows us that a dear one can be unfaithful to us, leave us, or die. The same concerns loss of professional status or wealth because of theft, disaster, or fire. We can lose all our money in a single night or constantly feel like we don't have enough, no matter how much effort we put into gaining it, as the example below shows.

I once found myself sitting in the lobby of a big bank, next to strangers that were waiting for their turn. The numbers projected signaled a long time of waiting, about an hour. It was raining heavily outside so I decided to wait. Suddenly, I began to see the images of reality from another place and time. I understood that I was participating in regression (a return to previous incarnation) but it wasn't mine. I looked around and saw a man sitting next to me on a bench. Most often, it is only me who sees such things but this time the man experiencing this regression was aware of what was happening and was very frightened.

I wasn't surprised by this phenomenon since I participated in many similar incidents before (independent regressions of someone's life). I sometimes saw a chain of previous incarnations as if I was watching a film, frame after frame. It most often happened when a particular person stood on the crossroads and needed help. When I discovered this was the cause of his problems, I immediately knew how to help him. Because I know the consequences of such insights (I personally had a lot of them in my life), I know that it is most often necessary to reach a helpful hand to a man who relives it so that the knowledge doesn't frighten him. Quite a few spend the rest of their lives on psychiatric wards because of such fear. It happens sometimes after hypnosis or regressions with inexperienced therapists.

I saw my neighbor as a very rich, influential man. As if in a film, before our eyes flowed his abundant professional and family life. During the great crisis in the twenties he suddenly lost everything he earned in London's stock market. He broke down and, not seeing a way out, jumped off of one of the London towers. „Now I understand," he mumbled in shock to himself, „why I constantly hear such a „bang" in my head and see myself hitting the pavement. That's where the fear of heights comes from." In the meantime, a group of onlookers surrounded us wanting to know what was happening to this man. He talked loudly to himself and his body began to convulse. In order to calm him down, I told him that I saw the exact same thing. I even added some things he overlooked because of his emotions. Together with the images he received necessary knowledge and a deep understanding followed on all the levels of his being. „What you told me and what I saw myself made me realize the roots of my uncertainty and a fear of loss, „he said in a more quiet voice. An ambulance arrived but he had already calmed down so they left without him. He jumped on his feet then and wanted to go home. I suggested that he didn't hurry and told him that there was still a lot that could happen. I was right. After a short while, we saw another incarnation in which this man lived in poverty and died young in pauperism. Both incarnations were strongly connected, of course. It was important for him to understand how they both influence his present life and so that the things he saw wouldn't influence him destructively.

He later told me on the phone that he couldn't make the ends meet in his present life, no matter how hard he tried. He earned a lot of money but he could never afford anything. He even lived in some luxury but he had never had a penny in his pocket. He had only enough to pay his bills and satisfy basic needs.

What is the lesson for him? I think that he has to understand that money is neutral in its nature—it is neither good nor bad. It is important how we relate to it, what we make of it, and that we don't sell our souls to it. We can buy food, clothes, and beautiful things for money but we can also use it in a very selfish or harmful way and lose a chance for a lesson that a particular situation brings us. Sooner or later, we will understand all the lessons in the school of life.

First of all, we should realize that the amount of money we have is not necessarily equal to our level of safety. I understood this when I was a young girl observing a very poor, happy family of my friend. Everyone around them was constantly worrying and fearing the next day but this family always felt safe and happy. The feeling of safety comes from inside exclusively and doesn't have anything to do with the quantity of material goods you possess. It is a spiritual trait, not material or earthly.

Money belongs to Earth and we can't take it with us when we leave for the spiritual world. If this is what our lesson is supposed to be about or if this is our destiny, we can lose everything in one night and get it back in one moment like the man in the previous example. Our reactions to loss determine how quickly we get back what we valued, if we get it back at all. We will certainly not get anything back if we fall into despair, fear, hatred, or other negative emotions like the man in the previous example.

A man that is truly rich doesn't break down when he goes bankrupt, he starts from the beginning. He has the knowledge and the ability to create his fortune anew. A man that earned his money by cheating and using others won't earn back what he lost. Although he gained wealth, there was the feeling of lacking in his consciousness from the very beginning, which is the same reason he cheated and lost his money. A truly rich man knows that the universe is a treasury of all wealth. He is not afraid of loss since he knows that he can get everything anew. Many so-called rich men (with the consciousness of poverty) think that there is not enough wealth for everybody. That's why they think that in order to possess anything they have to take away that „something" from others. A truly rich man knows that it is not that a poor man doesn't want wealth, he just can't attain it for himself because he constantly thinks of how he doesn't have it. If you want to be rich, you should think wealth. Analogically, whoever wants to be healthy must think of health, not diseases. Health is wealth, disease is poverty.

Life is a school that is intended to teach us how to avoid the negative results of our attachments and negative, harmful energies of other people. We are taught how to stop false symbols of power like money, sex, or external authorities from shaking your healthy self-esteem.

Although the example given above was based on an independent return to previous incarnations, you must know that the knowledge concerning former lives isn't necessary for making positive changes. The experiences of present incarnations contain all the elements of former incarnations (they are its sum) and are absolutely enough to get rid of all the limitations. The real key is understanding. When you understand your true nature and purpose *Who Are You in Essence*, your life will change permanently. You will be able then to mold not only your reality but the world around you, if you wish.

REINCARNATION – FURTHER CONSIDERATION

Let us consider again, dear reader, if reincarnation exists or not. If it does, why does the church denounce it? If it doesn't, how does it influence your life? On the basis of several dozen years of experience contacting the spiritual world, I would formulate it the following way: both people who believe in reincarnation and those who deny it are right. Many readers may be confused. How come both sides are right? I will try to explain it. In order to understand my point of view you must look at the matter with a fresh eye, without prejudice. This is what I know about reincarnation.

God created a perfect world in which every man, during his stay on Earth, should perfect himself and raise his vibrations so he can reach so-called Heaven. On one hand, he wouldn't like to return to Earth, but on the other, he wouldn't have a reason for that since his goal would have been reached. The ultimate human goal is reminding ourselves *Who We Are in Essence,* which ignites the desire to return Home to God, where we came from. In this scenario, it is the opponents of reincarnation that are right. Many probably wonder if the goal of ascension can be realized at all. It turns out that many saints reached it, not only those that were carried out to the altars, but many others the world has never heard of. You could consider if they accomplished it within one incarnation or if their success consists of a number of past incarnations. And what about everyone else? Did God make a mistake while creating everything? There are so few people that have accomplished the condition of enlightenment. Didn't God think of them?

God gave the possibility of returning to Earth to the vast number of people that have failed in ascending during their first trial on Earth, so that they can try again. It takes everyone a different amount of time to succeed.

Those who still don't want to believe in reincarnation should remind themselves thousands of cases noted in literature, especially those of children speaking unfamiliar languages that they have never had contact with. Or of people who have birthmarks in places where they were killed, often feeling pain in those body parts. What about children who knew where certain objects were hidden or buried, tens or hundreds of years before, in unfamiliar and far off places thousands miles away, where they have never been before? Doesn't it show that they have already existed on earth and have now come for their „treasures"?

Moreover, looking at life from the perspective of one incarnation only, many things can seem nonsense to us and God may seem unfair. We wonder why some people are healthy, beautiful, and have everything a soul can desire, while others lack literally everything. Every day they must struggle with new difficulties, diseases, miseries. On the other hand, we may ask why are those beautiful wise and rich people so very unhappy sometimes? Or why poor people are sometimes cheerful, filled with love, and fulfilled? Couldn't this be a consequence of earlier doings? From the perspective of a single incarnation in which we are presently stuck, it is very difficult to most of us to understand God, ourselves, or the meaning of life in general.

From the larger perspective, which I deal with on a daily basis, everything becomes suddenly clear, understandable, and re-possesses a completely different meaning. It is easy, then, to find the deep meaning of the universe's way of functioning and finding justice. Pretenses directed at God disappear since we begin to understand that the conditions of individual lives come from the wants of their souls and are their next lesson or a consequence of past actions. For example, if you destroy a natural environment, you will have to live in it when you are born in the future. This is just higher justice. Many people don't understand the fact that their grandchildren and grand, grand-children will have to live in awful conditions because they don't have them yet or don't care about them. When they finally understand, however, that they themselves are going to live in the destroyed environment, they change their myopic attitude (more in the chapter „Castaways").

RENEWED BIRTH

When a soul absorbs the experiences gathered during the physical life and gains new strengths, it begins to feel the need for material, sensual life that can be fulfilled in the physical world only. This manifests itself by causing a man to strive for sensations from the outside that prove that he exists. As we know, the need comes from earlier wishes that were not fulfilled. How do wishes form and what is the force that maintains them? When a man strongly identifies himself with some object, situation, person, etc. and his feelings and senses are activated, a small mark is being imprinted on his mind. This mark becomes the seed of a future wish to experience the same or a similar thing. The cycle constantly repeats this way: an experience, a mark, a wish. The wish that was formed this way and wasn't fulfilled in the previous life pulls us (like an addiction) back to Earth. When the decision to return is being made, the whole mechanism that once bound us to Earth is starting to activate.

In Heaven, a soul is free of suffering and grief of any
kind. All evil (as well as good), injustice, and inequality that
was perpetrated in the previous incarnation and hasn't burnt out
yet abides in hibernation. Do you remember, dear reader, how I
wrote that at the moment of death the life's net curls around
physical permanent atoms and is placed within the causal body?
It is kept intact there from the moment of death until the present
moment. The former aptitude for experiencing physical life,
including evil or being a victim begins to sprout then and slowly
forms a new personality in the next incarnation. From the
moment the wish is formed until it is manifested, the soul begins
to shoulder the burden of the past anew. In this way, the tendencies that were „shut down" in a sense until that time are being
awoken by the soul and expressed outwardly. If it stayed in
heaven a confrontation with the past would never occur. On the
other hand, it couldn't stay there since the wish to manifest is
stronger (once again, the analogy of addiction applies). Only the
man who is free from wishes can be certain that nothing will
pull him to earthly matters by force when he wants to stay in
higher worlds.

Although the soul returns to Earth, it has the memory of
this unspeakable bliss or happiness it tasted in Heaven. Many
people, after entering to the physical world, don't want to live
on Earth and they end up committing suicide because the
memory of that joyous, perfect life is still very vivid within
them. However, staying in the higher world is possible only
after working through every lesson. The aim of these lessons is
to liberate us form earthly striving such as the desire to be a
victim, exploiting others, etc. The point is to experience them
fully and consciously decide if we still want to have them,
which is why disowning them works to our disadvantage. The
soul free of any bonds of lower nature can grow further. If a man

of only partial spiritual growth wanted to stay in the higher world, he would feel like a first-year pupil at university. He wouldn't understand what's going on there and he would just vegetate. If you dream of getting there and staying there for good, start to grow spiritually today. The growth will give you wisdom so that you begin to break free of earthly wants. This has nothing to do, of course, with disowning them but with understanding their nature. Knowledge transformed into wisdom will guarantee that you ascend to the level of consciousness where you will understand that world, and it is only then that you would be able to grow further. Life is a constant growth, in this and every other world. If you didn't learn how to grow using pleasure in the spiritual world, you must grow using pain in physicality.

As you see, dear reader, every incarnation is unavoidable, automatic, and sublimely connected to all past incarnations and their unbroken course forms one great Life of the soul. We incarnate as long as we learn our lessons and pass the exam to reach the higher level. Reincarnation is essential since we gain greater knowledge, wisdom, and understanding because of it. When we realize this, it is easier for us to understand what we take with us from this world and what we have to leave behind. We understand why we are here and what we need to accomplish in order to go further in growth. We also recognize that we receive powerful help and guidance on this path and that our loved ones (enemies, too) come with us. They lessen our, as well as, we lessen their, burdens and finally bring forgiveness, amendment, healing, and balance of various forces.

Stupid (vulgar or low) thoughts, constantly thrown out without awareness or control bind you to the reincarnation wheel almost eternally, dear reader. It happens in accordance with the decision we made not to rule them. This will last until you cut this sequence, transform it, or disperse it. If you want to change anything about your experience, you must realize your own mistakes while you live physically because only you can get rid of them. Nobody will do it for you. Always remember— whatever „wrong" you would do, God always forgives. However, it is also people that have to forgive you if you hurt them consciously. If you became their victim, you must forgive both them and yourself. Forgiveness is a duty, not an option that you can either use or not. You have to forgive and strive to receive forgiveness. This is a necessity. If you don't do it in this life, you will bring the problem to the next incarnation, as you can see in the example below. You will have to experience everything that hurts you one more time, though under much more difficult conditions. I don't think you want that.

If you experience anything you don't like, you can change it any time. In order to do this, however, you must first forgive yourself for the past „wrong" choice and consciously choose something else to become your new desire. You don't have to be poor, ill, downhearted nor stuck in the role of victim forever. You can forgive yourself for that choice and choose richness, health, and control over every situation experienced.

If you find yourself in this or any other situation, it means that you want to be there. It may be caused by a feeling of guilt on the deeper level. You bring a punishment on yourself because you once couldn't forgive yourself for some deed. It can drag on behind you for many incarnations and last until you learn to forgive yourself first and then everyone else. Maybe you were too proud once to forgive. Or you need to be a victim and suffer so that you can feel sorry for yourself and for others. Whatever the reason for your present problems, forgive yourself for attracting them. You don't have to necessarily know what exactly caused them. Just forgive everything that comes to your mind and expect the change. You can say, „I, (put your name here), forgive myself and everyone else for everything." Sometimes the decision that you want changes is enough and causes them to happen.

However, know that without releasing anger and forgiving yourself and others, changes are not possible. You can release anger in different ways but the simplest way is to take a pile of loose papers and write down everything that lies heavy on your heart. For example, write „I, (put you name here), am furious that you, (the wrongdoer's name), did this or didn't do that, even though you promised you would." Then write down everything that comes to your mind. It is only after we release all the anger and regret that we are able to forgive another person. The process of forgiving goes analogically. We write, „I (put your name here) forgive you (the name of the wrongdoer) for..." and forgive everything that we earlier specified as the reason for anger or regret. Even more important is to go through the same process with ourselves. „I, (put your name here), am furious at myself that I let myself be cheated, got hurt, couldn't take care of myself, did this or that to others, didn't do what I promised, etc." And then, „I, (put your name here), forgive myself for allowing myself to be cheated, hurt, etc." I am writing about this in detail because many people find confusing how to forgive.

Forgiving yourself and others may not be simple for the underdeveloped soul. It is necessary to raise oneself to a certain level in order to understand what you forgive yourself for and that you do it for yourself in order to get rid of suffering caused by holding a grudge. The problem or reason we suffer is never the things others did to us or we did to ourselves. Suffering comes from cultivating a grudge, out of which anger, hatred, or lack of forgiveness result. Besides, many people forgive with no effect because they still have layers of anger within them.

Whatever your case, always remember that forgiveness doesn't mean forgetting or allowing others to mistreat you again. It doesn't mean that we are to meet the „wrongdoers" as if nothing happened. Forgiveness is understanding that we are all in school and whatever happens to us is a lesson we planned in advance. Nothing can happen that you didn't invite earlier. If you don't like what you experience, forgive yourself and cease inviting it into your life by refusing to pay attention to it. The one who hurt you did it out of concern for his wants, which form when you pay too much attention to something. This harm was done to make clear to you that you once paid attention to energy that can be painful now, e.g. you hurt someone identically. If you are well aware of your thoughts and emotions, you will know that you really pay attention to unhealthy energies that return to you multiplied. You will begin to gain all the more consciousness as the creator of your own reality and you will begin to walk away from the consciousness of a victim that is rooted in all of us to some degree.

Remember that if you still want to indulge in bad habits, you will bring them to your next life. It is only after you decide that you are strong enough to master the external problems that you won't have them in the next incarnation. Bringing unsolved lessons to the next life, you will be forced to work through things you don't want to confront, plus the lesson your soul has planned for this next incarnation. A soul residing in Heaven is most often overenthusiastic about its capabilities on the physical plane. If a soul was humble and accepted advice from older Brothers (that they met in Heaven), it would know that burdens come from chosen lessons and the additional weight of the lessons that were not processed in former lives will be too difficult to lift.

In a sense, one cannot be blamed for such a process. Heaven is free from all worries and troubles. Whatever one thinks of manifests at once, and many years have passed since the moment of physical death. It is easy to forget how hard it was to process the lessons once. Maybe you feel so miserable now because instead of one burden, you carry two or three or more. I assume that you don't want to make it even bigger in the next incarnation. This may be the case, though, if you don't start to forgive yourself and others.

To the next incarnation we bring also all the bad habits we adopted while in a physical body. They most often manifest as intangible, mysterious fondness. Patterns such as aggression can last for many incarnations if they are not recognized and dispersed in time. In my work I often meet such returning patterns. If you are in any relationship (husband/wife, child/parent, superior/subordinate, etc.) and you jump down your neighbors' throats with no reason, it can be rooted in the past incarnations. Here is an example.

A woman once called me asking to help a family she was a neighbor to. She claimed that it was a good, wise, helpful, and loving family with no addictions. Its members, however, had violent fights sometimes that could be heard on the whole street. The woman was afraid that they would hurt each other. I checked and there were many ghosts near them that left at once. But the fights still happened. It was not the ghosts that caused them, they just appeared when a chance to steal the energy of the fighting people arose, which is a common phenomenon. The woman must have told the family about me because its members came to one of my lectures. When we started to talk I saw or rather, had an impression that their tragedy dragged on for many incarnations. Each of the past incarnations ended with the killing of one of the family members. They attracted each other on grounds of mutual hatred. I told them that if they don't forgive each other in the present incarnation, the tragedy will happen again. They began a very difficult process of forgiveness. They started to remember many unpleasant, tragic events, such as someone being killed, including how and why it happened. When they finally finished the process of forgiving, they began healing. This family consisted of four people and this wasn't accidental. The whole story started innocently. Its beginning took place in times when duels came up because of trivial reasons. In one incarnation, one family member killed another and in the next it was exactly the other way round. In the next incarnation they understood for a while that they shouldn't drag their old conflicts behind and became close friends. They both, however, fell in love with the same beautiful girl. She chose one of them, and in the other an old hatred awoke. He couldn't forgive the lovers and killed them at the first opportunity. In the next incarnation the girl that was killed was a man and her assassin was a pregnant woman. The former stabbed the latter with a knife out of revenge. In the present incarnation, they were all together, the parents and two almost grown up children. You know the next part of the story already. Luckily, their neighbor offered a helpful hand and so what lasted for so many incarnations could finally be healed.

Destructive patterns don't necessarily lead to such big tragedies. They take many other forms that make life difficult. They should be searched one by one and healed. It is easier to break destructive patterns when we recognize the needs we have, e.g. the need to be a victim, an executioner, to feel sorry for oneself, etc. Many such needs were formed in past incarnations. Destructive habits, grudges, and relationships based on violence from past incarnations will often take new configurations e.g. an aggressive husband in the past incarnation is now a quick-tempered father or boss at work. Or a pair of people that didn't care for each other and had killed, cheated on, or hurt each other are now husband and wife or parent and child. When we recognize the returning pattern and understand its causes, we can dissolve it. There is no sense in bringing old suffering to the present incarnation. This is why it is so important to forgive oneself and others, not necessarily searching for deeper causes of troubles, saying, „I, (your name), forgive myself and others for everything."

It is normal for images or thoughts to come to your head that indicate what you need to forgive or help you understand how you were hurt. It happens that the „wrongdoer" is not around or that you see wrongdoing but you don't know who did it. You don't have any other choice but to forgive yourself and him, even blindly, in order to break free of the never-ending drama once and for all so the old tragedy doesn't influence your present life. Most serious diseases are caused by a lack of forgiveness. Unfortunately, most people would rather suffer than forgive. It is us who suffer, though, and not the „wrongdoer" because there is a thorn deep within us that often causes us constant pain that manifests itself in cancer, a heart attack, or some other problem.

And so you can see, dear reader, that on the subconscious level while in a physical body, we still remember relationships from many incarnations ago. We come together once more to try again and heal them with various results. Unfortunately, it happens quite often that instead of healing one of the sides driven by an old temptation, we strive to exploit or manhandle the other side. Whether the other side lets it happen will depend on whether or not the person has processed their lesson effectively during the ages. If it is not strong enough to oppose or break free, it will become a victim in the present life again. A person that has been manipulated over the course of many incarnations can still gain some self-respect and end the toxic relationship.

If you are in such situation, always consider what is truly important to you and strive for it without losing your courage. Stop fearing other people's anger, even if you are the cause of it. Take the risk of breaking free from the ruts you have been stuck in for perhaps many, many incarnations. Change your perspective. You probably feel that this scheme has been dragging on since long before this incarnation. The fear of anger stops you from making the right move and brings you much sadness. No matter the initial failures, trust that you will finally succeed.

Regarding incarnation: at the very moment the soul begins returning to physicality, it starts to attract the mental matter out of which it builds a new mental body. Substances that it presently attracts express exactly the same level of mental growth it had accomplished at the end of its last life on earth. They consist of abstract ideas, patterns of the mind, and intellectual faculties. So the soul undertakes its further growth at exactly the same point it was previously interrupted. Next, the soul (real human) attracts astral matter out of which a new astral body will be built. Now preferences, cravings, and passions it brought from past lives begin to appear.

The process of gathering matter sometimes goes quite quickly and sometimes very slowly, but I will write about it in a moment. When this process comes to an end, the soul is already clothed in a so-called karmic robe, consisting of all the conditionings it adopted in past lives. As you can see, dear reader, this process was its own choice, whether conscious or not. Nobody imposed it on it, although it was a consequence of its former actions.

It is only now that the soul is ready to receive its etheric double from the hands of Karma Lords. It is a model or copy determining the future shape, size, and traits of the physical body. Preparations for the journey to earth are more complex than it would seem because an adequate space for it must be formed. First of all, an adequate *energy* of the future mother must be found. This process is very complex and no birth is accidental, even if conception came out of a short, „accidental" relationship. No soul committed to the process of reincarnation can enter its body otherwise than through the body of another incarnated soul, its physical mother. The soul of the mother must reach a certain stage and „line up" with the soul being incarnated. The point is that not only an individual but all of humanity, and even all the beings on every plane of the universe, are obliged to „enter" or fit into the existing reality. It is not only the needs of the soul being incarnated that are important; the needs of the souls of the future family, friends, neighbors, and environment are taken into account as well.

This is an enormous task for the higher spiritual „energetic engineering." The soul must not only be fitted in the right family, it also has to find corresponding vibrations of friends (as well as foes), the place of birth, race, and sex, in order to best prepare karma for this particular period of life. In order to understand how difficult this task is, you should know that there are many kinds of karma or debts that must be squared. There is individual karma, concerning the obligations of an individual being. It connects in different ways to group karma, such as karma of the family, race, religion, nationality, etc. In group karma, individuals have to work debts off or repay them but also receive from others the favors they once accommodated. This is how not only „bad" but also good karma returns to us. On the higher level, there is also planetary karma that influences the destiny and the ultimate fate of the planet. Solving, balancing, or working the karma off concerns an individual, group, country, or the entire planet. This is why the soul being reincarnated is tasked with working many different kinds of karma off. It doesn't happen all at once or right after coming to the world, but over the course of an entire life span.

When the soul has already found the right place of birth and is absolutely ready, the situation is raised to the second evaluation, since some changes can happen in the meantime. If the soul entering a new body encounters any obstacle or has any change in energy, the incarnation can fall through and be delayed until conditions are right. Then the future incarnation would be subdued to a new evaluation on the plane of pure energy, hence it cannot be understood if from the level of reason or emotions.

When the soul incarnates, all the conditions and gifts that enable it to work through its karma are present. It is the opportunities, conditions, and meetings with other people but also the conditionings of the spirit, energy, and free will. We are already on Earth and we walk through life along the karmic path, we receive new gifts and opportunities necessary for the continuation of the journey.

THE QUESTION OF SEPARATION

I trust that you already understand why we should stop fearing death once and for all and lamenting our dead ones with so much despair. We never lose them, our souls are eternal. We always meet them at the other side and if the joint work hasn't been accomplished, we come back in human form again. We change roles if we need to in order to learn something, but as souls we are still the same and just as close to each other. We have met in physicality many times before. What's more is that we make spiritual families and are always together on the heart level.

Sometimes while carefully examining a new body we can recognize our identity from a past life. We can, for example, find stigmas in the places where scars once were. If you could look into past incarnations, you would see that your loved ones have been accompanying you for centuries, though the relationship changes in each life. The deeper self-consciousness makes many people feel, with all their being that they will meet again on the physical plane but in some other time and place. This is why we never lose our loved ones. We come back together and the energy of a new connection is love. When relationships lack love, the routes part. We can still meet but on another plane. We sometimes sense the past feeling, although we apparently talk to a complete stranger.

If you suffer over the loss, know that I understand your pain. I went through this myself. It lasted until the moment the understanding came, and then I broke free of suffering. Maybe your present pain is increased by previous losses you went through, which didn't lead you to any new understanding. Maybe you were many times separated from your loved ones during some of your incarnations and now you are more sensitive to the loss of love and you feel it more deeply. Every new loss evokes feelings earlier repressed or forgotten, which increases sadness.

All this suffering comes exclusively from the wrong belief that you have lost your loved ones forever. Death, however, is only a passing through the door leading to the next classroom. Although we leave, we also constantly return in order to learn particular lessons or traits such as love, compassion, forgiveness, understanding, patience, gentleness, etc. We must simultaneously unlearn vices such as fear, anger, greed, hatred, pride, etc., coming from old conditioning. When we master this, we can pass the exam and leave the school if we want. We have all the time in the world at our disposal in order to learn and feel. We are immortal, infinite, and full of God's nature. You suffer because you forgot about *Who You Are In Essence*.

I hope that with this knowledge you will look at loss from a different perspective and let the beloved soul continue its journey. You can always contact it in the astral body and on the heart level when you think of it with love. You may not always realize this but your soul knows.

THE ETHERIC DOUBLE

The etheric body (or etheric double) for the soul descending to Earth is built in advance by the right elemental being. Into this form the physical particles of the new body of the child are built-in next. The form resembles an infant's body in size and shape. Clairvoyants sometimes see this phenomenon as a doll residing next to the future Mom. This etheric body is sometimes mistaken for the child's soul. Actually, it is only a model of a new body. The soul doesn't participate in the process of building and it generally connects to the physical body later. It happens most often when the fetus has grown to the size of the etheric model and is ready for physical birth.

This is not an easy task because a being building the child's model must pick right the etheric matter that is to be a part of the etheric body of the future child. The choice is determined by karma formed in the past, and the future body must be adjusted to the needs of a particular man. Karma depends on the disposition, energy level, sensitivity, brilliancy, and beauty, among other factors. The elemental being possesses all the means and elements necessary to create and reside inside the mother's egg and father's sperm. It only chooses the components that are necessary in a particular case. It derives the etheric matter for the child from the mother's body, which is why the quality of her etheric body is so important.

If certain characteristics belonging to the child, such as unusual beauty or ugliness, haven't been determined before birth, they will be the product of the mother's thoughts and the thought forms surrounding her. If there are not many special characteristics in the future child, the builder can withdraw quite early, giving the soul power over its own body. If, however, the need to develop any special traits strengthening or limiting the body, the elemental being can stay in the child's body for as long as seven years after its born.

If a soul doesn't participate in this much, the new astral body connects to the etheric body very early on and strongly influences its shaping. Similarly, the mental body influences the nervous system. When the building of the body comes to an end, the force focusing the particles of the elemental being gets exhausted and withdraws. Further development of the child's body is under the soul's control at this point.

A NEW LIFE

Just like we should not despair over somebody's death, we should not celebrate birth, although it is good to see the soul back among us. Why? Because although the Earth is very beautiful and it lets us learn lessons, living here is very difficult compared to our true Home. The soul of the baby in Heaven lived in perfect conditions, free, full of carelessness and joy. At the moment of awakening of the desire to return to Earth, all of this began to disappear out of sight and the place began to fill with sadness, worry, regret, old limiting habits, and beliefs. For that reason, leaving Home and passing through spherical regions towards the physical Earth in order to penetrate the physical body is more traumatic to the soul than dying. The soul coming back to Earth cannot feel happy leaving such a perfect place. I think it is not right to celebrate since the soul of our dear child is sad and sometimes disoriented or frightened. It seems selfish and cruel to me. It doesn't mean, of course, that we shouldn't welcome the returning soul. It should be done with understanding of its new condition, though, with tenderness. A baby or child often gets frustrated and cries and we don't know why. This is due to its inability to find itself in the conditions of this new life. The soul of a baby tries to set a direction at the moment of birth that will be adequate for searching for the truth of its nature. Although the body is still tiny, the soul may already be afraid of how it will manage to deal with the tasks awaiting it in the future. We don't know what these tasks are, but our child does. This is why it is so important to show it as much love and care as possible in this wonderful, delicate, and difficult period.

At the moment we come into this world, the characteristics of the former life are not activated yet. They exist in the form of the old traits' seeds. Their development is strongly dependent on the influence of the environment the child finds itself in the first years of its life. Each of these seeds, both good and „bad", can easily be activated or annihilated in case there is no stimuli. If a child is vividly interested in a particular trait, it operates with much more strength than in the previous life. Annihilated, it remains an unfertilized germ that soon disappears in later incarnations. In both cases, the point is the real human's decision concerning a particular trait. It is his choice that determines the development or disappearing of a particular trait. The environment has only some influence over the activation of seeds of traits. Every child has a few years during which it can transform a big part of its tendencies, habits, and preferences. This in turn can change every aspect of the chosen earlier karmic path. Traits can be transformed also later, although it would need much more effort then.

A child doesn't have an organized astral and mental body yet, only a matter out of which these bodies were built. In order to understand it better I will use an example of an addict. Let's assume that a man was addicted in his past life and that the overwhelming desire to abuse alcohol (or sex, drugs, etc.) burned out in the astral world, where he broke free of these claws completely. The desire to drink disappeared, however the weakness or susceptibility of character that previously made him an alcoholic or drug addict (a smoker, a gambler, etc.) was still there. In the next life his astral body will contain the matter that will enable him to express the same desires in the form of seeds. It is up to the man only to express them in his new life, since he can presently manage the astral matter in a completely new way. Much depends on the upbringing in the first years of life. If the child realized that this desire will be an inconvenience to him, it can gain control over it, which will strip the astral matter of its fodder and cause it to diminish. Anyone that has developed any addiction can do the same. If they gain control over it (by recognizing the thoughts and emotions that lead to the addiction, the astral matter deprived of fodder will decline and an attraction to the addiction will fade in time.

The matter of all the subtle bodies gradually wears down and is exchanged for new matter. It is similar with the matter of the astral body. When particles with certain traits in latency fall away, much more subtle matter will take its place. In this way, one irreversibly swallows all the faults, bad habits, liabilities, and addictions. The virtue of control replaces the former weakness. As you can see, dear reader, emotional and psychosomatic disorders, destructive patterns such as drug abuse, alcoholism, and cigarette use, and problems in interpersonal relationships are often rooted in past incarnations.

That's why every child, until it turns seven years old, will manifest certain traits from the past life and the problems connected to it. During the first years of life, the soul poorly controls its bodies. That's why a child expects help from his parents in mastering control over latent negative tendencies and creating advantageous conditions to overcome them (and developing wanted traits). The parents should learn in advance and confront their child with the truth of its soul. Each child should realize the beauty contained not only within itself but in other people, too. For we are all beautiful souls with wonderful, priceless brilliance. It is necessary to remember it and not let yourself get dirty again as it happened in previous incarnations.

The astral and mental bodies react vividly to every vibration reaching them, both good and „bad." In the first years of their lives, children are susceptible and it is easy to mold them, but they also absorb unwanted habits that are hard to remove or change later once they are established. You can certainly say that the child's future is in the hands of its parents, but mostly depends on what the child brought to the world and on the decision that the soul made concerning its latent traits. The child's surroundings during childhood have a great impact on its development. In order to help lead the child out of its past conditioning, a perfect environment like the one I wrote about in the chapter „Life in the Lost Civilization" is necessary.

Unfortunately, it is difficult now to find such an environment. Remember, dear reader, that children should not be pressured. They need to be loved, guarded, and directed. Parents are supposed to guide them with kindness, light, and power. Every teacher's goal—I'm saying this in the universal meaning, and this is the role parents play—is to make each man realize his unique nature and help every growing soul realize its truth.. In the modern world, most people try to break their children's will in order to subordinate them. If it is a requirement of a lesson the child is supposed to learn, the parents don't cumulate the „bad" karma, though in all the other cases they do.

Most of what I wrote here concerns children that have

come into the world with unwanted preferences. Souls without seeds of negative tendencies or faults also come into the world. These children can live among low vibrations and not be contaminated by them. Such a child can be brought up in the most destructive family and grow up to be a good man. Other souls with negative tendencies, however, can be brought up in the most ideal family and still fall because of own tendencies or an extended environmental influence.

THE FACTORS DETERMINING MAN'S FUTURE BIRTH

In the very beginning of each incarnation, a great law of evolution operates that places a man in the conditions most suitable for him. It serves the development of characteristics the man needs most. I will write about this in the chapter „The Universal Laws."

Looking at the overall plan, we recognize that humanity was divided into great native races and that one after another inhabited the world and ruled it (more on this subject later). Through energy and power the human race realizes its dreams. As a part of a race, every individual can realize its goals. In order for it to be possible, every man must find a place where he can grow. There were many races in the past, and one of them is the Aryan race, also known as Caucasian. People that are the most advanced on the evolutionary road stem from this race. Before this there was the Mongolian race, which ruled from a location that was in the waters of the Atlantic Ocean. This race perished almost whole. Before it was the Negro race. Its descendants live even today, but not in a pure form. Each of the great races had many branches, called sub-races, and each sub-race divided into many smaller branches, e.g. Poles, Germans, Englishmen, Frenchmen, etc. The nationality division exists only to give every soul the widest choice of conditions and surroundings to experience its innumerable lessons. In every nation, there is an endless quantity of various conditions: richness and poverty, wonderful opportunities or their complete lack, and easy or difficult conditions. I will write more about this in the chapter called „Castaways." Each race developed various characteristics necessary for its own evolution. Among this variety the law of evolution leads a man to conditions or opportunities that will correspond best with his needs on a particular level of growth.

The members of a race and your soul's relationships with other souls can be compared to a large forest with powerful trees covered with thousands of leaves. As an individual, you are a single leaf. Your strongest connections are to those other leaves that are also on your little twig. This is your family, that you share your life with in joy and in sadness. You not only learn and experience together, but you also help each other in growth and in shouldering the burdens of life. There are other little twigs around you with the same or similar leaves. These are other families. You are, of course, connected to your own twig the most, but the others placed near you are still important to your well-being. Even if they are extremely close to you, they are not as close as the leaves on your twig. Together the leaves share a bigger twig, a branch, or even a limb. Moving further, you notice that together with other leaves you are still one big unity since you are the part of one trunk, but the leaves on the other side of the tree are not as close to you as are these in your neighborhood. The tree is your country but in this beautiful forest there are many other trees, meaning many other countries. Each connects to others through the root system lying underground. In this way we make a race. Even if the leaf on another tree seems completely different from yours and very distant, you are still connected to it. Indeed, you are connected to all the leaves in the whole forest. The biggest bond you have, however, is with the leaves on your tree. You are close to the leaves on your branch but closest to the leaves on your twig.

In your past lives, you probably met souls that were part of your tree, though more distant. They could relate to you in various ways and influence you for a long or short time. Such a meeting could help only yourself, another soul, or both, depending on a lesson you were supposed to learn. More people could participate in one lesson, if necessary. The meetings could be of different characters, repetitive or one-time, and even „accidental". One of the souls, for example, could be a man in need and you offered him the gift of your heart by helping him. Although you gave, you benefited because the gift enlarged your compassion and gave the knowledge of existing love, mercy, and help to the other side. You and that man could never meet again in this life but you have become a part of the drama. All those meetings could differ based on how long they last, but it is only the given or absorbed lessons or education that is important.

Evolution is God's will and it tries to give a man what is necessary. The law of evolution is limited by the law of cause and effect called the law of karma, which I will write more about later. The past deeds of a man can be unworthy of better conditions in the present. It is necessary then to bring about certain limitations counteracting the accomplishment of better results. That's why the working of the law of evolution that itself strives for perfection is necessarily limited by the past deeds of a particular man and the various relationships he once initiated.

At first glance, it can seem that the man becoming reincarnated could gather his experience in many other different situations. Why did he find himself in this one and not in some other? It could also seem that some souls do so many good things that they are liberated of at least some of their karmic obligations. However, with such a variety of opportunities that the soul has at its disposal, its choice will always be to stay in the family or in the neighborhood of the soul or souls that owe him favors or that he has a debt of love to repay. One thing should be explained here. For many people, karma means obligation, which is why they are so afraid of it. Karma, however, is not only our obligation toward others but our reception of debts of gratitude. That is why it is so important to constantly balance everything. The debt of good and bad deeds is an integral part of the universe. It is connected to the soul's growth and its responsibility for itself and for every other soul. I repeat once more that the debt is introduced not only by „bad" deeds but also by good ones.

First of all, each soul has to realize that if it hurts another soul, it hurts itself, too. Its own harm is experienced later and causes it to understand what it did and this is its lesson. In this way, each man learns why some of his actions are careless and divergent from the individual line of evolution. This is how the soul makes increasing progress. However, the debt must be paid in every case. As I said, not every debt concerns unwanted things since sometimes they concern proper ones. It can be concluded, dear reader, that karma never ends, which means that you can never repay it com-

THE FACTORS DETERMINING MAN'S ...   393

pletely. Karma equals actions so it exists always and constantly influences us.

In all of this there exists something more: the freedom of mind. You can gain it through forgiving yourself and others, so that it is not only you becoming free, but also freeing others from you.

This means that by balancing every deed, we can never meet again. If we meet in the future, it would be because we want it and not because we have to, and this, as you understand, dear reader, makes the fundamental difference. We can certainly say that the basic reason for meeting other souls again is some unsolved or unforgiven knot of past experiences. These can be bonds of love, hate, help, or harm. Sometimes it is many souls (of a bigger branch) incarnating at the same time, cooperating to repay karma to each other or people from another branch in order to gain new, broader spiritual knowledge. This can last for many incarnations.

Each soul being reincarnated must then take into account the factors mentioned before it decides where and how it is to be born anew. That's why citizens often die and reincarnate in the same neighborhood or place—they made bonds that attract them to the environment they used to live in.

I often hear the question, „If reincarnation exists, how much time passes before we come back to the Earth?" As you have probably figured out, dear reader, there is no explicit answer to this question. First of all, it depends on whether we leave behind the death curtain while dying, or hold on to dear life. We are often not aware that we have died already and we wander throughout the spiritual world. How long? Until we finally wake up and sometimes this takes ages. First, we have to acknowledge death and it is only then that we can return to Earth in the new physical body.

Physical life is not, as you can see, the effect of a coincidence, though many people think so. Incarnations are prepared with love and attention so that they make education and growth easier. We usually choose our parents from the souls we met in past incarnations. As we learn as children, adolescents, and grown-ups, we evolve spiritually while our bodies grow physically. When a soul leaves a body at the moment of physical death, education continues on higher planes that, in reality, are higher levels of consciousness.

In each life, there are some meetings built-in in advance. We usually don't pick up life's thread at exactly the same place where it was broken. First, we need to find ourselves. For this search we need more than normal human recognition abilities. In addition to a new body we get a new brain connected to the subconscious memory. That's why it is only souls that are able to recognize each other while meeting again. Then the game that we call life begins anew. The purposes of existence are connected to the attitudes and emotions towards other people, places, objects, and situations. We came to Earth to start something, finish, clean, eliminate, and harmonize. We implement the elements concerning people, places, and business from the past, present and future.

I hope you recognize more clearly, dear reader that things happening in your life are totally of your making, even what family or place you were born to. You may protest. You may say that there is so much disease, misery, and poverty around. You will ask how you could consciously choose alcoholic or drug addict parents, how you could want to live in pauperism, to be born as a cripple, or become an orphan right after coming into the world. Looking through the prism of our own feelings, it can seem impossible that we chose so wrongly. However, everyone that takes the trouble to realize their own deep emotions and thoughts will discover that this reality best serves the understanding of ourselves. The experience coming out of this reality shows us at every turn that we have the emotions and thoughts creating the situation in which we find ourselves.

There are as many reasons to come to this world as souls. If you don't like your choice, discover the reason and what you are to learn. You will soon recognize that your unconscious emotions and thoughts affirm or maintain the world you live in. Change them (as well as the internal affirmation) and you will change the reality.

Earlier, I often asked myself what determines our being. That's why I undertook my longstanding studies. What's more is that among the thousands of people that I helped, I didn't meet a case that didn't confirm the things I am writing about. And since we choose ourselves, we should consider what to do to make our choice better next time. In order to do it we must know right now what the general indicator or causal element in the process of choosing is.

We have various wants in the physical world. Some of them we manage to realize easily, others partially, and others are unavailable to us. The wants that were not achieved become the next impetus pushing us to be born in a certain place or family. It is this family that is to help us attain our wants. This is the reason that many people are born constantly in the same cities, conditions, and relationships, having no idea why they are there. The wants of single people within such groups are often completely different. Some get the impression that they came into the world for nothing.

I met a girl named Imogene once. I got the impression that she didn't live as she should have and that she was constantly waiting for something. Since this was a very persistent impression, I told her about it. Astonished, she asked me how I knew such information She confirmed that she had always had all her things packed as if she was about to set out on a journey. Of course, she didn't live out of suitcases, but all her things were put on shelves and in drawers in such a way that would allow her to pack quickly. Though she never left for long, she claimed that it was stronger than her. „I live, but it is of no importance to me whatsoever," she said. „I feel that I will leave here any moment and I don't want to get attached. I don't have the impression that I will leave this world only that I will meet someone important and I will bond with him forever." „I can see," I said, „that you have been waiting for *him* for many incarnations. He comes for a moment and leaves and you still wait." „God! You are right!" she exclaimed. „I met a man a few years ago and we spent just one evening together. We didn't even get close. We didn't make a date, there were no confessions or promises, and I'm still longing for him and waiting. My friends tell me that this is nonsense and try to get him out of my head. It is the only reason for me to stick to my partner for several years. He has eyes only for me, and I treat him indifferently since I wait for him. I even know that he has a family and kids, but I don't mind. I hope that we'll be together one day. Maybe they'll divorce. I don't know what I'm waiting for anymore." I told her what I saw. She once had a partner, a sailor that she loved him very much, but he set out for the sea and disappeared without a trace. She then died of grief and longing. The want to see him again brought her to Earth later, but he had other wants. They had met, but he was with someone else and their paths didn't cross for good. Nevertheless, she still waited for him. It was exactly the same in many other incarnations as it was in the present one. She subconsciously remembered her wish to wait for him. „You are right," she said. „This explains

my behavior throughout my whole life. I need to think it over."
Then we departed.

We met again after a few years and she told me how her
story developed. She told me: „When I heard your comments
then, I felt as if I had woken up from a very long sleep. I suddenly understood what didn't work in my present life. I came
back home, unpacked all my things for good, and started to live
at last. In the beginning, the desire came back to me as a boomerang but as you suggested, I started to forgive myself for
choosing wrong and everything else that came to mind. And
there were plenty of things. I forgave him, too. I thought that it
wouldn't end and that my feelings were stronger than me. At
one moment I noticed, however, that this memory grew pale
until it disappeared completely. Whatever I do now, I do for
good. I got involved with my partner for good and we made a
true family. I work permanently and despite my age I started
new studies. Mrs. Pratnicka, I was needlessly wasting my life
waiting. Thank you for your help."

As you can see, we sometimes become the captives of a
wish coming from many incarnations ago. The fact that you
created some situation by your desire doesn't mean that you
have to be stuck in it forever, though. We come to earth in order
to go through our experiences but we should remember that we
have free will that we can use any moment. This means that
each past desire can be changed into a new one. In order to
change the desire we're set to follow, it has to be determined
anew, clearly set. By changing earlier attitudes and expectations,
we can change all conditions. Even in the greatest trouble, a
change of perspective and a conscious, wise choice of thoughts
changes the frequency of vibrations emitted. Then doors open to
another way out from disadvantageous conditions in which
many readers may find themselves. We don't necessarily have to

stick to what we once planned.

A few words concerning the loss of dear people: if you can be born anew, this concerns your loved ones, too. We can all return in order to confront the joys, worries, victories, tragedies of living on Earth once more. This should lessen the suffering coming from the feeling of loss that many people feel so acutely. Parting is only of physical nature, since we never part spiritually. This is as certain as the fact that the sun will shine tomorrow. It shines always, and only sometimes it is covered by clouds just like sadness sometimes covers our understanding. I hope these words will disperse it.

WHY WE DO NOT REMEMBER OUR PAST INCARNATIONS?

Let us consider together: if reincarnation exists, why don't we remember our past lives? The explanation is very simple and you might have already found it yourself after reading the chapters describing life after death. Let us sum up what we know already. Everything we see around us in the physical world is an effect of vibrating energy slowing down in order for us to experience the surroundings of bigger density, meaning our three-dimensional world. In the same way, crystallization (or precipitation) operates to transform the objects of high vibration to a level of increasing density or bring them to a visible form to the observer in the three-dimensional world. The level of the highest density is the physical condition. Vibration is the slowest here. In this condition, time seems to run faster since it is in inverse proportion to the vibration level. When the level of vibration increases, time slows. It is sometimes the cause of the difficulties the soul has trying to get into the right body since the difference in time can cause it to overlook the chance. Time doesn't practically exist on the other side, and here a soul must adjust to a certain time period.

The mental, astral (also known as emotional), and physical body together with its etheric double are created by the soul for the time of a single incarnation. All those bodies are disposable, or mortal. The natural body, relatively permanent, is the causal body in which a soul sets out for a journey into its incarnations. The term relatively permanent means that you c cease to need it if you climb up in your journey and unite with higher worlds more and more.

All the bodies a soul puts on for the time of its earthly life serve as tools and vessels in order for it to be able to experiences its wishes. A soul coming back Home throws them away one after another—physical with etheric in the physical world, then the astral in the astral world, and then the mental in the mental world. After they all fall down, there is only the causal body left or the true Home in the causal world (Heaven, Paradise, or whatever a man calls it).

Until this moment, the length of a soul's stay in particular worlds depended on the quantity of matter it has gathered in its vessels (subtle bodies – the emotional and mental). In the causal world, its true Home, it could stay forever if it wanted to. However, often after a long or a short rest, the wishes begin to attract new experiences. Its journey begins anew. Nobody forces it to go nor throws it out of Paradise. It is its own and not a compulsory choice. While descending, it puts on completely new bodies, which means adopting a new brain and memories. If we wanted to find DNA traces on the body's new clothes, we wouldn't find anything though there would be plenty on the old clothes. The old clothes, however, don't exist anymore and the new ones don't remember anything. The bodies themselves (the clothes) cannot tell us anything about their past lives. Only the soul, our Self, the impersonal, immortal I, that has put on new clothes many times before (and has been incarnated many times) knows everything.

What's more is that the lack of memory is deliberate and fosters a lot of our growth. In this way we can learn new lessons and improve our fate. If we had the memory of past incarnations, we would also know how to balance or avoid certain causes. Every lesson in turn resembles the next game. When you play it the first time, it fascinates you greatly. If you played it many times, it would bore you because you would know in advance how to avoid all the traps and challenges awaiting you. Then we would have a stereotypic, boring life. We wouldn't be interested in it since we would know each next step. I will give an example: let us assume that somebody has to work through the lesson of losing a romantic love. Coming to the world without the memory of former losses, they will get involved in the relationship deeply. If they knew in advance that this relationship would break down, they wouldn't get involved in the first place or would do everything they could to avoid suffering. The parting experience, however, is very important since it lets us understand deeply that we never part with our loved ones and this liberates from the fear of loss.

Many people would have a complete breakdown if they knew all the „bad" or unreasonable things they did in their past lives. That's why it is absolutely not worth it to look into past incarnations out of pure curiosity. I know a great number of cases in which thrill-seeker people looked into their past incarnations. The first things that their subconscious showed them were the most traumatic experiences. Now, they cannot forgive themselves or others and instead of growing they are stuck in a complete resignation of life, sometimes even ending up in psychiatric wards. If you are not grown up enough to understand or forgive, don't dabble in seeing past lives since you might not be able to stand the truth which you will see. For example, you may perceive yourself as a compassionate person. What would your reaction be if you saw that you used to steal, torture, and kill others, even your loved one? Would you have as much respect for yourself? And what if you suddenly saw that the loved ones you happily live with now tortured you earlier and maybe even killed you? Would you love them the same way? Subconscious lead to the most traumatic experiences first because these emotions become imprinted deeply in our psyche and are being carried by the soul to the next incarnations. When you are ready, meaning conscious enough, the insights will show themselves (as it was with me and many others). You don't need to regress to this.

However, if you looked into past incarnations and the memory of it is very traumatic and filled with emotions, it is good to return to it a second and third time. Although we are often afraid of memories (in most cases, fear paralyzes common sense completely), every return eases negative emotions. Then a man remembers more and more details and begins to understand cause and effect. On account of this, the emotional blockages disappear as well as physical obstacles some time after and we learn something new about ourselves.

Although there are many levels of consciousness and many vibrating states, not everybody has to know them all. The physical level, the first of seven, is the most important to all of us. It is important to feel on the physical first plane and refrain from entering into higher planes by force (some wrongly think that you can do it via drugs) if you are not mature enough yet. It can cause panic. That's why one should never explain the facts to unprepared people since you can easily harm them deeply. Everyone experiences higher levels eventually and since we are not conscious of them yet, it can't be helped. The fundamental task on Earth is to learn to live in happiness on the basis of one's own experiences. Others should be allowed to do the same. The aim is to transform one's own beliefs into experience. Then the learning becomes complete since experience exceeds faith. It is necessary to learn to experience and remove one's fear at the same time. It is necessary to love and accept ourselves so that we can know how to love others. We are here also to help each other. It demands not only our own free will but the free will of other people. Whatever you do, reach deep inside you where love reigns. Then you will easily relate to other people with love or compassion, which will enable mutual growth and coexistence with others. We cannot exist without helping each other. We can, however, help others only when they are ready for help and want to receive it. Otherwise, it is only disharmony that will come out of our good intentions, or „evil" that we should avoid at all costs.

Coming back to the subject—when a soul changes bodies it changes personality, too. It is different with every new incarnation. The dictionary says that the term *personality* derives from the word *person, which means „mask" in Latin*. This dependency is vividly presented by actors of ancient theatre, who *personified* the characters they played by putting masks on. We create our personality ourselves. It is a mask put on by a character shaped by habits. Thanks to the insight into subconscious we can change our habits and what follows influences our character and personality. In order to change habits it is necessary to describe the present situation and recognize the true purpose we strive for. It is simply achieving perfection. Looking deeply inside, we realize the level of our (im)perfection, which prompts us to gain an increasing influence on the mind. If our actions and thoughts remain constantly on the same level unchanged, our personality becomes unstable or crazed since it lacks cohesion of body, mind, thought, and action in the constant striving forward.

Each personality is only a part, different every time, performed by an actor (the real human, true Self, or soul) during a particular drama (one incarnation). That is why a conscious earthly mind doesn't memorize past lives, though the Higher Self that really lived it knows them all and remembers very well.

In the new incarnation, a soul develops memory and registers only the events of the present incarnation. Higher traits such as love, kindness, compassion, mercy, and many higher feelings are permanent characteristics of every soul, rooting themselves and reflecting divine traits in man. All other traits bringing forward karmic effects are transient and don't imprint themselves on the new physical brain or personality. However, all such marks (splits or impressions) are kept deep inside the soul.

This faculty is the only true memory of a soul. It is this that gives man (whether he understands it or not) a faint impression or flashes of his previous lives and of many incarnations awaiting him in the future. Tendencies, characteristics, or attributes of personality (including memory) disappear after the incarnation ends like a mark on water, leaving only memories behind within the soul.

As you can see, dear reader, the ability to remember isn't the function of the physical brain. Rather, it is connected to intuition and is called by the spiritual Self, always present within us. These are visions of all kinds—the inspired visions of a genius, flashes, smaller insights or hallucinations in fever or madness, though these are often degraded by science to the rank of fantasies or delusions.

Why doesn't the real human, soul, or true Self with former memories pass this knowledge to the new personality? Well, it does, but we often don't want to believe in those flashes or premonitions. Intuition guides us constantly but we often don't want to listen. There are many reasons for that.

Everybody has the memory of the soul, though only some have access to it. How could we otherwise explain the phenomenon occurring with many people during hypnosis or a deep trance, when they are able to do things they cannot do while awake? They can, for example, play an instrument perfectly or speak a language fluently, even though they are unfamiliar with it in their present life. Many experts confirm that the spiritual Self can influence the brain only when the personal „self" is hushed or immobilized. If a man can consciously maintain this connection, he has permanent insight into his intuition. Otherwise, intuition reaches him in the form of flashes, which as I mentioned already, he often ignores.

All knowledge is the attribute of the highest Self of a man, while personality is the product of an environment and a captive of the physical memory of the brain. If the Higher Self could manifest itself on Earth constantly and without obstacles, people wouldn't be here. We would all live like gods.

Don't follow your fear but instead lovingly listen to your intuition, which is the internal feeling and heart of your soul. When it passes something to you and knows something you were not previously aware of without a doubt, listen to it and don't let other people's arguments influence you. They are most often based on fear. Some people want to help you, but will end up misguiding you because they are influenced by fear. If you rely on other peoples' advice only, you can make serious mistakes. Only your heart knows for sure what you need. People have different goals and can even unintentionally pull you back from a road chosen by your soul.

Many people have memories of past incarnations, but only a few believe in their stories. We usually perceive those sensitive people as crazy visionaries or frauds. Many people don't believe in the soul's existence. They say mockingly, „And what is soul? Can you prove its existence?" There is no use, of course, in persuading such a person. You can ask him if he remembers what he was like and what he did as a baby. Has he kept even the faintest memory of his thoughts or sensations from the first few years of his life? And since he doesn't remember, you can ask him analogically why he doesn't question the fact that he existed during that time.

I will also remind you that the time between two incarnations encompasses sometimes ten, twenty, or even more centuries while the physical consciousness is totally inactive. It didn't have the organs to act nor exist, so it is obvious that we cannot have this memory.

In order to gain the belief or proof that incarnation and past lives are undeniable facts, it is necessary to contact your inner being, the perennial Self, first instead of putting your trust in the transient personality.

THE END OF THE SECOND VOLUME

As I end, dear reader, I wish to remind you to remind yourself every day of *Who You Are in Essence.* Never forget this. You are a unique, powerful Spiritual Being who entered the physical body in order to experience human life. It is time to reshape your life and to regain the memory of *Who You Are in Essence,* and not delude yourself with false perceptions of what you are. It has been the intention of this book since the beginning to reunite you with this Highest Truth. If you have achieved this, that is wonderful. If you haven't, read this book again. Understanding may come to you when you read about the people in Earth's older civilizations and you are able to translate this knowledge into everyday life. You will learn about this in the third volume only, however. In the meantime, dear reader, consider who you really are. Not from the perspective of a small earthly personality, but from a powerful Self, with many earthly incarnations behind you. You may not realize that you are an unusual being already, filled with knowledge and wisdom. Who knows? Maybe you should believe it first. Try to realize the true beauty of your soul. Let your Higher Self, the golden part of you, remind your personality of all of your virtues and of the great Love you were born from. Your soul is also that Love, the whole depth of Love. You are connected to the whole universe through pure and unblemished love. You exist only because you love deep in your soul. If you forgot about it, it was only on the personality level. Love, among other things, is a condition or process of souls touching each other. Your soul, like all other souls, is powerful. Compassion and love rest inside of it. When you come to this world you are perfect, beautiful, brilliant, shimmering with numerous facets, and unblemished by any defect. You are like an unwritten, clear piece of paper. In the depth of your being rests love, peace, balance, and harmony. Every man is deeply compassionate, caring, and kind. You don't have to become such a person since you are it already. God made you this way. First of all, you are a wonderful soul and not only a physical body. God loves you and lives deeply inside of you. He is inside you and in each man without exception. You don't have to deserve Him. He is even in the man that seems to be the meanest according to our human understanding. The baseness is only his actions, but a soul is not just acts of personality. Actions are only experiences through which a soul learns what it is to be what we, people, think of as „evil." Someone's mean attitude may even teach us what goodness is. Perhaps we would never see or appreciate goodness if it wasn't for that „evil." People often don't respect or appreciate what they have; they may even despise it. It is only when they lose this „something" that they wake up, as if from a dream, and see that they needed it very much, though it is often too late.

Everyone was given intuitive forces that they should follow and not resist. Marauders and rebels against the Inner Being are threatened with serious danger since they get lost and lose orientation of where they are and what they do. They oppose it since they wrongly think that they are a physical body only, forgetting about everything else. It is as if an iceberg claimed it is just a peak standing above the water's surface while 90% of its being is hidden below it.

If you got lost long ago, know that despite whatever bad things happen to you, somebody loves you always and will always guards you. You don't feel it because you closeted yourself to it and forgot that it was possible. You don't feel worthy. You are never alone; this is completely impossible and downright infeasible. That's why you cannot be forgotten, overlooked, or ignored by God. Divine Love is all that exists.

Sense it and always remember that you are part of the divine energy, the being of light, wisdom, and love, and not a separate lonely personality. Maybe you don't realize it, but you are never truly alone since your soul touches every other soul plugged into the net of the universe. We all comprise one Unity, and Love is the ultimate means to feel and understand it. So you are not a body, brain, or even a mind. You are a soul, or rather, a Spirit with a capital S. You need to wake up and remember this always. From this perspective you will see that as a Spirit you have no limits of the physical body, intellect, or mind. When you have accepted this, you will eventually understand that you as a soul live forever and you will begin to live the highest potential of your spiritual growth. In order for this to happen you must love yourself. Love is not an abstraction but a real energy or range of energy that you can generate and maintain within you. Feel what it's like to be loved by connecting to the love that many beings close to you are sending you at this very moment and express love in return. This will cause everything in your life to change for the better.

In order to accomplish it more easily, you need to remember what has disturbed or soiled your wonderful treasure of a soul and clean it. Maybe your soul has been damaged by the opinions of the people you met on our path. You should take into account all the persons surrounding you in your childhood—Dad, Mom, grandparents, siblings, uncles, aunts, neighbors, teachers, colleagues from school, friends, foes, and even a priest at church. What you consume from the media also counts since it influences us daily, whether we realize it or not.

Remember, though: the past needs to be remembered in order for us to understand what soiled us, and then we should totally forget it and let it go. This concerns traumas of childhood and past incarnations, as well as attitudes, misunderstandings, belief systems, and accidental thoughts. It is not possible to see clearly and distinctly through all those thoughts. You came to the world to learn something new and look at things from a new perspective.

All the opinions that other people have about us or through which they want to influence us shape our reality. During your entire life you have gathered many positive, constructive opinions. Many of them, however, were negative and destroyed your self-confidence and dignity. They presently bring disharmony to your experience and chart the wrong direction leading to worthlessness. That's why many people carry the subconscious belief of their unworthiness within them. The stronger it is, the more it makes life difficult since it takes away our confidence and faith in our strength. It is only when our self-respect balances our belief in unworthiness that we can start to moderately prosper, relax, and stop fearing the future. And it is only the lack of existential fears that allows us to look deep inside ourselves and find our inner being.

We should remember that other peoples' opinions influence us only when we allow them to. We are influenced not by what we experienced but by our attitude towards it. That's why a man brought up in a so called „good" family with the best parents, schools, and role models can be weak and passive. Even the slightest, innocent commentary will fluster him and he will instantly take what he hears personally. So this is not an arduous, hard life that shapes our fate and character, but what we believe to be our truth and what we let enter our reality. If we once heard negative commentaries concerning us and we acknowledged them as true, this „truth" becomes our limitation and an increasingly deep rut. Meanwhile, life realizes or externalizes our beliefs and it constantly helps us prove that we are right. It is going to be this way until the moment we wake up from this nightmare and admit to ourselves that we were wrong. All those opinions heard and acknowledged to be our own shape our self-beliefs. This is how we sometimes pretend in following incarnations that we are only what we think we are. Many walk through life in rage, fear, uncertainty, guilt, and self-doubt because we forgot long ago Who We really Are, and we began to live according to the images created by our environment and ourselves. This happens most often when we rely exclusively on other peoples' advice without realizing that they can have totally different goals than ours. I wrote more on this question in the chapter „Beliefs."

No man needs to learn love, balance, peace, compassion, forgiveness, and faith. We have all known them always and carried them within us; they have been the content of our inner being. So the burning task we face as humanity is unlearning as quickly as possible the negative, harmful emotions and attitudes that cause us all so much suffering. By throwing away the negative traits we will finally regain our true nature that is positive and filled with love Self and has always been with us, even though it can be hidden or forgotten. When you remove external layers of dirt from your energetic shell made of negative thoughts and emotions, you will be able to find the connection to the diamond that is your wonderful, inner being deep inside you. You have always been it but you forgot about it long ago. It is only when you discover it anew the understanding will come to you that you are an immortal, divine being, heading Home together with other souls.

You may be afraid of discovering the Divine Self. Maybe you don't believe in It or it seems too hard for you. Your beautiful inside becomes encased in a shell made of fear, anger, bitterness, jealousy, hatred, sadness, uncertainty, and many other negative thoughts and emotions. You brought them all as seeds from past incarnations and your upbringing in childhood. Current life experiences enlarge and consolidate this external covering of the shell.

Do you know that your soul participates in everything that you do and that is present in every moment of your life? All your thoughts and decisions reflect the condition of the spirit and influence your health. You came to the physical world free and unlimited. It is still this way. Unfortunately, most people don't see it or feel it. They allowed their upbringing and education to impose predetermined ways of acting upon them. These set schemes of various kinds don't let us see clearly. Exist in an unlimited manner and you have the full right to see clearly. Most of us grew up like an eagle among hens. Even though we are the king of birds, we stayed on the ground because the other hens showed us that we couldn't. This is how most people think. They grew up with people that have been the victims of limitations and have passed them onto you.

When you feel these limitations acting in your life you do nothing to change them.. You soon forget about it and life goes on in the same patterns.

However, I know, dear reader that you are not really able to forget what you carry deep within. Who knows? Maybe over the course of your life you've just learned to cheat yourself better. You are like this eagle. Always restless and dissatisfied with yourself. Deep inside you know that you once possessed this illimitability but you lost grasp of it at some point. This is the only thing you are truly searching and longing for but you cannot realize it since this is a very subtle impression and hard to catch. How can you realize a thing that is not a part of our physical reality? When you feel the wish again and decide to do everything you can to reach this illimitability, you will find a way to do it. Don't be afraid, try it, you won't lose anything (besides limitations). You are an endless energy created in the image and likeness of God.

The main task after coming to the Earth in the physical body is to find what you know already deep inside. It is not what you want to believe or what someone else wants you to believe, but what you feel deep inside. While remembering *Who You Are in Essence,* you will understand your part in life. It will become something more than eating, sleeping, working, and entertaining. The obligation of the present moment is an increasingly deep faith in what you feel inside already because it connects you to God, the Highest Creator.

The task facing all of humanity is not gathering all the new information but remembering your own depth. We find ourselves in the transient stage now, learning a very important lesson concerning the change in the earth vibration. This is why our shared lesson is to realize our connection to God, the Highest Creator of everything that lives. Everything unites us

414   IN THE WHEEL OF LIFE, VOLUME II

and each one of us is a part of the Whole.

At some point, we will remember that before we came to this world we decided that we will abundantly share what we have inside with others while depending on our own abilities. Everything will be easier to understand when you realize this. We should also remind ourselves that life should be about self-discovery, self-expression, and self-realization since it is only when we are fully happy that we can imbue others with ourselves. This task is holy. If you fulfil it, you gain power. If you don't, you lose it. Did you forget it? When you remember this, you will know what the purpose of your stay on Earth is—you came in order to fulfil your task and fulfill a promise you made to yourself and others. When you remember, you will set an example for those who have gone so far in experiencing that they have forgotten *Who They Are in Essence*. They immersed themselves in chaos, fear, uncertainty, or hatred.

You may be considering where I know all this from and if what I write is true. Well, my work concerns people that are possessed as well as ghosts that do the possessing. Studies on cause and effect in this domain have taught me the most. Every day, ghosts confirm my inner knowledge that death in human understanding doesn't exist and that we are all on a journey in the school called life. No matter how we live our lives, this journey or lesson is different for each man. Some travel or learn very slowly. Learning is not easy for them, while the others tackle all the homework instantly. The first group is slowed down even more because it is exhausted from carrying the weight of prior experiences that increases exponentially all the time without realizing it. The second group walks through life lightly, getting rid of luggage and never picking up any more.

However, no matter the ease or difficulty of this work,

each soul without exception feels more or less separated from the Source, God, Home while in the physical world. This delusion of separation causes many people to feel lost, wandering as if in a fog. This is a lesson itself. We should not only remember but embody this knowledge. Separation is only a delusion. You cannot separate from the thing you are united with, e.g. an eye from a head. This is impossible. You will rightly say that everything comes down to the senses. No doubt. However, the eye cells cannot operate without the rest of the body. This is just the way it is but you agreed to it being this way before you came into the world.

Separation is in a sense „pretended" and serves the soul by showing it *Who It is in Essence*. In this way you can learn the lessons stemming from your own and other peoples' experiences. A soul can be compared to an actor on a stage. He knows that he is not the character he is playing but he enters into his part in order to play it well. If he didn't enter it with all his senses, he wouldn't play it believably and authentically and he wouldn't be fulfilled as an actor. You are such an actor, too, only the stage is life. Do you want to enter the part you took earlier, or have you decided that playing it is harmful to you? If so, you will have to leave this world empty handed. While being „there" you had to try very hard to get here because there are more willing souls than bodies that can be inhabited on Earth. During this casting, many souls were eager to take your place.

So instead of complaining about your hard life, remember why you came to the world as a soul and what do you want to learn. Don't be afraid that you will fail. It is always a success, you always achieve the result of your desires, and you always succeed. By limiting yourself you succeed, though in failure, but you want to experience the limiting. Know that you are always protected and safe so give yourself over the thing you want to happen in full trust.

People surrounding you came to the world for the same reason you did. You are together in order to make experiencing possible to each other. You will play your parts together as long as you need each other. When one of you learns your lesson (or part) faster, you will either pass away or sacrifice yourself to the other person and stay. It is neither good nor desired for both sides. Even if it is a spiritual partner, such a relationship can be very toxic and disadvantageous to the soul's growth.

A man that is unawakened makes decisions based on the mind's directions and his own fears and prejudices. Unfortunately, this often leads to the heart's suffering. The more awakened the couple is, the bigger the probability that it will make decisions based on love. The spiritual partner that is not awakened is a tragic figure and can cause a lot of pain. If one soul is less advanced than the other, some elements of violence, greed, envy, hatred, fear etc. can be brought to relationship that is subsequently toxic to a more advanced partner.

The unawakened partner is the one that doesn't have knowledge of souls, isn't conscious of higher levels of existence, and can't see clearly. The everyday mind usually prevents the awakening. Maybe you are in such a situation and when suggest to your partner that they awaken, you hear the following justifications: I am too young, I need more experience, I am not ready to settle down yet, I represent something else (religion, race, region, social class, intellectual level, cultural background). Don't let yourself be misled; these are only excuses. The soul doesn't own any of the attributes your partner hides behind. The more advanced partner often wishes to help the other to grow. If the other, however, doesn't let themselves be helped and chooses to remain stagnant, the relationship is doomed to fail.

Maybe there will be another opportunity in another incarnation. There is a chance, of course, that the partner awakes in this incarnation, but the more advanced side risks a lot if this happens. It is very probable that it fails in helping the partner and its own growth will be blocked. Only the couple that is equally awakened makes decisions based on love, which fosters their collective growth.

When the more advanced partner decides to leave, acknowledging that the present part doesn't serve them well, another person will take their place and the education of the less advanced side will continue. That is why you shouldn't worry that you will be lonely or make your partner lonely if you leave. This is absolutely impossible. Lonely people are stuck in isolation because they don't let anyone come close to them. Their fear of abandonment is often so big that they are afraid to try one more time. Some even think that if they once failed, it will be forever. As soon as they muster the courage to try, the empty place next to them will be filled.

Remember, dear reader, that each of our stories began a long time ago when we left Home, Source, God. While in the physical body we don't remember what we came here for and what causes the feeling of being far away from Home. As I wrote before, this is just a delusion. Out of the body, every soul functions because of energy filled with light in the void of threads along which energy is constantly flowing and cooperating perfectly as a whole. If one of the threads loses sync, we all feel it.

The apparent separation from the Source and all other lifeforms happens only to encourage us to develop a separate personality or ego. It is necessary to learn through various experiences. Because of this apparent separation we begin to think that personality is all that we are. This is a lesson itself. We have to learn how to correct it. In that sense, the earthly plan gives soul opportunities to learn. Remember, though, that you are connected to your Higher Self. Don't believe me? You have lived in so many bodies already, so many times. Ask your present self why it is filled with fear. Why is it so much afraid of taking a reasonable risk? Why does a personal self-worry so much about its reputation and what others would think? It may be that those fears come from childhood or maybe they were born much, much earlier. Ask yourself the following questions: what can I lose? What is the worst thing that can happen to me? Am I absolutely satisfied with this life? Are changes that risky compared to the death that every one of us will have to go through?

Working with ghosts helped me to understand that the feeling of separation is the cause of all the difficulties that people experience in their earthly life as personality or ego. When they leave their physical body behind and pass to the more subtle condition, they still struggle with identical difficulties. What they haven't learned in their physical bodies they have to learn now in the astral body though the suffering is much, much deeper. The absence of the physical body means a lack of a barrier protecting from astral (or emotional) energies. A man feels those energies in the physical body much less intensively. It reminds me of a situation as if he was behind a soundproof wall. Feeling without physical body in the astral body is direct and much more intensive and painful. As I wrote earlier, our learning proceeds with the help of pleasure or suffering. If we cannot walk the first path ourselves, the second one forces us to, so the dose of offering is bigger.

When we are in the physical body, our daily experiences radiate from us as aura energies. More specifically, these rays are the energetic (emotional and mental) reactions to those experiences. It may seem to you that if you didn't experience anything, you would radiate white light. Idleness and laziness are experiences, and they too color the aura (not white of course).

Auras (I will write about these in the third volume) are not the hallucinations of mentally disturbed people, but emanations of chakras and subtle bodies through which you experience life. A soul put them on one after another while descending to Earth in order to be able to experience, learn, and grow. When a soul takes on a journey back to Home, Source, God, it begins to throw them away in reverse order.

Staying in the physical body, you may doubt that you have subtle bodies. You will no longer doubt that when you lack the physical body. You will have a new understanding of what you truly needed them for. If you were to deal daily with the souls that have left their physical body, you would know exactly what I'm talking about. I truly hope that it won't encourage you to contact the ghosts of the dead, however. You would probably become possessed very soon and would share the tragic fate of people calling you every day, asking for help. My first book *Possessed by Ghosts* tells about it in detail.

It is worth it for you to always remember that we as people find ourselves on the ascending evolutionary arc and the elementary essence of our cells (not only physical, but astral and mental, too) are on the descending arc, also known as involution. I wrote about this in the first volume while discussing addictions. We ascend with the evolutionary wave and they go down. That's why we need everything that is noble in our growth and they need what is low, heavy, and „evil." It is, in spite of appearances, very important information since knowing it makes it easier for us to persist in resisting low energies such as anger, hatred, or fear. The deceased that cannot pass to the other side of the death curtain are in this very condition. They are still influenced by the elementary essence of their subtle bodies' cells. They became subdued to this influence completely and let themselves be wrapped in a cocoon.

We have free will, of course, and we can do whatever we want but by subduing ourselves to this descending tendency we place ourselves in opposition to ourselves. However, the permanent war with our own bodies is a failure on both sides. We can behave differently and more wisely and acknowledge the physical and subtle bodies cells as our younger brothers. Instead of submitting to them, we can lead them higher so that everybody benefits. We will stop fighting with addiction, since together with our cells we will wish the same.

Considering those questions can be difficult for many. For we were taught to think of life in the pure physical terms. Scientists haven't yet discovered what I am writing about. I hope that this book will help you break prejudice and stereotypes and allow you to look at life from a wider perspective. You may not have to lose your physical body in order to see and understand what you can do now while you still have it.

I wish for you to become aware of your whole being (not only the physical body) and to understand how you were constructed. Everything is a multilevel matrix of light, including yourself. Other people are such a matrix too and everything taken together is Universe, God. You know all that already, you only need to bring it out from the deeper levels of memory (your Holy Self).

THE END OF THE SECOND VOLUME

HELP

Dear reader, if you are in a situation where you cannot cope you may turn to me and ask me to help at the following address:

Wanda Pratnicka
P.O. Box 257
81-963 Gdynia 1
Poland
e-mail: office@TheExorcisms.com
www.TheExorcisms.com

You may also phone my office at:

Phone in Poland: +48 58 555 9815
Fax in Poland: +48 58 550 6812

Phone in the United States: 631 402 1254
Phone in the United Kingdom: 02032 984727

Please take a look at our website ("Contact") for current phone numbers in the country of your residence.

I will need to have the following information:

1) Forenames and surname
2) Date of birth
3) Place of permanent stay

For the help to be effective I will most often need to have the details of all the people residing in the house/apartment because in the majority of cases the whole family is in need of help.

If you are a public person or for any reason you are unwilling / unable to pass to me your personal data (which I fully under-stand and respect) you still can use my services (checking and cleansing of you and your near ones) without passing to me or to my associates any of your personal information.
That option is certainly making it more difficult for me and I am willing to grant that option only in rare, justified cases and for a higher fee. Please call to receive more information on that matter.

Please note that I am also giving private consultations for problems not connected to the presence of ghosts. Ask my staff to receive more information about that option.

If the subject of this book has aroused your interest then I will be happy to hear your opinion of it.

BOOK ORDERING

You can order this book at the following address:

Centrum Publishers
P.O. Box 257
81-963 Gdynia
Poland
e-mail: info@TheExorcisms.com
or use our ordering page at
www.TheExorcisms.com/shop.html

You may also phone my office at:

Phone in Poland: +48 58 555 9815
Fax in Poland: +48 58 550 6812

Phone in the United States: 631 402 1254
Phone in the United Kingdom: 02032 984727

Wanda Pratnicka
Possessed by Ghosts – Exorcisms in XXI century

This book is aimed at all readers, not just those who are interested in the esoteric arts. It presents in an accessible and surprisingly clear way the causes of the toxic associations that arise between people and ghosts. It contains a large dose of the psy-

chology of soul. Ghosts are the souls of people who, for various reasons, overlooked their own death, did not have the courage to depart for the other world or were detained, or even dragged from the road, by their dear ones weeping for those souls. When they remain in the world of the living they possess people and this can be the cause of very unfortunate, and sometimes even tragic, experiences. The presence of ghosts within a person causes powerful mood swings from strong negative emotional outbursts to profound depression. They evoke powerful anxiety attacks, persuade those who are possessed to commit suicide, have strong influences on the psyche and are the cause of mental illnesses. Additionally, the physical illnesses of the person who died are very often transferred by the ghost to the person possessed.

The subject of this book could be a panacea for very many of our world's misfortunes. From various states of mental disturbance, deviations, dependencies, severe psychiatric illnesses including those requiring isolation, through to chronic diseases or those that are considered to be incurable.

The question of ghosts also applies to various everyday situations like the demanding behavior of a family member, difficulties with learning, with people close to one, work colleagues or business associates. They often lead to helplessness, loneliness, isolation, or to difficult financial, health and social situations.

What is a frequent cause of various diseases, misfortunes, lesser or greater failures? How can one deal with them, how can one guard against them in the future? That's what this book is about. It is also a reply to the endless questions asked by people turning to Wanda Pratnicka for help. They often believe that the things that have happened to them are unique, they happened only to them. They wonder why they are suffering so much. They think that maybe they did something bad and that now they're being punished. Or maybe it's the work of some curse or black magic.

Possessed by Ghosts is a very exceptional work. Nobody before has described the dependencies that exist between the world of ghosts and that of people in such an extensive, comprehensible and profound way. It allows you to understand the causes of these dependencies and shows how to free yourself from them. It is a guide that leads to a life of peace, satisfaction, enthusiasm and wealth.

It is a handbook for anyone who is pursuing personal and spiritual development. It shows the universal laws that govern our world and is a testament to the author's spiritual maturity.

Wanda Pratnicka about her book:

"For many years I really wanted to read a good book about exorcisms, but I never found one. Unfortunately, till now nobody had written one. So I had to do it myself. In it there are answers to questions asked every day by my patients, but also answers to questions I asked myself.

In it, I address those who have tried everything, every method, every remedy to ease their problems or those of their near ones. Unfortunately, none of them worked or if they did work they did so for only a short time. I wrote it also for those who are only at the beginning, they sense that something bad is happening to them or their families, or that not everything is as it should be. I wrote it for those who are healthy and happy, too, those who have nothing wrong with them or their nearest. They are the very ones who could help in many tragedies which are taking place inside their neighbors' homes, or to an unhappy family nearby, or to some hooligan or drug addict in the street where they live. Sometimes one can help simply with a piece of advice about what can be done in a given situation or with the information that something can be done at all.

Usually, the fact is that the person who is possessed is unaware of his or her state. By helping such a person we are really helping ourselves since we no longer hear the fights the other side of the wall, or our neighborhood becomes quieter. In extreme cases we may even prevent a suicide, a rape or even worse. It affects, therefore, not just the individual but most often all of us."

Wanda Pratnicka
In the Wheel
of Life
Volume II

Wanda Pratnicka presents the Universal Laws ruling our Universe over the span of approximately **two thousand pages** in her new book **consisting of four volumes.** These laws have the same impact on our daily lives as they do on our overarching concepts of

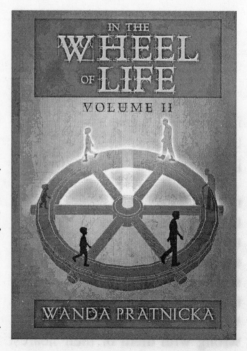

spiritual development. The author often raises extremely complicated and deep questions, presenting them in an exceptionally simple way. Her work is easily comprehended by experts in the esoteric field and novices alike. An expert will find the correct way to interpret the studies of the greatest Teachers of humanity, and the beginner will find explanations full of truth, peace, and light concerning all areas of daily life. The book discusses the entire range of what human experiences consist of. It raises questions corresponding to physical space, as well as higher worlds including the etheric, astral, mental, causal, and higher. This work is intended for people interested in spiritual development, as well as people who constantly work on improving their situation, whether it be emotional, material, interpersonal, etc.

Volume I and II contain further explanation of all phenomena mentioned in the author's previous book, Possessed by Ghosts: Exorcisms in the 21st Century.

A note from the author regarding **Volumes I-IV** of *In the Wheel of Life*:

"Dear reader, in this book I would like to present Life from a broader perspective and lead you step by step through all its stages. I talk extensively about a soul, to make it clear to you Who You Are in Essence and to let you know what caused you to come to Earth.

This knowledge will help you discover meaning in your experiences and what the purpose of your life and the lives of those close to you is. You will find out how the distant past influences your present life and what will happen with you when you are separated from your physical body. These are very essential matters because this knowledge has an influence not only on your journey here on Earth, but on the entire range of experiences each human shares while going through the transition commonly known as death of the physical body.

Information contained in this book will allow you to look at life from a completely different perspective, free of fear and the illusions you have accepted as the truth until this point. Everything that I present here is already known to you on the deeper levels of Your Being. Hence, my role is only to remind you of what you already know."

Wanda Pratnicka about **Volume II**:

"In Volume II, I present Life from an even broader perspective. I wrote Volume I assuming that you lived on Earth only once. In this book, I describe your Life from the perspective of many incarnations and gently lead you step-by-step from life here on Earth, through so-called death and all levels of existence that follow, and into the next life in physicality.

Essentially, it will help you realize what we commonly call death is not the end of life, but a transition from one state to another. This will lead you to the conclusion that you never die, you only exchange bodies like clothes, and as a soul you exist eternally.

This knowledge will spontaneously and completely change your view on Life and free you from both fear of death and life. It will also free you from the fear of a dangerous, vengeful, unjust God.

Taking a look at one's own life from the perspective of many lives answers a very essential question about ostensible injustice. Who knows? Perhaps you will stop blaming God for injustice when you will realize why He, who ultimately is only Love, put people on earth in such extreme diverse conditions.

By accepting this broadened perspective you will come to understand why some people are happy, healthy, beautiful, and wealthy, while others lack everything. People in the latter group struggle greatly every day and deceive themselves into believing that there is no chance for a better future. You will become convinced that you are not a victim of your life, but your life's creator. This will allow you to take responsibility for your life. The knowledge contained in my book gives you this responsibility, but also the tools to introduce your psyche to changes that will lead to a better, happier, more secure and wealthy life on all fronts. I wish you this from the bottom of my heart."

Wanda Pratnicka
Know the Truth
And Be Free
A note from the author:
I am addressing this book to everyone irrespective of race or religion because one day we will all deal with our own or someone else's death. We should adequately prepare for this event, especially when we are sick, elderly or have someone in our family who is rapidly approaching the

transition we call "death". If you have lost a loved one and have been grieving then this book is perfect for you. The wisdom contained here will also help you to heal from past traumatic experiences that followed the passing of loved ones.

Most people fear death. Do you realize that the fear of death is the cause for most, if not all, misfortunes in this world? It is not caused by death itself, but rather from a lack of information on this subject. Therefore, knowledge about death while you are alive is as important as the air that you breathe.

By familiarizing yourself with this text you will stop living your life with constant frustration. If on a deep level of your being you adapt to guidance from this book, you will get rid of your fear of death once and for all. And having rid yourself of this fear you will begin to make different, more conscious choices. Then it's not out of the question that you will become amazingly wise and happy.

From the chapter "Preface":

"Do you realize that the fear of death is the primary cause of most, if not all of our internal adversities? The fear of death is like the interior of a simmering volcano. It is that hidden, constant fear that no amount of money or superficial effort can neutralize. This fear is the essence of all things. It is a fear that emanates not only from death itself, but also from a lack of understanding of this very emotional subject. Traditional media is not making it any easier to understand death. Death is either not shown or, for example in movies and video games it is presented in a banal or unrealistic way.

Therefore most people leave things up to chance, not

knowing how to control their life on Earth as well as after death. When you familiarize yourself with the information introduced in this book you will no longer waste your life. You will begin to make different, more conscious choices. Who knows, maybe you will become amazingly wise and happy. Once and for all you will get rid of your fears and stop living in constant frustration. You will understand that what you fear the most (most often unconsciously) doesn't even exist, because what you call death is just taking off your body in the same way that you take off and throw away the old clothes that you don't need anymore. Meanwhile you, the essence of you, moves forward. Where? Well, to understand this is extraordinarily important because what you know about death, what you think about it during your life and what you expect from it, will determine what you will experience in the future. Therefore, the knowledge you acquire about death in your lifetime is as important as the air that you breathe because your future depends on it. I hope that you will come to understand that everything that happens to you depends only and solely of you. You must take your life into your own hands because nobody else will help you with it.

Nobody can get by in life without the knowledge provided in this book. It is especially important when you are sick, aged or you have someone in your family who is quickly approaching the transition commonly known as "death". If you have lost someone close to you and you are mourning then this book is appropriate for you. This book will explain every tragedy and it will help you heal any wounds in your heart caused by the loss of someone dear to you."

WANDA PRATNICKA is a psychologist M.A., parapsychologist, psychic, spiritual teacher and exorcist. During her 45 years of practice she has helped tens of thousands of people around the world. Her first book *Possessed by Ghosts – Exorcisms in XXI century* became a bestseller in Poland shortly after publication of its first edition. The book was translated to English, German, Spanish, Russian, Japanese and currently other translations are being prepared.

Wanda Pratnicka's next literary work *In the Wheel of Life* consists of four volumes and around 2,000 pages. Her books are aimed to all readers, not just those who are interested in the esoteric arts.

These books present, in an accessible and surprisingly clear way, the universal laws of the Universe, a soul's psychology, deep matters in regards to true human origin and the causes of toxic associations that arise between people and ghosts. Ghosts are the souls of people who, for various reasons, overlooked their own death, did not have the courage to depart for the other world or were detained by their dear ones weeping for those souls. When they remain in the world of the living, they possess people and this can be the cause of very unfortunate and sometimes even tragic experiences. Starting from the mildest symptoms, the presence of ghosts within a person causes powerful mood swings from strong negative emotional outbursts to profound depression. They evoke powerful anxiety attacks, persuade those who are possessed to commit suicide, have strong influence on psyche and are the cause of mental illnesses. Additionally, the physical illnesses of the person who died are often transferred by the ghost to the person possessed.

Wanda Pratnicka's newest book is *Know the Truth and Be Free* which cures such problems as fear of death/life or traumatic experiences that result from loved ones' loss/death.